UXBRIDGE
COLLEGE

of related interest

The Child's World
Assessing Children in Need
Edited by Jan Horwath
ISBN 1 85302 957 2

Child Welfare Policy and Practice Issues and Lessons Emerging from Current Research
Edited by Dorota Iwaniec and Malcolm Hill
ISBN 1 85302 812 6

Effective Ways of Working with Children and their Families
Edited by Malcolm Hill
ISBN 1 85302 619 0

Child Development for Child Care and Protection Workers
Brigid Daniel, Sally Wassell and Robbie Gilligan
Foreword by Jim Ennis
ISBN 1 85302 633 6

Social Work with Children and Families
Getting into Practice
Ian Butler and Gwenda Roberts
ISBN 1 85302 365 5

Child Welfare Services
Developments in Law, Policy Practice and Research
Edited by Malcolm Hill and Jane Aldgate
ISBN 1 85302 316 7

Making an Impact – Children and Domestic Violence
A Reader
Marianne Hester, Chris Pearson and Nicola Harwin
ISBN 1 85302 844 4

Engaging with Fathers
Practice Issues for Health and Social Care
Brigid Daniel and Julie Taylor
ISBN 1 85302 794 4

Approaches to Needs Assessment in Children's Services

Edited by Harriet Ward and Wendy Rose

Jessica Kingsley Publishers
London and Philadelphia

First published in the United Kingdom in 2002
by Jessica Kingsley Publishers Ltd
116 Pentonville Road
London N1 9JB, England
and
325 Chestnut Street
Philadelphia, PA 19106, USA

www.jkp.com

Library of Congress Cataloging in Publication Data
A CIP catalog record for this book is available from the Library of Congress

British Library Cataloguing in Publication Data
A CIP catalogue record for this book is available from the British Library

ISBN 1 85302 780 4

Printed and Bound in Great Britain by
Athenaeum Press, Gateshead, Tyne and Wear

Contents

List of Figures

List of Tables

Foreword

Under the new Labour government, children at last appear to be receiving the priority that they deserve in government policy. They are our most precious resource, and their health, wellbeing and prosperity are vital for the future success of our nation.

One of the central tenets of the NHS Plan announced by the Secretary of State, in July 2001, is the delivery of services that are integrated, appropriate, evidence-based and focussed on the needs of the individual.

I welcome the publication of this comprehensive volume with its important contributions from highly respected authorities in the fields of Child Life and Health. Assessing the needs of children is the fundamental starting point in delivering appropriate services to match those needs. The authors are to be thanked for having contributed to a unique volume on this aspect of the implementation of policy.

Professor A Aynsley-Green MA Dhc DPhil FRCP FRCP(Edin) FRCPCH FMedSci
Nuffield Professor of Child Health and Director of Clinical Research and Development

Preface

Interest in how we assess need and make sense of what is happening to some of our most vulnerable children has been gathering momentum since the implementation of the Children Act 1989. Two particular sets of concerns account for the attention being given to the systems and processes used for ascertaining children's needs. First, increasing doubts have been voiced, among policy makers and child welfare professionals alike, that we have not always been effective in our interventions in the lives of children in need. The services provided have clearly often not had the beneficial results intended. Accounts by children and families have confirmed that the impact of policies and practice on the current wellbeing of children and on their longer term progress into adulthood has been insufficiently addressed. Sir William Utting and Sir Ronald Waterhouse are among many who have chronicled some of the more public failures of the child welfare system in this respect. The Government has responded by setting objectives for children's social services and by launching initiatives such as Quality Protects in England and Children First in Wales, aimed at improving the outcomes for the most vulnerable child population.

The second set of concerns has been focused on the quality of information which has informed decisions about the services which should be provided to children. Time after time reports in the 1990s, by the Social Services Inspectorate and by researchers, identified the absence of recorded assessments and plans for individual children with whom social services were working. These findings begged a number of important questions. What information had practitioners regarded as significant in the critical decisions they were making? How had they reached these decisions? Similar concerns about the information base for children's services planning were being expressed at the same time, including the technical challenges for social services departments of separating measures of need from measures of supply in order to map need in a local community. Children's services plans were found, as a consequence, to be extremely variable in content and effectiveness. Latterly, such concerns were being aired in the context of a radical programme of government reform to modernise and improve social services, with increasing emphasis placed on their performance and delivery of Government objectives.

The response has been the generation of some remarkable partnerships between service managers and academics, and between policy makers and professionals, to work on the theory and practice of assessing need. These collaborations have been marked by a high degree of creativity, enthusiasm and commitment to developing new conceptual frameworks for identifying and understanding need at both an individual and community level and to testing out their application in practice. Our purpose in this book has been to chart the progress which has been made in developing different approaches and to record the experience of their use in practice. Whilst the chapters reflect the striving for more effective and rigorous processes in assessment, they also document a bumpy ride with uneven progress, often two steps forward and one step back.

The book falls naturally into two parts. The first is concerned with populations of children and the identification and analysis of their needs as the basis for service planning in a community. The second focuses on the issues involved in assessing the needs of individual children and their families within a developmental/ecological framework as the basis for more effective intervention. The challenge is how these two processes can be integrated within a coherent overall framework. All the authors have contributed to, and are continuing to contribute to, the review and formulation of government policy about children's services. Some have done so as the result of commissions from the Department of Health, others by the influence their work has had on deliberations by policy makers or through their roles as advisers to government projects. Jenny Gray provides an authoritative view from the Department of Health.

We are inevitably indebted, as editors, to many people in the production of this book. Our authors have worked with us steadfastly and optimistically since the proposal for the book was originally conceived, and have ensured that they have reflected new and emerging issues against a fast changing policy backcloth. We wish to acknowledge with gratitude the fine administrative and clerical support of Suzanne Dexter, Lyn Swanevelder and Julie Stock. In particular we are grateful to Amy Lankester-Owen at Jessica Kingsley Publishers for her support and advice throughout. Most of all we are indebted to Christopher Rose and Christopher Ward, without whose patience, encouragement and forbearance this book would never have seen the light of day.

We hope that the ideas, experiences and reflections in this book will assist and support those who face the challenge of improving the assessment processes of their agencies in order to provide more effective services for children in need.

Harriet Ward and Wendy Rose

Authors' Note

Over the last year or so there has been a change in the terminology used to describe local units of administration in England and Wales. The term 'council' has begun to replace 'local authority' as the generic term for local government units through which social services are provided. In this period of transition, the editors have decided to retain the term 'local authority' for the sake of consistency.

CHAPTER ONE

Introduction

Harriet Ward

This introductory chapter explains how the book explores how local authorities in England and Wales have engaged in the task of identifying children who are in need and planning appropriate services for them. The task of needs assessment inevitably draws all those involved into an ongoing debate on a number of perennial issues such as the question of less eligibility, the respective merits of child rescue versus family support, and the purpose of promoting children's wellbeing. The changing response to these political and moral questions forms the context within which agencies grapple with the difficulties of providing a co-ordinated needs-led service.

The Children Act 1989

In England and Wales, Part III of the Children Act 1989 forms the basis in law for the provision of local services to children in need. The legislation states that:

> It shall be the general duty of every local authority...
>
> (a) to safeguard and promote the welfare of children within their area who are in need; and
>
> (b) so far as is consistent with that duty, to promote the upbringing of such children by their families, by providing a range and level of services appropriate to those children's needs. (Children Act 1989, s.17.1)

Local authorities are also required to facilitate the provision of services for children in need by other agencies (particularly voluntary organisations) (s.17.5), make efforts to identify the extent of children in need in their area (Schedule 2, para. 1.1) and publicise the services that are available, taking reasonable steps to ensure that the relevant information reaches those children and families who might benefit from it (Schedule 2, para. 1.2).

This book aims to explore some of the many initiatives introduced by local authorities and other child welfare agencies in England and Wales as they engage in the task of identifying children who, under the terms of the Children Act 1989, are regarded as being 'in need', and plan how to provide the appropriate 'range and level of services'. The assessment of need is undertaken at both an aggregate level, through procedures which attempt to identify and assess the needs of populations of children who are likely to require additional supportive services, or who have already received extra help, and at an individual level through initiatives which aim to provide practitioners with the skills and tools that are necessary if they are to make accurate assessments of the needs of particular children and their families. The chapters in Part One of this book explore the assessment of need at an aggregate level, while those in Part Two focus on the individual level.

Many of the initiatives explored in the chapters in Part One were introduced in response to the increasing duties laid on local authorities to make and publish strategic plans for the development of children's services, introduced in the *Children Act 1989 (Amendment) Children's Services Planning Order 1996*, and then extended through the requirement to produce annual Management Action Plans as part of the extensive Quality Protects programme to modernise and improve the delivery of social services. Chapter 2 sets the scene, identifying areas where children are vulnerable and exploring the direction of policy under New Labour designed to offer better opportunities for change. Chapters 4 and 7 describe, from very different perspectives, the local authority response to the new requirements, and Chapters 3, 5 and 6 discuss in greater detail some of the specific initiatives designed both to help planners improve their conceptual grasp of how needs may be assessed and to provide practical methodologies that can be used to help them in their task.

Many of the initiatives described in Part Two are underpinned by the *Framework for the Assessment of Children in Need and their Families*, new government guidance launched by the Department of Health in 2000 and implemented in England in 2001 and in Wales from April 2002 (Department of Health, Department for Education and Employment, Home Office 2000a). Chapter 8 describes this guidance and explains why it was introduced, Chapters 9 and 12 consider some of the risk and protective factors associated with children's vulnerability and Chapters 10, 11 and 13 explore specific programmes designed to help practitioners identify and assess children who are in need and monitor the effectiveness of services.

Why should family support services be provided?

The assessment of need in children's services inevitably touches on a number of perennial themes with which policy makers continually have to grapple, and which emerge in various different forms in many of the chapters in the book. Some of the most important questions to be answered in the development of social policy in this area revolve around the reasons why it should be the responsibility of the state to provide services to families. Should not parents be responsible for safeguarding and promoting the wellbeing of their children? In what areas should the state become involved, and where would its intervention be unjustifiable or intrusive? Should children be rescued from unsatisfactory parents or should parents be helped to develop better skills? Is it legitimate for the state to provide services to some families and not to others? Do those families that receive services become unnecessarily dependent, and unwilling to shoulder their responsibilities towards their children? These are both moral and political questions and they are answered differently as circumstances or administrations change. As Hardiker and colleagues discuss in Chapter 3, the changing responses to such questions form the social policy context within which need is understood and levels of intervention planned within different models of welfare.

Ever since it was recommended in the *Report of the Royal Commission on the Poor Laws* in 1834 (Poor Law Commissioners 1834) the principle of less eligibility has dogged the debate on the provision of services for children in need. This principle, that '[the pauper's] situation...shall not be made really or apparently so eligible as the situation of the independent labourer of the lowest class', was introduced as a means of reducing dependence on the state. It meant that, for at least the following century, statutory agencies could not offer family support services to children who were living at home with their parents. Able-bodied adults were expected to bring up their families, initially without assistance, and later only with help from universal services such as education, which became compulsory in 1870, or the school medical service, introduced in a rudimentary form in 1907. Those who needed extra help were regarded as seeking an unfair advantage over those who managed alone.

However, such a principle ignores the reality that:

> some children's special needs are so extensive that they cannot be adequately met by parents working together with the universal services; other families require support...because the circumstances of the parents are such that they cannot meet their children's needs without additional assistance. (Ward 1998, p.204)

The development of child welfare law over the last century demonstrates both a gradual acceptance of the view that the state does have a role to play in ensuring the wellbeing of children and an acknowledgement that some parents will require more support than others in helping them achieve satisfactory outcomes (Ward 1999). However this has been a long drawn-out process. The Children Act 1948, one of the cornerstones of the welfare state, marked the beginning of a change from a punitive attitude to destitute children to one which placed an emphasis on affording them the 'opportunity for the proper development of [their] character and abilities'. Nevertheless, it only laid on local authorities a duty to offer support services to children who were separated from their families, and not to those who were living at home, whose parents might otherwise shirk their responsibilities.

However, by the early 1950s, both financial considerations and the work of child development experts such as John Bowlby began to push policy towards preventing children being separated from their parents in the first place. The Ingleby Report (Committee on Children and Young Persons 1960) reflected pressure from several lobbies and recommended early detection of families at risk. It led to the Children and Young Person's Act 1963, Section 1, which, for the first time gave local authorities permissive powers to offer advice, guidance and assistance – including in exceptional circumstances assistance in cash or kind – to children living within their own families in order to prevent the need for them to be taken into care.

The relatively recent Children Act 1989 takes the argument much further: it introduces the principle that statutory agencies should work in partnership with parents (Department of Health 1990), thus establishing a theoretical position where the state is given a new duty: to offer a range of services designed to supplement the efforts of parents in order to promote the wellbeing of children who might not otherwise reach their full potential.

Indeed, under Section 17.3 of this Act, services may be provided to the *family* of a child in need, rather than specifically to the child, if their purpose is to safeguard and promote his or her welfare. The 'Grid' described by Hardiker and colleagues in Chapter 3 offers a conceptual model which is now used by a number of authorities to identify and plan the range of services they require to meet children's different levels of need.

Nevertheless the Children Act 1989 continues to reflect the tension between different political and moral imperatives. The fear that, in providing services designed to promote the wellbeing of children who might otherwise not have sufficient opportunities to fulfill their potential, the state will encourage an undesirable dependency in their parents, has not been eradicated. The Act was implemented in 1991 by a government determined to reduce dependency. The Act makes it clear that parents have enduring responsibilities for their children that cannot be transferred, although they may be shared (s.2). It also gives local authorities the power to demand whole or partial repayment of assistance offered to families with children in need (s.17.7).

Considerations of 'less eligibility' are not the only reasons why, for many years, policymakers have been reluctant to provide family support services to children in need. The corollary to the view that the state should not encourage dependency by helping parents to bring up their children is the opinion that children should be rescued from parents who are unable to meet their needs. This is another perennial issue whose resolution tends to change according to the political and economic climate. The close relationship between those factors which precipitate children into need and the experience of poverty has been extensively explored (Bradshaw 1990, 2001a; Kumar 1993; Utting 1995; Social Exclusion Unit 1998a, 2001; Ward 2000). In times of relative affluence, families which are struggling tend to become more apparent; it is always easier to blame them for their situation than to address the structural causes which create social exclusion. Recent years have seen a demise of the doctrine that a key function of government is to take money from the rich to protect the poor. In his analysis of the current 'Culture of Contentment', Galbraith (1993) argues that if urban discontent, crime and violence increase 'this will be attributed not to the social situation but to the inferior, even criminal, disposition of the people involved' (p.172).

England and Wales both have a long tradition of separating children from parents whose actions or lifestyles have been thought to be detrimental to their welfare. However the numbers of children looked after tend to increase when economic conditions are good, and decrease as they deteriorate. Although a number of children clearly need permanent protection from abusive parents, others are placed away from home because adequate family support services are not forthcoming. One group for whom this is particularly apparent are children with disabilities. Child rescue carries within it an element of blame, and it has sometimes proved easier to remove children from parents who can be labelled as undeserving of assistance than to provide support services such as washing machines or holidays for families under stress.

The Children Act 1989 introduced a number of changes that attempted to move the debate away from a polarisation between those who thought children should be rescued and those who thought parents should be helped to meet their needs. The requirement that, unless it was clearly detrimental to their welfare, children looked after away from home would be allowed 'reasonable' contact with their parents (s.34), the introduction of accommodation as a family support service (s.20), and the principle that local authorities would work in partnership with parents (Department of Health 1990), all tend to blur the distinction between children looked after away from home and other children in need and reduce the rescue element in child welfare interventions.

Services to promote wellbeing

If we accept that the state has a legitimate duty to provide services designed to safeguard and promote the welfare of children, the next issue to resolve is the grounds on which children might be regarded as being 'in need'. England and Wales are both signatories to the United Nations Convention on the Rights of the Child (United Nations 1989), which requires them to recognise, amongst others: children's inherent rights to life (Article 6), to protection from abuse (Articles 34–37), to the enjoyment of the highest attainable standard of health (Article 24), to a standard of living adequate to their physical, mental, spiritual, moral and social development (Article 27), to education (Article 28), and to rest and leisure (Article 31). Part III of the Children Act 1989 can be seen as one of the primary ways in which the UN convention may be implemented in England and Wales. Both are predicated on the view that it is the responsibility of the state to ensure that children's *developmental* needs are met; indeed, the Act states that a child shall be taken to be in need if:

(a) he is unlikely to achieve or maintain or to have the opportunity of achieving or maintaining, a reasonable standard of health or development without the provision for him of services by a local authority...

(b) his health or development is likely to be significantly impaired, or further impaired, without the provision for him of such services; or

(c) he is disabled. (Children Act 1989, s.17.10)

This principle that the state should provide services designed to promote and safeguard children's wellbeing has not, of course, been introduced purely from motives of altruism. While the importance of making sure that, as far as possible, all children should have a happy childhood may be claimed as a laudable objective, there are also many strong, pragmatic reasons why it is in the interests of societies to ensure that their children attain a reasonable standard of health and development. The draft Guidance on Children's Services Planning made it explicit that 'The government seeks to support families to bring up children safely and effectively *so that they become active adult participants, both socially and economically*' (Department of Health 2000a, p.11 (my italics)). As Page points out in Chapter 2, childhood disadvantages lead to poor health, poor employment prospects, social exclusion and increased dependence on statutory services at key stages in the life cycle. All of these outcomes are not only undesirable, they are also expensive. It costs £223 to provide one day's in-patient hospital care; £1612 to provide a week in a children's residential unit; £419 for a week in a residential care home for the elderly and £27,566 for a year in prison (Netten and Curtis 2000, p.67, p.28, p.73; Home Office 2001, p.129). In economic terms it is therefore very much in the interests of the wider society to ensure that services are provided to safeguard and promote the wellbeing of children who are 'in need'.

Planning needs-led services

Authorities given the task of providing services to promote children's satisfactory development need a substantial amount of information if they are to provide the appropriate range and level of services. At a strategic level they need to know the likely prevalence of specific types of need in particular localities, and at a front-line level they need to know how to identify individual children who might require additional support. Since at least the mid-nineteenth century, administrative data from, for instance, the census, the Poor Law returns and the registration of births, marriages and deaths have made it possible to identify need on a population basis. Data on, for instance, the ages, occupations and death rates of the population, the numbers who are financially dependent on the state and their concentration in a given locality, provide crude indicators of need on both a national and a local basis. The data are so comprehensive that it is possible to map changes in the geographical distribution of poverty in England and Wales on at least three indicators (infant mortality, overcrowding and unemployment) for a century or more (Gregory, Southall and Dorling 2000). As the role of the state has expanded, so has the amount of administrative data available, and this has been complemented by the development of large-scale social surveys such as the Family Expenditure Survey, the General Household Survey and the Family Resources Survey (Smith and Noble 2000). The publication *Social Trends*, which summarises much of these data to give a picture of long-term social change, has been published annually since 1970.

Developments in information technology since the mid-1970s have revolutionised the availability and transfer of data as well as its aggregation and analysis. As Pinnock and Garnett demonstrate in Chapter 4, local authorities make increasing use of this population-based information in planning their services. The development of a Geographical Information System in north Lincolnshire, for instance, has made it possible to measure the distance between areas of greatest need and the provision of relevant services. This type of population-based information also makes it easier to identify with greater precision areas where children in need would most benefit from targeted initiatives such as Sure Start or the creation of a Health Improvement Zone.

However, while information such as that described above provides a broad picture which can facilitate strategic planning, other data present in the files of social services departments on the reasons why individual children are referred as being in need should provide a rich source of evidence that could be used to identify those services which it would be most appropriate to develop. At present such initiatives are in their infancy: few local authorities have the resources to search through files for key indicators of need in parents, children or the environment in which they live, and few management information systems are designed in such a way that these data can be easily input and aggregated.

The *Looking After Children* materials (Parker *et al.* 1991; Ward 1995; Department of Health 1995a) were introduced in order to provide local authorities with a systematic means of gathering similar relevant information about children looked after away from home, but patchy implementation, together with the inadequacies of a mainly paper-based system have meant that much of the data are insufficiently accurate or comprehensive for this purpose (Skuse, Macdonald and Ward 2001; Ward, forthcoming). The Integrated Children's System (Chapter 14) will be designed to address some of these issues. At an individual level it links *Looking After Children* with the *Assessment Framework* (see below) to provide a unified system for assessment, planning, intervention and review for all children in need. At an aggregate level it will also form an integral part of another initiative intended to help local authorities improve their use of management information: the *Children's Social Services Core Information Requirements: Process Model and Data Model* (Department of Health 2001a, 2001b).

The Integrated Children's System will be produced as a specification for the development of a software programme that allows for the input, transfer and aggregation of data and the production of reports. It will be linked to the database on children in need in their area held by social services. However the creation and scrutiny of large databases are by no means the only way in which local authorities can identify and aggregate need and plan appropriate services. Moreover for many the development of an appropriate information technology system is still some way in the future. Other, simpler initiatives, such as *Matching Needs and Services* (Chapter 5) have been developed to introduce at a grass-roots level the concept of aggregating data on individual case files in order to inform service planning.

The *Matching Needs and Services* exercise provides a simple methodology which enables social workers and their managers to establish whether enough referral or active cases display sufficiently similar profiles to be categorised as specific needs groups that can then be offered a particular tailor-made service. In a context within which practitioners work intensively with individual children and try to address needs which will be perceived as unique by each family, the view that children can be grouped according to particular characteristics is not always readily accepted. However a methodology for grouping children with common needs is a prerequisite for assessing the effectiveness of services as a whole. As Sinclair and Little demonstrate (Chapter 6) a robust taxonomy of need would be of immense value in developing both evidence-based service planning and the monitoring of outcomes. Information about groups of children in need can be of immense assistance in the strategic planning of services. One of the most useful sources of data in this area will be the *Children in Need Census* (Department of Health 2000b), which collates information on all children receiving support from social services within a given week. However, this comprehensive database relies on retrospective data; it can show which children received support at a particular time, but it does not help agencies decide which children are most likely to require support or how they can be identified.

Identifying and assessing children in need

The *Children in Need Census* (Department of Health 2000b) found that for 35 per cent of children receiving support from social services, the primary cause of need was neglect or abuse. Obviously the first priority in providing services is to offer protection to those children 'whose health or development is likely to be significantly impaired, or further impaired'. However, since the mid-1990s, there have been increasing concerns that the overwhelming emphasis on investigating possible cases of abuse tends to obscure the evidence of extensive need in other families where child protection is not an issue. The Department of Health (1995b) overview of research on child abuse found that only about 20 per cent of child protection investigations led to a child being placed on the child protection register, and only 5 per cent led directly to an admission to care or accommodation. Many families where children were thought to be at risk of suffering significant harm went through intensive investigations but did not receive a service, and there were concerns that time and resources might have been better spent on providing more extensive family support. Such findings have led to a policy initiative to introduce a new focus, encouraging authorities to develop services for children who are unlikely to achieve or maintain a reasonable standard of health or development in the hope that fewer will reach a situation where they are at risk of significant harm.

However Aldgate (Chapter 7) demonstrates that local authorities have often found it difficult to adopt this broader approach in the provision of services. Children at risk of abuse are more likely to receive services, regardless of whether the ill-treatment is likely to impact on their long-term development. Such decisions often disregard the competing demands of other children whose needs are greater, though they do not involve abuse, or whose needs could be addressed before their situation deteriorates to the point at which they require protection. Notwithstanding their inclusion in the legal definition of children who are in need, disabled children have often been denied services unless they are maltreated. Research undertaken by Tunstill and Aldgate (2000) also found little evidence of consistency in the manner in which children in need were assessed or services provided, either between authorities or, sometimes, between practitioners working in the same authorities.

The new *Framework for the Assessment of Children in Need and their Families* (Department of Health, Department for Education and Employment, Home Office 2000a) (Chapter 8) adopts a broad approach that seeks, among other objectives, to address some of the findings from the Aldgate and Tunstill research (1995; Tunstill and Aldgate 2000). The Assessment Framework is designed to provide a consistent methodology that will help practitioners identify, at an individual level, children who are in need. It takes forward and clarifies some of the conceptual thinking that underpinned the Children Act 1989 and the development of the *Looking After Children* materials (Parker *et al.* 1991). Perhaps its most significant feature is the expectation that, in undertaking assessments, practitioners will focus on the complex inter-relationship between children's developmental progress, the capacity of parents and caregivers to respond appropriately to their needs and the impact of a number of factors within their wider family and environment. Implementation of the Framework is intended to help practitioners move away from a narrow focus on risk towards a more holistic assessment of need in the three domains of child development, parenting capacity and the wider family and the environment.

Two issues are of particular significance here. First, in making assessments, practitioners are advised to look for strengths as well as weaknesses. This moves the thinking on needs assessment still further away from the earlier concentration on child rescue, and should serve to reinforce the view that effective interventions are most likely to be those undertaken in partnership with parents and children rather than in the face of their opposition. Some of the complementary work that underpins the Framework, aimed at providing practitioners with the knowledge base that they need in order to understand the inter-relationship between the three domains, explores in greater depth the delicate balance between the protective and risk factors present in families where children are in need (Chapters 9 and 12).

The second issue of particular relevance to the theme of this chapter is the emphasis given by the Framework on the inter-relationship between the three domains. Once the focus broadens from a somewhat narrow concentration on risk to a more holistic, complementary assessment – of the manner in which factors affecting the parent's capacity or the wider family and immediate environment are impacting on the child's developmental progress, then the inter-relationship between interventions becomes apparent. In particular, the emphasis on parenting capacity reinforces the argument that one way in which the state can safeguard the wellbeing of children is by addressing the needs of parents. The Framework is not concerned with conflicting ideologies around parental responsibility and dependency, but rather with the need to promote and safeguard the wellbeing of children, regardless of the political context. However if social workers are to understand the relationships between the three domains, they need a more robust knowledge base. In particular they need better information concerning how the difficulties with which some parents struggle may or may not affect their capacity to support their children. Cleaver explores a number of these questions in Chapter 12.

Fragmentation of services

Holistic assessments of need requiring practitioners to analyse the inter-relationships between factors across three domains will inevitably demonstrate the complexity of the issues addressed by social services departments. They will also demonstrate the interdependence of a range of different services, some of which address parents' needs or family or community issues, but all of which aim, directly or indirectly, to improve the wellbeing of children in need. Such an imperative requires close co-operation between the various service providers and yet, in England and Wales, there is a long history of fragmentation. The introduction of children's departments in the 1950s; the establishment of social services departments in the 1970s; the more recent creation of joint departments such as social services and housing (Kensington and Chelsea) or children's services with education and early years and community and economic development in the Learning and Development Directorate (Milton Keynes) are all designed to reduce divisions between different service providers. Nevertheless, services remain disappointingly fragmented, both between and within agencies, where providers of adult services often have little contact with child welfare practitioners. Such divisions are exacerbated by differences in ideological perspective, in training requirements and in levels of responsibility, all of which make it harder for practitioners to work together to a common end, and which often work to the detriment of the service provided. Perhaps one reason why inter-agency co-operation has proved difficult to achieve lies in the short-term approach to so many social issues. If services only address a particular stage in the life cycle, such as childhood, adolescence or adulthood, it is possible to be ignorant of the consequences of the presence or absence of earlier provision, for when service users move to a different budget they cease to be the responsibility or concern of previous providers.

Falkov demonstrates (Chapter 11) how poor communication between adult and children's service providers may obstruct attempts to provide support to families where a parent is mentally ill. Adult service providers may be unaware that their clients have parental responsibilities; children's service providers may lack the knowledge to make rational judgements concerning the extent to which parents' difficulties may, or perhaps may not, affect their capacity to provide satisfactory care. From a different perspective, as Ward and Peel point out (Chapter 10), most children in need are first known to universal service providers such as health authorities or education departments before they come to the attention of social services. Identifying commonly-held indicators of need to which all agencies can subscribe and establishing agreed thresholds of concern proves a far easier task than helping agencies overcome long-held distrust and mutual suspicion sufficiently to collaborate on a joint purpose.

There is, however, some evidence that the requirement for agencies to work together to produce a Children's Services Plan (Department of Health and Department for Education and Employment 1996), the creation of identical objectives for children in need to be shared across agencies (Department of Health 1999a) and the introduction of joint funding under the Health Act 1999 may have begun to sow the seeds of improved co-operation (Department of Health 2001c).

Assessing the outcome of interventions

The corollary to the identification and assessment of need is the assessment of outcome. An improved understanding of need should lead to more appropriate and effective interventions which, in turn, should lead to better outcomes for children and young people. Attempts to assess outcome are by no means new to children's services. Dr Parson's Report to the 1909 Royal Commission on the Poor Laws compared the physical condition of children in need who were placed with foster carers against that of children living on outdoor relief (income support) with their own parents. Easily measured variables such as height, weight, physical development and clothing supply were used and, on every one, the findings were more satisfactory for children living with their parents (Parsons 1910). While this may be one of the earlier outcome investigations, from at least the mid-1970s onwards there has been a plethora of research studies designed to assess outcomes of different parts of the service for children in need, particularly for those who are placed away from home.

From the 1980s onwards a growing body of research has demonstrated how the extensive developmental needs of children who become looked after are often ignored following admission to care or accommodation or are exacerbated by their subsequent experiences. Young people who have been brought up in the care system may experience inadequate health care, particularly when they have mental health needs (Bamford and Wolkind 1988; Butler and Payne 1997; Ward and Skuse 1999), and behavioural difficulties may deteriorate (Keane 1983; Sinclair and Gibbs 1998). Those looked after by local authorities are substantially less likely than their peers to leave school with educational qualifications, and substantially more likely to become homeless, become involved in prostitution or enter the prison population (Jackson 1989; Acheson 1998; Wade *et al.* 1998). They may lose contact with their families while in the care system (Milham *et al.* 1986) and, at eighteen or younger, they may be expected to cope with premature independence when most of their peers would expect to be supported by their families for several more years (Stein and Carey 1986; Stein 1990; Biehal *et al.* 1995). There is also evidence that a number of children who are placed away from home for their own protection, nevertheless continue to be abused while in the care of local authorities (Utting 1997; Waterhouse 2000).

A number of significant initiatives such as the Children (Leaving Care) Act 2000 and the accompanying *Regulations and Guidance* (Department of Health 2001d) and the *Guidance on the Education of Children in the Public Care* (Department of Health and Department for Education and Employment 2000) have been introduced to address particular issues raised by specific research studies. Yet sporadic research findings, however plentiful, are no substitute for routine monitoring of outcome for all children who receive a particular service. In its absence, there is no way of ascertaining which children with which needs are more (or less) likely to benefit from which interventions, or whether the needs of children are changing or the quality of interventions improving over time.

The implementation of the *Looking After Children* materials, and particularly the Assessment and Action Records, in almost all local authorities in England and Wales between 1996 and 1998, represented the first systematic attempt to introduce a routine method of outcome measurement into children's services, although it was restricted to those looked after away from home for substantial periods (Ward 1998; Jones *et al.* 1998). A subsequent programme of extensive consultation, auditing and further research has revealed weaknesses in the materials and in the process of implementation, which it is intended will be addressed when they are linked with the Assessment Framework Recording Forms (Department of Health and Cleaver 2000) and developed to form the Integrated Children's System (Chapter 14). However among the major findings from the current phase of research and development in this area are those which focus on the difficulties of obtaining time series data from *Looking After Children* (or indeed from other sources) of sufficient validity and reliability to produce viable comparisons. Quinton and Murray (Chapter 13) describe an initiative designed to improve the quality of data on the emotional and behavioural development of looked after children, gathered through the *Looking After Children* system. The prevalence of emotional and behavioural difficulties in this population is known to be high (McCann *et al.* 1996) and it is important to ascertain whether appropriate interventions are provided and if they are associated with improvement or deterioration. The absence of baseline information, together with the paucity of accurate, objective data make it well-nigh impossible to assess routinely the outcome of services in this area.

Since *Looking After Children* was launched in 1995, the information technology that can support the aggregation and analysis of data has greatly improved. Better technology has been behind ever increasing demands for local authorities to provide routine statistical returns to central government. Although criticised for its seeming obsession with measurement in the public sector, the New Labour government has introduced a number of initiatives that bring outcome assessment firmly into focus. The requirement for local authorities to demonstrate their performance on a number of child wellbeing indicators within the *Performance Assessment Framework*

(Department of Health 1999b) may appear onerous and can lead to numerous perverse incentives and other anomalies (see Ward and Skuse 2001). Nevertheless it has meant that local authorities are becoming more aware of issues of great significance to the children for whom they are responsible. When the requirement to produce data on educational outcomes for looked after children was first introduced only 30 per cent of authorities were able to provide the GCSE results for this population (Department of Health 1999c); now such ignorance is regarded as unacceptable. One of the major advances has been to relate the performance indicators to a number of identical government objectives for all children, regardless of whether they are looked after, otherwise in need, or living in the community (Department of Health 1999a). This has, for the first time, made it explicit that certain basic aspirations should be held for all children, and has done much to eradicate the remaining vestiges of the principle of less eligibility which, for so long, made it difficult to introduce measures designed to improve outcomes for this vulnerable population.

Part 1

Assessing the Needs of Populations of Children

CHAPTER TWO

Towards Social Inclusion

Can Childhood Disadvantages be Overcome?

Robert M. Page

This chapter charts the disadvantages that many children in the UK face in terms of income, health, education and housing. It also explores New Labour's approach to social inclusion and its attempts to devise effective policies to counter social exclusion. It is concluded that while many of New Labour's policies will undoubtedly improve the lives of poorer children, a broader egalitarian vision is needed if more far-reaching change is to be achieved.

Introduction

Following its landslide electoral success in 1997, the New Labour government placed great store by its desire to establish a more socially inclusive society:

> We seek a diverse but inclusive society, promoting tolerance within agreed norms, promoting civic activism as a complement to (but not a replacement for) modern government. An inclusive society imposes duties on individuals and parents as well as on society as a whole. (Blair 1998, p.12)

This chapter will focus first on the roots of social exclusion. What types of disadvantage are children exposed to and what are the consequences? Second, consideration will be given to New Labour's social inclusion strategy. Third, a brief and provisional assessment of this strategy will be offered.

Childhood disadvantage

Poverty

Unquestionably the major form of disadvantage that has blighted the lives of successive generations of children is poverty.

The economic position of children is inextricably linked to the financial situation of their parents or guardians. According to the *Households Below Average Income* (HBAI) statistical series (in which a household with below half average income is deemed to be poor) some 32 per cent of children were found to be in poverty in 1999/2000 compared with 10 per cent in 1968 and 12.6 per cent in 1979 (Department of Social Security 1997; 1998a; 1999a; 2001; Gregg, Harkness and Machin 1999). Certain groups of children are particularly likely to experience poverty. According to the 1999–2000 HBAI survey, children living in workless households (2 million), single parent families, larger family units or in a household headed by a member of an ethnic minority were markedly more likely to experience income deprivation (Department of Social Security 2001; Howarth *et al.* 1998). A similar picture emerges from New Labour's first Annual Report on poverty and social exclusion, *Opportunity for All* (Department of Social Security 1999b), in which children from the following types of household were identified as having a 50 per cent or greater possibility of being in *the bottom third of the income distribution*:

- larger families (4 or more children): 73%
- young mother (16 to 24): 68%
- ethnic minority family: 65%
- single mother family: 79%
- divorced/separated mother family: 66%
- parent(s) without educational qualifications: 54%.

This propensity to poverty is also demonstrated by the fact that children as a group are over-represented in the bottom fifth (25%) rather than the top fifth (14%) of the income distribution (Howarth *et al.* 1998, p.41; Joseph Rowntree Foundation 1995).

The fact that so many children live in poverty should not, as Middleton, Ashworth and Braithwaite (1997) make clear, lead one to conclude that parental neglect is a causal factor here. It merely reflects the extreme difficulty that adults living on means-tested social security benefits have in meeting even the most basic of their children's needs because of the inadequacy of state allowances. The failure of successive post-war governments to link benefit rates to any notion of adequacy (Veit Wilson 1994, 1998) has led to a situation in which claimants find it extremely difficult to achieve even a modest living standard (Piachaud 1979,1981; Oldfield and Yu 1993). Such households often have to rely on the financial support of relatives and friends in order to provide minimal support for their children. If these additional sources of support are unavailable, as is often the case in lone parent households, this deprivation is likely to be particularly acute.

The need to tackle childhood poverty is all the more crucial given the way in which it is linked to ill-health, poor housing and impaired educational development with all the consequent adverse effects these have later in life.

Ill-health and mortality

Despite the continued reduction in infant mortality in the post-1945 period, noticeable class divisions in relation to age-specific deaths and ill health in the case of children and young people persist (Townsend and Davidson 1982; Whitehead 1988; Shaw *et al.* 1999; Gordon *et al.* 1999). For example, low birthweight is associated with poorer health during early childhood, impaired physical and mental development and increased possibility of premature death from coronary heart disease (Carr-Hill 1990; Botting and Crawley 1995; Spencer 1996). The negative consequences associated with low birthweight are more likely to be borne by those in social classes IV and V. The incidence of low birthweight in these groups is some 25 per cent higher than in Classes I to III (see Macfarlane and Mugford 1984; Howarth *et al.* 1998, ch.2).

Children in the lowest social classes are also more likely to be under-nourished and have poorer diets than their better off peers. In addition there is evidence that poorer children are less likely to be immunised or screened for impaired sight or hearing (Blaxter 1981; Bennett and Smith 1992). Moreover, children from social classes IV and V are twice as likely to be the victims of accidents (which are responsible for 50% of all deaths amongst one to nineteen-year-olds) than those in Social Classes I to III. As Erskine (1996) has noted, the lack of safe play spaces for working class children makes this group particularly vulnerable to road traffic fatalities. Class factors are also a significant explanatory variable in relation to the disproportionately high death rate of poorer children from fire within the home. In poorer households the heating system is often intrinsically more unsafe and furnishings are less likely to be flame resistant (Gordon *et al.* 1999, p.53).

Of course it has been argued that the adverse situation of working class children is a reflection of poor parental knowledge or decision making rather than inadequate resources. It has been argued that if parents were properly informed about the dietary needs of their children they would purchase more 'nutritious' foodstuffs for them. However the purchasing decisions of many low-income parents can be defended. The decision to purchase biscuits rather than fruit for instance is perfectly understandable if one focuses on the need to maximise calorific intake and avoid waste. Moreover the apparent unwillingness to use preventative services can be better understood as a rational response to time and resource constraints. As Graham (1984) notes:

> Where money is short, the costs and benefits of any action must be carefully weighed. Where the costs, however marginally, outweigh the benefits, a mother cannot always afford to take advantage of health services for herself and her family. Even with a National Health Service, which is free at the time of use, the indirect costs can be prohibitive. (p.54)

It is clear that the disproportionately high levels of mortality and morbidity amongst poorer children can best be explained by adverse economic and social factors. A number of studies have confirmed the positive correlation between adverse social and economic conditions (such as unemployment and overcrowding) and various health indices such as higher standardised mortality rates and rates of sickness and low birthweight (Blackburn 1991; Whitehead 1988; Townsend, Phillimore and Beattie 1988; Phillimore, Beattie and Townsend 1994; Eames, Ben-Shlomo and Marmot 1993). Such an association is hardly surprising. Adults and children forced to subsist on low incomes in cramped sub-standard accommodation in neighbourhoods with few amenities are clearly vulnerable to episodes of ill-health (Best 1995; Benzeval and Webb 1995; Oppenheim and Harker 1996).

Finally, it should be noted that the health disadvantages of childhood carry over into adulthood. A poor health status in childhood is a good predictor of increased rates of adult morbidity and premature death. (Townsend and Davidson 1982; Acheson 1998; Shaw *et al.* 1999).

Education

Although there has been increased educational opportunity for poorer children in the post-1945 period, and this has led to some modest upward mobility, it remains the case that children from social classes IV and V tend to leave school earlier with fewer qualifications than those in classes I and II (Halsey, Heath and Judge 1980; Sanderson 1999). As a result they run the risk of insecure and low-paid employment with the consequent probability of poverty in later life (Atkinson and Hills 1998). Moreover in a study by Gregg, Harkness and Machin (1999) a clear link was found between adverse childhood experiences and poor educational outcome. As the authors note:

> Educational attainment by age 23 is very strongly related to childhood factors, and children growing up in relatively disadvantaged situations have strikingly worse levels of educational attainment, even taking account of ability at age 7. As such, education plays a potentially important role as a transmission mechanism, underpinning the link between childhood development and economic success or failure as an adult. (pp.24 and 26)

More generally, the financial barriers to continued study (lack of proper financial support for 16 to 18-year-olds and the introduction of student loans and tuition fees) continue to limit educational opportunity for poorer children.

Given that structural changes in the labour market have made it even more important to obtain appropriate academic and vocational qualifications in order to secure reasonably well paid work, it is disconcerting to find that around 220,000 students still leave school each year with no GCSEs above grade D.

The number of fixed term (around 100,000 a year) and permanent exclusions (12,500 in 1995–96) from school also exacerbates this problem, not least because children subjected to this sanction often fail to return to mainstream schooling (see Donovan 1998). According to a report by the Social Exclusion Unit (1998a) these exclusions are:

- rising most quickly in the primary sector (up by 18% in 1995–96)
- disproportionately high amongst black pupils (six times more likely), children in care (ten times more likely) and those with statements of special education need (six times more likely)

- heavily concentrated in particular areas (the rate in Hammersmith and Fulham is six times greater than in Oxfordshire)
- linked to juvenile crime.

Poorer children have also gained little from the changes made to the education system by the Conservatives during the 1980s. Increasing levels of school autonomy and parental choice often resulted in an intensification of disadvantage. Middle class exit from neighbourhood schools has resulted in an ever-greater concentration of poorer children in schools with inadequate resource levels in relation to their needs (Halsey *et al.* 1997).

Housing

Poorer children are also likely to be living in unsatisfactory forms of accommodation. For example, according to the 1991 census, some 1.3 million children live in densely occupied households (i.e. more than one person per room). In addition, some 43,000 children live in households where there is enforced sharing of a basic amenity such as a bath or toilet with another family. Moreover, according to Dorling (1993), some 25,000 children are living in non-permanent forms of accommodation such as a mobile home or a caravan. Even when poorer children reside in permanent accommodation they are more likely to be found on unpopular 'sink' estates with few amenities (Power 1987).

Although it is difficult to gain an accurate figure of homelessness in Britain, it is estimated that nearly 200,000 children a year experience the involuntary loss of their home. Over half (57.2%) of all the 100,000 households accepted as homeless in 1997 contained children. Child homelessness has been linked to impaired physical and mental development, poor health, behavioural and mental health problems and adverse educational consequences (Daniel and Ivatts 1998, ch.5). For example, in a study of mental health, Vostanis *et al.* (1996) found that 30 per cent of the children living in a Midlands hostel for homeless families displayed a mental health problem that warranted a social services referral. In terms of the school environment homeless children often find it difficult to make and retain friendships or participate fully in the life of the school. They often lack adequate space to complete homework and find it difficult to progress in their studies because of the frequent need to move school (Power, Whitty and Youdell 1995).

Disadvantaged young people are particularly prone to homelessness. They often lack the resources to rent accommodation and find themselves excluded from council house tenancies. Many local authorities will not lease properties to those aged under 21 (Howarth *et al.* 1998). In addition, young people leaving care have a one in five chance of becoming homeless within the following two years (Department of Social Security 1999b, p.71).

The disadvantages and prospects for looked after children are particularly worthy of note. It is estimated that 26 per cent of looked after children have a statement of special educational need compared with around 3 per cent in the general population. Around 25 per cent of looked after children aged between 14 and 16 do not attend school regularly; 70 per cent fail to obtain any educational qualifications; 67 per cent have an identifiable mental health problem (Department of Social Security 1999b; Department of Health 2001e). It comes as no surprise that the Government White Paper *Modernising Social Services* (Department of Health 1998a) concluded that 'the life chances of children in care are unacceptably low, with poor opportunities while in care and low chances of successful settled lives once they leave care' (para. 3,31, p.57).

More generally, it is clear that the various childhood disadvantages discussed so far lead to further difficulties later in the life cycle. Children who fail to obtain formal qualifications will find it increasingly difficult to obtain paid work. At present, around 30 per cent of working men without formal qualifications are economically inactive. Consequent periods of unemployment are likely to have an adverse effect on family relationships and long-term health. In terms of the former it has been estimated that 'marriage break-up is 75% more common' for those out of work than for those with a secure job (Howarth *et al.* 1998, p.93). In the case of health, those who are long-term unemployed are 50 per cent more likely to die of lung cancer and respiratory diseases than those who are in secure employment. Such individuals also have a heightened susceptibility both to bouts of depression (27% of unemployed people have reported feeling depressed or anxious compared with 14% in a salaried job) and suicide. Moreover adult homeless people aged between 45 and 64 will experience mortality rates 25 times higher than the national average (Howarth *et al.* 1998, p.107).

Towards social inclusion

The fact that post-1945 welfare reforms have only played a modest role in countering some of these disadvantages (Le Grand 1982; Page 1991; Glennerster 1995) naturally raises questions about the extent to which government intervention can bring about positive change in these areas. However the New Labour government is convinced that purposeful, well-targeted forms of intervention can play a key part in tackling long-standing forms of disadvantage. For example, Peter Mandelson (1997), one of the key architects of the New Labour project, argued that a fresh approach would have a positive effect:

> One challenge above all stands out...tackling the scourge and waste of social exclusion. It is this area where the case against the Tories was most telling. It is this area where Labour can show how we are different and prove that we can make a difference. (p.6)

Since its success at the May 1997 general election, New Labour has signalled its desire to create a more inclusive society. Importantly, New Labour does not believe that a return to the redistributionist welfare strategy of 'classic' post-1945 social democracy can create an inclusive society (Page 1999). As the party's 1997 general election manifesto made clear:

> In each area of policy a new and distinctive approach has been mapped out that differs from the solutions of the old left. We believe in the strength of our values, but we recognise also that the policies of 1997 cannot be those of 1947 or 1967. (Labour Party 1997, p.3)

In terms of economic policy, New Labour has sought to dissociate itself from the laissez faire approach of New Right Conservatism and the overt egalitarianism of classic social democracy. For New Labour, a modern government must acknowledge the dynamism of global economic forces, which has given rise to increased deregulation and a shift from manufacturing to service sector employment. In this changed environment circumspect forms of intervention are seen as more appropriate. While New Labour has signed up for the EU Social Chapter, introduced a 'competitive' minimum wage and increased the level of employment protection, it has proved unwilling to introduce egalitarian regulatory and financial regimes, which are seen as a burden, rather than a necessary restraint on enterprise.

In terms of social policy, New Labour believes that the post-war welfare state has proved to be not only structurally deficient and producer-dominated but also economically and socially regressive. Like the Commission on Social Justice, New Labour believes there is now a need for an 'intelligent' welfare state more suited to current circumstances:

> Instead of a welfare state designed for old risks, old industries and old family structures, there is a need for an intelligent welfare state that will be active throughout our lives, helping people to negotiate unpredictable change at work and home. Instead of a safety net to relieve poverty, we need a social security system that can help to prevent poverty. Instead of a health service designed primarily to treat illness, we need a health policy whose priority is to promote better health. In other words, the welfare state must not only look after people when they cannot look after themselves; it must also enable them to achieve self-improvement and self-support. The welfare state must offer a hand-up rather than a handout. (Commission on Social Justice 1994, pp.223–224)

The dramatic shift in traditional employment and family patterns has led New Labour to undertake a rethink on underlying welfare principles as well as policy (Halpern and Mikosz 1998). For example, New Labour now accepts that ever rising levels of public spending are potentially damaging for economic prosperity (Layard 1997). Moreover New Labour has also accepted that traditional state welfare provision can have adverse effects on both individuals and communities. For example, Frank Field (1995), who served briefly as Minister for Social Reform in the first New Labour government, wanted to reform the social security system because its administrative structures tended to encourage claimants to act 'dishonestly'. Concerns have also been raised about welfare providers, who have been criticised for failing to provide services of a sufficiently high standard (Piachaud 1991; Meadows 1996; Wright 1996). Like others, New Labour also highlights the fact that the classic welfare state has failed to meet one of its prime objectives: the creation of a more equal society (Le Grand 1982; Glennerster 1995).

Although New Labour's welfare strategy is still evolving, it can already be distinguished from previous approaches (Giddens 1998; Driver and Martell 1998; Blair 1998; Powell 1999). Crucially, it makes no pretence to pursue equality of *outcome* though it is determined to ensure that there is far greater equality of *opportunity*. As Gordon Brown has stated:

> Predetermined results imposed, as they would have to be, by a central authority and decided irrespective of work, effort or contribution to the community, is not a socialist dream but other people's nightmare of socialism.
>
> It denies humanity rather than liberates it. It is to make people something they are not, rather than helping them to make the most of what they can be. What people resent about Britain is not that some people who have worked hard have done well. What angers people is that millions have been denied the opportunity to realise their potential and are powerless to do so. It is this inequality that must be addressed. (Brown 1999, p.42)

New Labour also wishes to restore the link between social rights and responsibilities and to promote a greater degree of public and private co-operation. Moreover, successful reform is deemed to be dependent more on organisational and cultural change rather than higher levels of public spending.

For New Labour, increased levels of opportunity and participation are vital if a fairer society is to be created. The establishment of a Social Exclusion Unit in December 1997, located in the Cabinet Office, attests to New Labour's determination to develop effective policies to counter long-standing disadvantage by ensuring that all citizens can play a full part in society. This is to be achieved by the provision of effective education and training opportunities; better targeted benefit and tax policies; the regeneration of run down neighbourhoods and communities; increased opportunities for participation; and the development of better functioning social networks (6, Perri 1997). Crucially, inclusionary policies of this kind are seen as vital to improve the position of children and young people. In a speech at Toynbee Hall in March 1999, the Prime Minister set out a twenty year programme, involving a mixture of universalist and selectivist measures, to eradicate child poverty and tackle associated problems such as poor educational performance, truancy, youth crime and teenage pregnancies (Blair 1999).

New Labour has recognised that its attack on childhood disadvantage must include policies that improve the position of parents as well as children. Various forms of support are being offered to poorer parents. For example, efforts are being made to ensure that poor parents have both the opportunity and incentive to return to the labour market through the introduction of the minimum wage and the Working Families Tax Credit (WFTC) which incorporates a childcare element. It is estimated that families receiving WFTC in 2000/01 will receive an additional £31 per week on average under this scheme compared with the former Family Credit scheme (Department of Social Security 2000). Moreover the real value of child benefit (payable to all families) has increased by 26 per cent compared with the position in 1997, while the weekly allowance for children payable to recipients of Income Support has also increased significantly. A couple with two children under 11 is nearly £30 per week better off than they would have been in 1997.

New Labour recognises that increased labour market participation necessitates an improvement in the supply of childcare. As part of its National Childcare Strategy some £470 million has been earmarked for the development of 'out of school childcare, after-hours clubs, literacy schemes and kids' clubs' (The Government's Annual Report 97/98, p.61). In addition, as part of its *Supporting Families* initiative (Home Office 1998), New Labour has introduced a National Family and Parenting Institute, a national parenting helpline and a Sure Start programme. Established in April 1999, the Sure Start programme will provide various health and support services to families with young children (under fours) living in deprived neighbourhoods throughout the UK. By 2004 some 500 programmes of this kind will be operating (Department of Social Security 2000).

New Labour believes that poor or inadequate schooling is a major contributor to adult social exclusion. Given that social class disparities in educational development emerge so rapidly, New Labour is determined to provide enhanced educational opportunities for disadvantaged families at the earliest possible stage. To this end a guaranteed free nursery education place for every four-year-old has been introduced. Moreover all schools will be expected to ensure that large proportions of their pupils have attained national standards in numeracy and literacy by the age of eleven. The introduction of a literacy hour and a daily mathematics lesson in primary schools from 1999 is intended to ensure that there is a realistic chance of meeting these targets.

A Standards and Effectiveness Unit has been established to improve educational performance whilst a National Schools Standards Task Force has been formed to deal with 'failing schools'. Moreover initiatives such as Education Action Zones and Excellence in Cities (launched in 1999 to transform education performance in major cities) are intended to raise educational standards in a number of deprived areas. Efforts are also being taken to ensure that exclusions and truancy levels are reduced, including investment of £140 million through the Standards Fund grant, which provides schools with funds to tackle the behavioural problems of pupils (Department of Social Security 2000).

New Labour is also determined to improve the situation of school leavers entering the world of work. Their five-year *New Deal for Young People* programme is aimed specifically at improving the employability of young people (18–24) who have been out of work for six months or more (those with a special need such as literacy difficulties can join the scheme earlier, Convery 1997). Under this scheme, which was introduced in April 1998, young people are expected, following preliminary guidance and advice, to undertake subsidised employment, full-time education or training (which will enhance their employment prospects), or work with an environmental taskforce or a voluntary sector organisation. By the end of June 1999 'over 300,000 young people had joined the programme and 123,000 of these had entered jobs (91,000 had been working for 13 weeks or more). (Department of Social Security 1999b, p.86)

New Labour has also expressed concern about the numbers of teenage pregnancies and births in the UK, which are now the highest in Western Europe (Social Exclusion Unit 1999, 2001). In 1997 nearly 90,000 teenage women became pregnant of whom 7700 were aged under 16. Early pregnancy can be both a cause and a consequence of social exclusion. Young women from social class V are ten times more likely to become teenage parents than their social class I peers. In addition women who have been brought up in care or accommodation are two and a half times more likely to become teenage mothers than those who lived with their natural parents (Social Exclusion Unit 1999). Given that early motherhood is linked with a vast array of adverse life circumstances such as low income, poor job prospects and relationship breakdowns, New Labour is aiming to halve the rate of conceptions amongst under-eighteen-year-olds by 2010. The attainment of this goal is deemed to necessitate not just improved health and contraceptive provision for all teenagers (such as the appointment of area-based teenage pregnancy co-ordinators), but also the development of attractive 'diversionary' policies such as high quality education and training so that labour market opportunities are enhanced.

New Labour is also keen to improve the life chances of looked after children, who have been one of the most neglected groups since the establishment of the post-1945 welfare state. As part of its Quality Protects initiative, a concerted attempt is being made to improve provision for vulnerable children and young people. In the case of looked after children, New Labour is encouraging local education authorities and social services departments to collaborate more closely to ensure that the educational and health needs of this group are addressed. Moreover in their White Paper on the modernisation of social services (Department of Health 1998a), it was stipulated that 'public care services must be improved in order to help looked after young people move into fulfilling independent lives in as stable a fashion as possible' (para. 3.39, p.60). Under the Children (Leaving Care) Act 2000, those leaving care must have a 'pathway to independence' plan and better support, particularly in relation to their accommodation needs. National performance indicators have been developed to ensure that local authorities meet their obligations in this regard. Much of the work on needs assessment described particularly in Chapters 4, 8 and 13 is designed to improve outcomes for all children in need, including those looked after by local authorities.

New Labour also believes that community initiatives are necessary in order to tackle social exclusion. It contends that successful regeneration requires enhanced community involvement in decision making and service provision at the local level (Social Exclusion Unit 1998b, 2001). New Labour's *New Deal for Communities* in England aims 'to regenerate the most deprived areas through improving job prospects, reducing crime, improving educational attainment and reducing poor health' (Department of Social Security 1999b, p.148). Importantly, New Labour is persuaded of the idea that even relatively modest initiatives, for instance the introduction of measures instigated by the community to reduce problems such as litter or speeding traffic can do much to improve the quality of life for residents in disadvantaged areas (see Forrest and Kearns 1999).

Green shoots?

Given New Labour's relatively short time in government it is premature to offer any definitive conclusions about their progress in countering childhood disadvantage. However, it is possible to make some preliminary observations. In its second annual report on poverty and social exclusion, *Opportunity for All – One Year On: Making a Difference* (Department of Social Security 2000), the New Labour government highlighted some of the positive developments that could be linked to their first term policies

(1997–2001). For example, as a result of the various changes to the tax and benefits system, some 1.2 million children have been lifted out of poverty (defined as above 60% of median income after housing costs) since 1997 (see also Bradshaw 2001b; Piachaud and Sutherland 2001). Although it might prove difficult to match this achievement in subsequent years as attempts are made to help some of the more acutely disadvantaged families, New Labour's aim to abolish child poverty within 20 years is well on course. Moreover some of the proposals highlighted in the party's manifesto for the June 2001 election, *Ambitions for Britain* (Labour Party 2001), such as the integrated child credit scheme (which is due to come on stream in 2003) and the Child Trust Fund, which will provide government sponsored endowments favouring poorer children (see Nissan and Le Grand 2000), suggest that New Labour is determined to achieve real change in this area.

The New Labour government can also point to positive changes in other areas. For example, in 2000 over 70 per cent of eleven-year-olds were achieving level 4 or above in Key Stage 2 tests for literacy (75%) and numeracy (72%) compared with 63 per cent and 62 per cent respectively in 1997. The introduction of Education Maintenance Allowances in fifteen pilot areas in 1999 also appears to be improving the staying-on rate of children from low income households. School exclusions are declining (down from 0.17% of pupils in 1996/97 to 0.14% in 1998/99) while the participation rate of teenage parents in education, employment or training is improving. Finally, although it is too early to assess the impact of initiatives such as Sure Start, it is clear that the Government is keen to ensure that its various initiatives are closely monitored and that its record of achievement or otherwise is available for critically scrutiny (see Bradshaw 2001b).

Conclusion

New Labour's positive commitment to social inclusion is likely to result in some improvement in the position of disadvantaged children in the immediate future and beyond. However, the new government's determination to distance itself from the more overt forms of egalitarianism associated with previous post-war Labour governments leaves it vulnerable to the charge that it is more concerned with preventing the emergence of a dispossessed 'underclass' than the pursuit of a more wide-ranging form of social justice. Given its success in gaining the electoral support of the middle classes in two general elections, New Labour has been keen to pursue policies which resonate with aspirational citizens who live in communities such as Woking in Surrey, identified by leading strategist Philip Gould (1998) as 'neither privileged nor deprived' (p.46). The fact that such a strategy will not lead to a more equitable distribution of resources in society (Reich 1999) is unproblematic for those New Labour supporters who are more concerned with ensuring that citizens receive equal respect rather than equal incomes. For example, Kellner (1999) believes that the attainment of income equality is a far less important objective than goals such as political and civic equality, good access to key services, the abolition of poverty, or the ending of gender and ethnic discrimination. Indeed, it appears that New Labour's strategy of social inclusion is intended to produce a contented, meritocratic society (Collins 2001) in which those who prosper should be able to enjoy the fruits of their success without a sense of guilt.

Whether New Labour will be successful in creating a climate of contentment amongst the less advantaged is more difficult to predict. Certainly, the introduction of minimum standards coupled with opportunities for personal advancement and community participation could engender feelings of social inclusion, especially if this leads to a marked increase in social mobility. However, New Labour's unwillingness to tackle the growing disparity in income and wealth in British society (Goodman, Johnson and Webb 1997) or the institutions that sustain it such as private schools (Brighouse 2000) suggests that there is limited prospect of greater mobility. If New Labour is really determined to create a fairer society for future generations of children, it will need to adopt a much more robust approach to the more fundamental causes of the inequalities that continue to blight British society.

CHAPTER THREE

A Framework for Conceptualising Need and its Application to Planning and Providing Services

Pauline Hardiker

with Brian Atkins, Mary Barker, Sue Brunton-Reed, Kenneth Exton, Mary Perry and Mike Pinnock

This chapter outlines a framework for conceptualising need in child welfare services. First formulated in 1989 in a feasibility study for the Department of Health, the framework (or Grid) has subsequently been developed through a variety of dissemination and developmental activities in the child welfare community. Examples are outlined of the ways in which four local authorities have used the Grid in planning and providing services during the 1990s. Work using the Grid continues.

Introduction

This chapter argues that *need* is a multi-dimensional and contested concept. Need is, therefore, used in different ways to make political claims (Fraser 1989). One way of exploring these is to examine need in the context of social policies. A broad framework for conceptualising need is outlined alongside ways in which it has been used in planning and providing children's services.

Original purpose of the Grid

Figure 3.1 outlines a framework which locates different dimensions of children's services. This is the fifteenth version of the Grid that has been developed through dissemination and developmental activities in the child welfare community (Hardiker, Exton and Barker 1991a, 1991b, 1996; Hardiker 1997). A *brief* exposition of the Grid follows.

The Enabling Authority

LEVEL OF INTERVENTION	WELFARE MODEL: ROLE OF THE STATE		
	Last Resort Safety Net	Addressing Needs	Combating Social Disadvantage
BASE (populations)			
FIRST (vulnerable groups and communities: diversion)			Community Development
SECOND (early stresses)		Social Casework / Social Care Planning	
THIRD (severe stresses)	Remedial Interventions		
FOURTH (social breakdown: 'in care')			

Figure 3.1 The Social Policy Contexts of Social Welfare
© University of Leicester School of Social Work: Gridlocks (1997)

Models of welfare (horizontal axis)

The value systems which legitimate welfare interventions may be understood in relation to the role of the state:

- In a *last resort* approach, the state is given a minimal role in welfare as the needs of children are not seen to be its proper business until situations reach damaging levels. This approach is one of surveillance and control in which children are rescued and parents punished. The Poor Law (1834) encapsulated this approach, which also becomes manifest if family support services are not developed in line with the enabling philosophies of the Children Act 1989. If children are placed in care or accommodation because of child protection concerns but no work is undertaken with them and their families, this is a latter-day version of last resort.
- The welfare state developed as a major institution to *address needs*: social science and professional knowledge recognised a wide range of psychosocial needs; the normality of stresses in rearing children in a complex, multi-cultural society plus life transitions and vulnerabilities are acknowledged; services aim to reintegrate children and families into society rather than to rescue children and punish parents. Family support services are given a high profile.
- *Combating social disadvantages* is a bolder approach to needs; problems are located in social structures and social policies rather than solely in the circumstances of individual families; the state is given a proactive role in child welfare through corporate strategies in relation to anti-poverty, safer cities and urban regeneration.

Levels of intervention (vertical axis)

These levels address different stages in problem development and targets for intervention. In the history of health care and child welfare, needs have been interpreted in relation to prevention. The 'what' of prevention is conceptualised in health care through three levels:

- primary – prevent disease arising in the first place
- secondary – provide help once problems have arisen
- tertiary – avoid the worst consequences of treatment, or chronic/terminal illness.

Hardiker *et al.* (1991b) used the term 'levels of intervention' rather than 'prevention'. Five levels have been subsequently identified (Hardiker 1997):

1. The *base* level identifies needs in the general population for whom universal services are provided. The ideology of the British welfare state claimed that universal services could prevent many needs developing at subsequent levels (Hardiker 1997). Children's services managers find the base level a useful distinction as it avoids the confusion with primary care as used by health professionals. It is essential to remove this confusion if the Grid is to be used between agencies as a model for mapping services. It is also a reminder that social services departments typically prioritise their *direct* services at second and subsequent levels of intervention. Nevertheless, the retraction of base level services generates needs for significant groups at subsequent levels. Changes in political economy in the 1980s and 1990s produced increased fragmentation of services for children and families through education and NHS reforms plus changes in social security and housing policies (Sutton 1995, 1997); this was reflected in rising numbers of school exclusions and youth homelessness As Robert Page has argued (Chapter 2) the present Labour government is attempting to reverse these trends through its base level social policies such as the Working Families Tax Credit, the New Deal, and a number of education and welfare reforms.
2. *First levels* target vulnerable groups and communities through programmes such as Sure Start: families are diverted from social services departments and enabled to use universal and community-based resources wherever possible. It is important for community facilities to be well-publicised and accessible.
3. *Second levels* address early stresses and families in temporary crisis through short-term, task-centred interventions and resources; children 'in need' appear here. The aim is to restore personal and

social functioning so that direct social services interventions are no longer required.

4. *Third levels* address serious stresses including the risks of significant harm, family breakdown and entry into the looked after system; difficulties may be acute or well-established. The aim is to mitigate the effects and to restore family functioning and 'good enough' parenting.

5. *Fourth levels* cover a diverse group of issues: social breakdown, children looked after, children abused within the care system; methods include therapy, damage limitation and permanency planning. Some authorities divide this level into two, distinguishing between rehabilitation and permanent substitute care.

The diagonal

The diagonal demonstrates how models of welfare and levels of intervention must be considered together. The value base of a service indicates the preferred level of intervention: last resort/third level, combating social disadvantages/first level. These in turn indicate specific welfare approaches:

- first level – community development
- second level – social casework and social care planning
- third level – remedial interventions.

As Mike Pinnock and Louise Garnett argue in Chapter 4, in areas of structural disadvantage, such as Britain's largest cities, prioritising early level services exposes large scales of unmet needs. This calls for robust corporate and community development strategies to combat social disadvantages through base and first level services for vulnerable populations.

Children's services workers readily grasp and use the levels axis of the Grid but sometimes struggle over the models of welfare; debates about the latter often take place in council chambers and community forums. The diagonal makes the links between policy, practice and politics imperative and explicit.

The enabling authority

There has always been a mixed economy of social care in child welfare: the state, the market, voluntary and not-for-profit organisations and informal carers provided services, albeit in different proportions, over many centuries. The mixed economy gained prominence in the Thatcher years and is being promoted by the current Labour administration. History reminds us that this is not new. Bright's factory in Rochdale opened the first and largest privately-run day nursery in the world in 1887 (Catlow and Cole 1992). This nursery was acquired by the social services department in the 1970s, and became the site of a famous NSPCC project in child protection (Dale *et al.* 1986).

Contested needs

As the concept of need is used in political contexts, child welfare services are often seen to meet contrasting interests. For example, childcare provision for young children is seen to serve contrasting needs by different groups (Fraser 1989):

- the needs for enrichment and moral supervision for poor children
- the needs of taxpayers to remove mothers from welfare rolls
- the needs of employers to increase productivity
- the need to redistribute income and resources to women
- the need to provide respite to families under stress.

The vested interests of feminist, welfare and children's rights groups, business, trades unions and educationalists are clearly recognisable.

The Enabling Authority

LEVEL OF INTERVENTION	NEEDS		
	Basic Survival	Psychosocial	Structural
BASE (populations)			
FIRST (vulnerable groups and communities: diversion)			Community Development
SECOND (early stresses)		Social Casework Social Care Planning	
THIRD (severe stresses)	Remedial Interventions		
FOURTH (social breakdown: 'in care')			

Figure 3.2 Needs and Levels of Interventions

Different types of needs are contested under different models of welfare (Figure 3.2). The 1834 Poor Law reforms adopted a safety net approach in relation to *basic survival* needs. The principle of less eligibility illustrated this precisely:

> The situation of the relief recipient on the whole shall not be made really or apparently so eligible (i.e. desirable) as the situation of the independent labourer of the lowest class. (Poor Law Commissioners 1834: p.228)

The workhouse was held out as a threat to able-bodied applicants for relief with the aims of reducing destitution, pauperism and costs. This was contested. In the north of England, and Rochdale in particular, the Act was reacted to with horror, fierce resistance and mass protest (Catlow and Cole 1992). Political representations were made and government commissioners visited the town demanding the construction of a single Union workhouse to replace the existing, more informal arrangements. It was not until 1877 that a single Union workhouse was built. This workhouse subsequently became a hospital under different administrations. The author (Pauline Hardiker) and most of her family were born there, and many of them were treated for illnesses or died there.

The welfare state began to address a wide range of *psychosocial and structural needs* through social security, health, education, employment and housing policies. The concept of need in contemporary children's and community care legislation is used partly as a lever to ration resources and stem broader interpretations (Hardiker and Barker 1999). Need in child protection has also been contested through the threshold requirements of risk and significant harm (Seden, Hardiker and Barker 1996). Need has also been used developmentally to promote corporate strategies in services for disabled children and young people (Hardiker 1999).

Structural needs take us to one forefront of welfare provisions which aim to combat social disadvantages. Corporate strategies in local authorities are an obvious site where the boundaries of these needs are contested. The *mixed economy of welfare* is a site of contest, where the respective roles of the family, the state and the market are regularly negotiated.

Using the Grid in children's services planning

The Grid is a framework for exploring issues in relation to needs; it is not prescriptive. The Grid should never be used like a stencil because it must be related to local contexts and mandates. These typologies are theoretically elementary and provide initial stages in analyses. Each concept should be developed further (Doyal and Gough 1991; Plant, Lesser and Taylor-Gooby 1980; Ware and Goodin 1990). Nevertheless, as children's services manager Mike Pinnock observed, '...its beauty lies in its simple utility'. Though need is a contested concept, this does not mean that it is unusable in theory or practice. Set out below are examples of the diverse and flexible ways in which the Grid has been used in children's services planning.

North Lincolnshire Council

Level	Description	Examples
Universal provision	Services which are available to all childcarers regardless of the existence of problems.	Ordinary school provision, the sensitive design of play areas and pedestrian areas, local authority housing, church and religious groups.
Primary provision	Services which exist to prevent problems arising in families. Action to reduce the need for formal intervention.	Immunisation programmes, playgroups, advice bureaux, community centres.
Secondary provision	Early identification of and action to resolve problems, intervention aimed at speedily restoring non-client status.	Sponsored playgroup placements, GP services, 'Well person' clinics, day centres, Homestart services.
Third level provision	Action to prevent the worst effects of established chronic welfare problems. Action to prevent clients from being drawn into increasingly intrusive and damaging interventions.	Special needs education, acute hospital services, child protection services, Homestart services.
Fourth level provision	Action to restore separated families.	Social work services, community support teams.
Fifth level provision	Action to prevent damage arising from long-term substitute care. Permanency planning.	Adoption services, post-adoption services, leaving care services.

Figure 3.3 Children's Services Plan 1998–2000
Developed from Policies and Practices in Preventive Child Care Hardiker, Exton & Barker 1991

Figure 3.3 outlines a version of the Grid, which introduces base level universal services for populations plus the distinction coined by Northamptonshire County Council between fourth and fifth level provision (see below). This Grid maps and illustrates service provision at six levels of intervention. It shows ways in which the needs of children are indivisible and interdependent; this makes an inter-agency approach to services imperative. The social services directorate tends to provide services from second to fifth levels and plans to improve provision at the second level. This is in line with refocusing initiatives, based on a broad hypothesis that improved provision at earlier levels may eventually reduce the need for services at subsequent ones (see Ward and Peel, Chapter 10).

The Grid has been used in this authority to introduce the idea to practitioners and managers that family support should be seen as a broad-based activity. Seen in these terms, family support can range from those formal and informal networks that are universal and, therefore, available to the whole community through to those services that are highly specialised and exist to benefit a relatively small proportion of the community. This inclusive conceptualisation of family support has encouraged staff to see different family support services as complementary rather than competing, contradictory or duplicating.

Managers find the Grid to be an extremely effective way of exploring the role and purpose of family support resources with teams in staff training sessions. These teams have been encouraged to locate the value base of their service by using the three contrasting models of welfare on the horizontal axis. The Grid has been used in these sessions as a floor game – rather like the game of 'Twister'. Staff have been encouraged to plot themselves on the Grid. This has proved to be an illuminating (and memorable!) exercise.

The diagonal has been used by managers to demonstrate how the existing resources of agencies are distributed and how they might be realigned as part of the authority's refocusing initiatives. By thinking of family support in this way, managers and elected members are encouraged to see promotional and protective services not as competing claims on the agencies' scarce resources but as complementary activities, targeted at needs-based subgroups within the local population.

More recently, the Grid has been used to map management information needs. Putting the levels of intervention down the vertical axis and the dimensions of management information across the horizontal has allowed staff to draw a picture of the strengths and weaknesses of their existing information systems against the different levels of intervention (see Pinnock and Garnett, Chapter 4). This plan is embedded in a social policy context, which identifies government themes relevant to child welfare: social exclusion, education, safer communities, healthy lifestyles and supporting family life. This provides a common agenda for inter-agency work. This agenda is further underpinned by values enshrined in the UN Convention on the Rights of the Child and local policy and democratic forums. In this authority, the use of the Grid is linked to a robust approach to the identification of need and strategic planning (see Pinnock and Garnett, Chapter 4).

Nottinghamshire County Council

This Council explicitly used the levels of intervention framework in developing its family support strategy. The need to develop a continuum of services between all levels was stressed, highlighting their functions in relation to promotion, safeguarding and rehabilitation plus the importance of balancing universal and targeted provision.

Age/stage of Child	**LEVEL 1**	**LEVEL 2**		**LEVEL 3**	**LEVEL 4**
	Universal Needs of Parents/ Carers	**Common Difficulties / Nneeds**	**Services /Advice**	**Specialist /Advice**	**In Care**
Pre-conception					
Before birth					
Post-natal care					
Pre-school (1–4 yrs)					
5–8 yrs					
9–12 yrs					
13–18 yrs					
Transition: school/work					

Figure 3.4 Family Support Strategy

One aspect of the ongoing work of the inter-agency family support strategy illustrates another creative use of the Grid: a life cycle approach in relation to levels of intervention (Figure 3.4). This had the positive result of providing a common, usable language for diverse agencies in relation to the meaning of family support. It also enabled the roles and responsibilities of different agencies to be clarified in relation to the respective levels of intervention and co-ordination issues; this highlighted the need for developments at earlier levels of intervention. A focus for work was identified in relation to support for parents and carers rather than services for children per se. Early discussions focused on sharing understandings and mapping current service provision. Current work focuses on specific targets and actions. The Grid provided a useful starting point for the work of this group; once underway, they no longer needed such a framework.

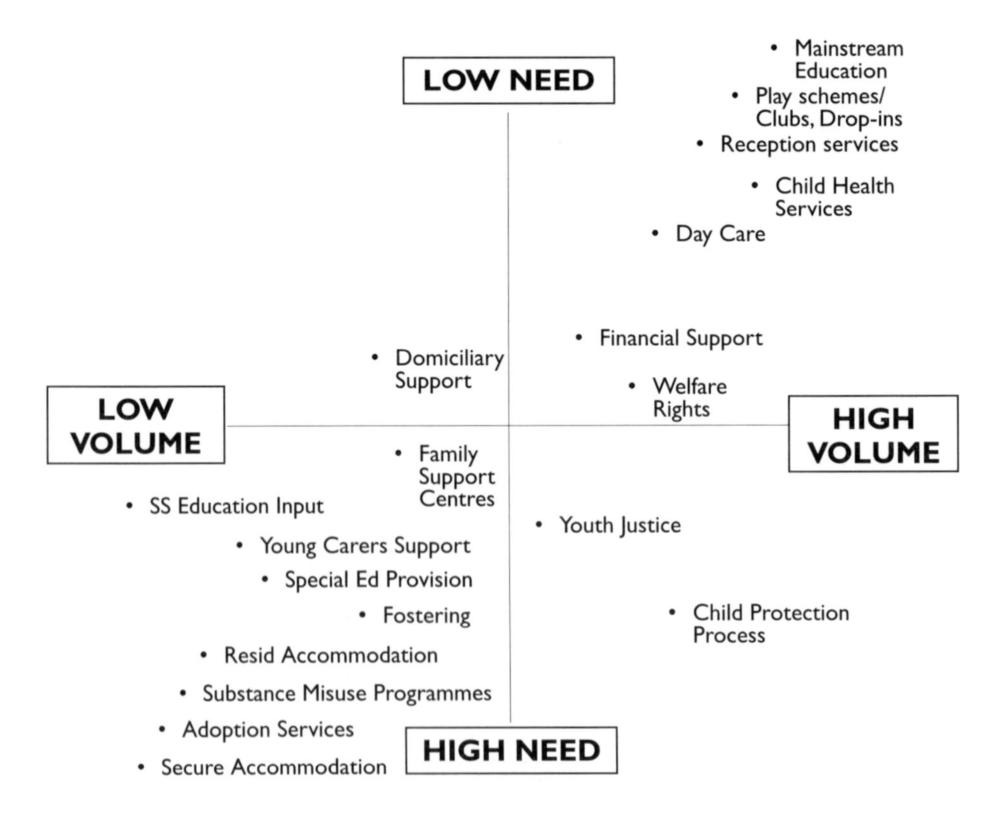

Figure 3.5 East Midlands/Report to ADSS, 1997

Members of the social services department participated in an East Midlands Project (Association of Directors of Social Services 1997). This group found contrasts between participating agencies in relation to their preferences about levels and targets of intervention. The group undertook an exercise relating resources to needs and volume, producing a matrix in relation to budget allocation and need (Figure 3.5). This indicated the possibility of a trade-off in resource allocation such as shifts in the balance between low volume/high cost and high volume/low cost services. These shifts are obviously not straightforward, particularly in the short term, and resources provided by other agencies need to be added to the equation. This kind of matrix could be usefully considered in relation to the Grid.

Northamptonshire County Council

Northamptonshire County Council was associated with the development of the Grid from its earliest days (Hardiker *et al.* 1991a). Its professional assignment groups focused on the value base of the service which legitimated interventions in discussion with political interest groups in the authority. The Grid was used to locate the boundaries of interventions. For example, one function of review panels was seen in terms of controlling the psychosocial variables presented by practitioners. Limits were thus placed around broad need interpretations.

Level of Intervention	Child Welfare	Child Protection	Youth Justice
1. Diversion			
2. Early Risks			
3. Serious Risks			
4. Rehabilitation			
5. Permanence			

Figure 3.6 The Monitoring and Information Framework
©Northamptonshire County Council, SSD

This authority used the Grid flexibly to develop a framework for planning and monitoring children's services (Figure 3.6). The fourth level of intervention was divided into two: rehabilitation and permanent substitute care. The horizontal axis distinguishes between child welfare, child protection and youth justice contexts. Thorpe's research examined rates of diversion from child protection and youth justice to child welfare (Thorpe *et al.* 1998).

Clarity about the purposes of local authority social services departments is stressed, given restricted resources and higher expectations of the quality of public services. This is epitomised in directives regarding a more business-like approach to children's service planning. The Grid is a useful tool for enabling the authority to set its objectives and to monitor outcomes on case and service levels. The Grid is also used to help position and reposition services, in relation to universal and targeted interventions and the relative balance in mixed economy provision. This is used with service users, purchasers and providers and in local democratic forums. For example:

- specifying the balance of services in relation to levels of intervention and contexts of work
- mapping service objectives at appropriate levels of intervention
- reaching agreement about thresholds
- measuring the effect of refocusing in relation to child protection and family support
- inter-agency planning
- resource distribution
- workload distribution.

Second level services are provided in partnership with voluntary organisations. Eligibility criteria tend to restrict direct services to third level interventions. The issue of service context is important in the area of refocusing. Attempts are made to ensure that families receive a service whether need is presented in welfare or protection terms. If referring agencies are confident about this, there is less need to invoke Section 47 enquiries, under the Children Act 1989.

Northamptonshire's plan is embedded in a corporate policy context in relation to: safer communities, educational achievement, health promotion, environmental protection and reducing inequality and poverty. These objectives are reinforced by the County Council's performance plan. The Grid is used as a basis for computerised case audit data to monitor objectives. This exercise has not been without its teething troubles, but it is facilitating robust developments in relation to the future shape of services. These quantitative measures are accompanied by a commitment to quality in-services provision, such as:

- promotion of welfare and independence and minimum intrusion into family life
- acting as a good parent to children looked after
- ensuring good quality services.

The aim is to restrict entry to more intrusive levels of intervention and ensure that service users receive the level of service appropriate to, but not exceeding, their needs, for instance, ensuring that users are not offered residential care when intensive domiciliary support is required. This is underpinned by a commitment to quality, for 'minimum necessary intervention without a concomitant commitment to quality in-services provision would be meaningless'.

City of York Council

This local authority initiated a project in relation to refocusing its children's services. The intention of the project is

> ...to explore the potential for combining existing services with a new and innovative approach to meeting the support needs of vulnerable families through the development of a more comprehensive and integrated social work service.

The first stage was implemented in 1998, when a social work team in the Children's Division of the Community Services Department moved into a family centre.

The *aims* are:

1. to explore the feasibility of refocusing family support services
2. to assess the potential for developing a more integrated approach across key statutory and voluntary sector services to support the needs of vulnerable families, whether or not they are the subject of a formal referral to the service unit
3. to test the hypothesis that the provision of an extended range of support services to vulnerable families will have the longer term effect of reducing the number of referrals of families in severe

crisis or with long-standing chronic problems; these often require intensive casework support and/or the protection of vulnerable children through the courts.

The following *objectives* are outlined:

1. to build on existing services and good practice, and develop greater use of co-working arrangements between social workers, family centre workers and family aides
2. to provide a wider range of services, thereby increasing customer choice and the range of options
3. to make services more widely and informally available in the community
4. to promote self-help, mutual support and equality, and to lessen stigma and coercion
5. to publicise and promote the update of services
6. to provide prompt initial assessments and offer fast-track access to support services
7. to offer individual casework support on a time-limited basis within a framework of written agreements
8. to enable the most vulnerable families to access and use less formal, community-based family support services
9. to develop new partnerships and multi-agency initiatives with other statutory and voluntary sector services
10. to evaluate performance.

Evaluation is explored in three areas:

1. caseloads or workloads
2. the style and shape of service offered
3. customer perception.

The Grid is used as a tool to map the shape of existing services and to identify a baseline against which changes are identified, using individual case data and aggregate profiles. This is repeated after one year. Two other service units in the city are used as controls.

The following examples illustrate some ways in which the integrated team of social workers, family centre practitioners and family aides began to affect service delivery:

- When families have been in crisis and social workers have been unable to respond within a reasonable timescale, family centre workers have made home visits to assess situations, resolve difficulties or offer advice and guidance until a social worker can respond.
- Communication between practitioners has greatly improved; this has increased customer satisfaction because more fluid roles enable customers to receive a service if their social worker is unavailable.
- A more creative and less intensive service has been offered through a range of projects for which formal referrals are unnecessary; a menu of services is offered from which customers choose which best suits their needs. This appears to be a less stigmatising approach, which also responds to customers who might previously have been given low priority or no service.
- This approach facilitates friendships and social networking which, hopefully, makes parents less dependent on social services.
- If customers need more formal intervention subsequently, they may more readily seek support from the department.
- A rolling programme of support groups, based on the needs of families, has been developed; these interdisciplinary services may be offered on an open-ended basis or to supplement a more formal services package.

Using the Grid to illustrate the service response to specific needs

The Grid has also been used by some social services departments to illuminate the service response to specific needs such as child abuse and disability. An illustration is given of its use in relation to the development of family centres as a specific service response.

Family centres

The Enabling Authority

LEVEL OF INTERVENTION	WELFARE MODEL: ROLE OF THE STATE		
	Last Resort Safety Net	Addressing Needs	Combating Social Disadvantages
BASE (populations)			
FIRST (vulnerable groups and communities: diversion)			Resource for local community networking campaigning
SECOND (early stresses)		Multiple interventions. Professional model partnerships	
THIRD (severe stresses)	Surveillance (coercive interventions)	Focused assessment of childcare interactions and work to reduce risks.	
FOURTH (social breakdown: 'in care')	Warehousing: discharge	Professional rehabilitation attempt for child in substitute care for protection	

Figure 3.7 The Social Policy Contexts of Family Centres

Family centres are a vivid illustration of one of the Grid assumptions: it is not the name of a service which indicates its nature and functions, rather, its location denotes its purpose (Figures 3.7 and 3.8). Many local authorities in the 1980s and 1990s changed the functions of their family centres from a community-orientated and multi-intervention approach towards more focused assessments and interventions in relation to risks and prospects for rehabilitation. This sometimes resulted in unfilled placements, therefore centres refocused towards work with disabled children and/or market provision.

Some local authorities in the early phases of children's services planning map their family centres and day nurseries geographically. Such an approach needs to be underpinned by Geographical Information Systems (GIS) and identification of the purpose and functions of these services. This has allowed some local authorities to explore the relationship between needs and services and adopt a more rational approach to resource allocation and prioritisation (see Chapter 4).

The major voluntary organisations, for example Barnardos, refocused many of their family centres towards a multi-professional and community development approach (Figure 3.8). Stones (1996) illustrates the values, skills and knowledge required for such innovations.

The aim of developing *integrated* services may produce tensions in relation to service-level agreements and partnerships with local authorities. Local authority requirements may change relatively rapidly in response to mandates from central and local government (e.g. child protection, Sure Start, targeting, Best Value, performance assessment). Different local authorities may contract for contrasting services from the same family centre. Some may contract for focused assessments for referred families, others for a more community networking approach for non-referred families. Families may not necessarily move freely between these approaches, even though they may have similar needs (Smith 1996).

These examples illustrate ways in which local authorities and their planning partners have used the Grid flexibly in children's services planning; many are continuing to do so. The Grid also illuminates the use of family centres as a service response to need. The Grid has been used to map, plan and evaluate services. This facilitates clarity regarding the refocusing debate in relation to current locations of service, areas requiring development and the need to examine the value base of the service. The figures outlined have been used in training and service-development exercises across the United Kingdom.

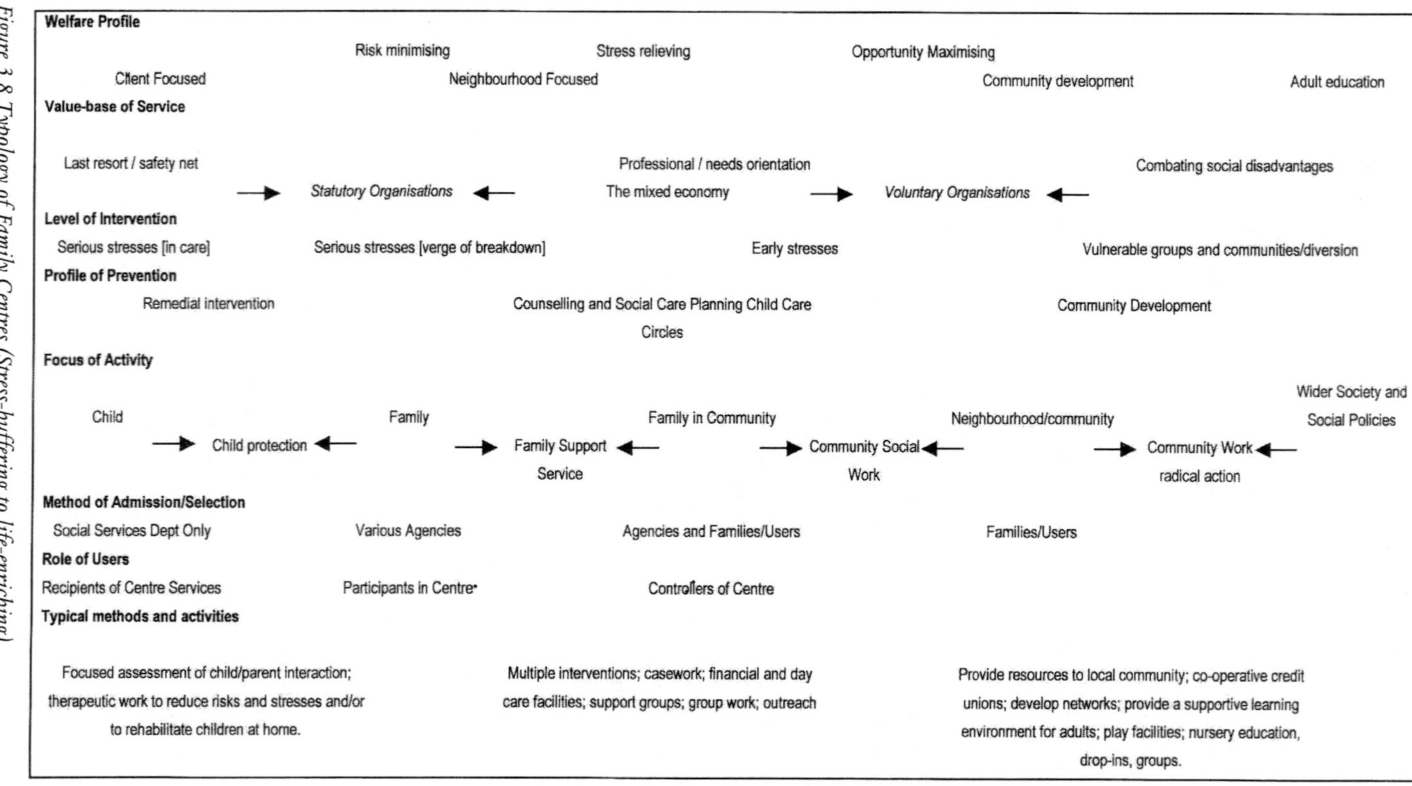

Figure 3.8 Typology of Family Centres (Stress-buffering to life-enriching)

Conclusion

This chapter illustrates the different versions of the Grid developed since 1989. The Grid is only one conceptual framework amongst many, but its axes are fundamental and overlay other variables in children's services planning. It is generic and is also relevant to community care, disability, crime prevention and health care. The Grid locates relevant issues, makes implicit developments explicit, and clarifies the axes of children's services. The original Grid was based on theoretically-grounded empirical research and evolved through regular testing of policies and practices. It has, therefore, the capacity to illuminate policy and practice issues and to facilitate strategic planning. Some authorities have been using the framework flexibly in formulating their Quality Protects management action plans since 1999.

CHAPTER FOUR

Needs-Led or Needs Must?

The Use of Needs-Based Information in Planning Children's Services

Mike Pinnock and Louise Garnett

> Need is a vernacular of justification, specifying the claims of necessity that those who lack may rightfully address to those who have. Without the language of need, and the language of right that derives from it, the human world would scarcely be human: between powerful and powerless only the law of the hammer and the anvil, master and slave would rule. (Ignatieff 1984, p.27)

In this chapter we describe how agencies might bring about better outcomes for children in need by improving the use of needs-based information within their joint planning processes. We examine the potential benefits of a needs-based approach to planning and assess its viability within partnership working. We outline the practical approaches that some agencies are adopting in gathering needs-based information and consider their applications in service shaping and strategic planning.

Introduction

The past decade has seen a resurgence of interest in the idea of rational planning in social care. This development has been accompanied by a corresponding revival of interest in the concept of social need as a medium for explaining and categorising social problems and for prioritising the claims that these needs make on the scarce resources of social welfare agencies (Percy-Smith 1996).

Increasing attention is also now being paid to the study of effectiveness in child welfare services. For example, in addition to formal evaluative research, initiatives such as Best Value require public sector agencies to extend their traditional concerns beyond inputs and efficiency factors towards effectiveness and outcomes (Department of the Environment, Transport and the Regions 1998). Policy goals expressed as outcomes have become a trademark of the Blair government and outcome-based targets for health and social care are now routinely attached to major initiatives such as, for example, National Priorities Guidance 2000/01–2002/03, Sure Start and Quality Protects.

Few would argue against the appliance of more science in the planning and evaluation of children's services. However, in reality the objectification of both need and outcome in social care is a complex undertaking that is fraught with the sort of conceptual and practical difficulties with which most local authorities are ill-equipped to engage.

It is clear that the introduction of Children's Services Plans (CSPs) in the early 1990s and the subsequent launch of the Quality Protects initiative in 1998 have led to substantial improvements in the way that child welfare services are planned. Agencies now routinely invest significant amounts of energy and resources into producing plans and supporting planning processes. Much of this effort has gone into collecting information about the needs of local children. In this chapter we identify three principal sources for this information:

- the views of prospective, existing and past users of services
- population data on risk factors known to be associated with poor outcomes for children and families, as well as agency information on service utilisation and unit costs
- the views of key stakeholders and 'experts' such as local voluntary groups concerned with child welfare, and local professionals, as well as research evidence on 'what works'.

We will argue that the process of needs assessment should not be seen as a remote statistical exercise that can be conducted from a desk at county hall. Instead, it should be an inclusive process that draws on both qualitative and quantitative research methods.

By arguing for an inclusive process in which service users and stakeholders play an active part, we recognise that our attempts to assess needs inevitably stray into assessing outcomes. Thus, whilst it is necessary to make a theoretical distinction between the concepts of need and outcome, this is not easily sustained on the ground – for example, in a lively discussion with a group of care leavers or parents of children with disabilities. Indeed, we recognise that the process is not about counting up sets of ready calibrated, neatly labelled needs so much as following the muddy footprints that past policies and practices have left on peoples' lives.

This chapter is based on our involvement in planning in an inter-agency setting over the past ten years. We should point out that it is not intended to be a 'how to' guide so much as an introduction to the sorts of ideas and insights that we have found useful in helping to make sense of what is undoubtedly a difficult and complex area.

Background

All the early studies suggested that local authorities were slow in responding to the statutory duty laid on them by the Children Act 1989, Schedule 2, implemented in 1991, to 'identify the extent to which there are children in need living within their area' (Aldgate and Tunstill 1995; Audit Commission 1994; Colton, Drury and Williams 1995; Department of Health 1994a; Social Information Systems 1993). The impression given by many local authorities was that of 'keen but nervous'. Keen to introduce the concept of need as a medium through which to develop a more rational approach to planning, but nervous of the practical and conceptual difficulties involved. They have also been cautious of stimulating an even greater call on their services at a time when they are struggling to meet existing levels of demand.

In November 1992, the Department of Health published its first circular on Children's Services Planning (Department of Health 1992). It was clear from the Social Services Inspectorate (SSI) study that followed a year later, that the idea of a CSP had given a purpose to the requirement in Schedule 2 of the Children Act 1989. The study revealed that 80 per cent of respondents '...had or would have undertaken some form of needs assessment by the time that the plan was published and will have identified service priorities linked to resources' (Department of Health 1994b, p.10). A study undertaken twelve months later confirmed that progress was being made. It concluded, however, that the mapping of need was still a relatively underdeveloped and unsophisticated activity within most local authorities (Department of Health 1995c).

In 1996 the Guidance on Children's Services Planning further encouraged local authorities to take a more rational, comprehensive and systematic approach by recommending that:

> Local authorities need to demonstrate their strategic approach to providing children's services based on: a reliable and updated comprehensive knowledge base; a thorough analysis of need and supply; the views of service users and the local community; consultation with other agencies; monitoring and feedback. (Department of Health and Department for Education and Employment 1996, p.2)

By 1998, a survey undertaken by the National Children's Bureau was able to conclude that some local authorities had '...made great strides in gathering information more systematically but that a number of key issues remain to be resolved' (Hearn and Sinclair 1998, p.36). These centred on the problems that agencies faced in analysing needs-based information and using it to effect changes in service provision. A further SSI inspection in the same year observed that 'overall, children's services planning had only limited information on levels of need in their area, and consequently on resource implications, to inform decision making' (Department of Health 1999d, p.25).

In 1998, the Government launched its Quality Protects initiative requiring local authorities to produce a Management Action Plan (MAP) that:

> sets out your arrangements for establishing and monitoring the number of children in your community who need your services, stating in a statistical summary the number and proportions of children in need. (Department of Health 1998a, Annex 3)

The evaluation of the MAPs published in 1999 reported mixed findings:

> The first round demonstrated again how fundamental good data collection is to all effective management. Without it, local authorities could not provide baseline information about their populations and could not project future need; they could not monitor what was happening to children they looked after, nor follow the careers of children who had left their care... There were good examples of systems, or plans for systems across the country, but far more examples of weak or patchy arrangements that were only half doing the job. Inspectors everywhere identified this as a priority for development. (Department of Health 1999c, p.17)

The introduction of the duty of Best Value now requires local authorities to provide evidence to demonstrate the validity of the relationship between the services that they provide and the needs of the community that they serve. Both Best Value (Department of the Environment, Transport and the Regions 1998) and the White Paper, *Modernising Social Services* (Department of Health 1998a), emphasise the importance of grounding plans on evidence of need and outcome. Indeed this evidence is central to the test of the 'Four C's' of Best Value: Challenge, Compare, Consult and Compete. In order to meet these challenges, local authorities will need to demonstrate that they have a knowledge of the needs of local children, and that they have used this knowledge to commission services they believe will be effective in producing desired outcomes. For social services departments, this duty suggests that in the future, the relationship between local needs, services and outcomes will have to be far more transparent than it has been in the past.

Clearly there are now compelling legal, professional, political and financial reasons why a local authority should want to ground its plans on evidence of need and effectiveness. The problem for those involved in the planning of children's services is how to achieve this. How can the notoriously difficult concepts of need and outcome act as a foundation for helping shape agency goals? How can we begin to classify, categorise and prioritise the needs of children in a systematic way? How can we develop and apply appropriate methodologies for gathering need and outcome-based information; and how can we use this information to good effect within the local planning process?

Needs and outcomes: partners in time

Over the past ten years the term 'needs-based planning' has come to serve both a rhetorical and a practical purpose. At a rhetorical level, the call for needs-based public services is analogous to the exhortation for 'customer-driven' services in the private sector. In this sense, the term is used as shorthand for focusing the efforts of the organisation on meeting the expressed needs and preferences of users.

At a practical level, the idea of needs-based planning has encouraged organisations to experiment with different ways of gathering information and using it within their planning systems. The simple logic is that better information will lead to better decisions, which in turn will lead to better outcomes for children and families. The immediate problem facing the planner is one of definition: how to go about putting a face on the idea of need. In theory, needs should provide us with a useful way of talking about the human condition, a way of comparing and explaining our observations and experiences of life. In reality, we often find that needs are a messy and difficult starting place for planning.

Part of the problem lies in the way that we talk about needs. Gough points out that, typically '...needs statements conform to the relational structure "A needs X in order to achieve Y"' (Percy-Smith and Sanderson 1992, p.6). Traditionally, plans for developing services for children and families have been couched in the language of 'service needs' – the 'X' in Gough's formula. Inevitably, these plans tended to support the status quo rather than lead to innovation and change. They also limited the contribution that existing and prospective service users made to the planning process. Simply assessing the need for existing services does not lead agencies to discover unmet need, nor does it reflect the capacity of families to meet needs in other informal ways. For example, would such an approach have been capable of revealing the existence of young carers, let alone tell us anything about their needs or coping strategies? Nor does it stimulate thinking around new and innovative ways of meeting existing needs.

Throughout the 1990s, changes to the structure of CSPs signalled the ways in which agencies have tried to break out of this 'grooved thinking'. Many authorities shifted from structuring their plans around services, such as foster care or youth court services, towards sub-groups of children who might benefit from interventions, for example, children in need of protection, in trouble with the law, or needing substitute care (the 'A' in Gough's formula). This began to open the way for children, young people and their families to talk about their needs and service preferences.

A further approach favoured by many in the United States has been to focus planning on outcomes (the 'Y' of Gough's formula). In this model, agencies are seen not just as producers of services but as co-producers of desired outcomes. This focus has important implications for the way that we approach the process of needs assessment. Logically, it suggests that we must:

- have a clear understanding of the outcomes that we want to achieve in terms of the overall health and wellbeing of our communities

- possess knowledge of which interventions are likely to be effective in achieving these outcomes, including the processes through which services are delivered
- be able to identify those children in the population who are likely to benefit from these services; and
- have the means for measuring the impact of our efforts.

In Vermont in the United States, Hogan and Murphey have demonstrated the practical benefits of a results-based model of partnership planning (www.ahs.state.vt.us/publs.htm#data). They have shown how the focus on outcomes can begin to tackle the so-called 'wicked issues' of government and suggest that such an approach can bring clarity and consistency of purpose to partnership working. They advocate that the process begin by engaging local communities in a debate about their main concerns and the sort of outcomes they want for themselves. In Vermont, this has led to a vision that, over time, has been distilled into nine clearly defined objectives relating to children and families:

- families, youths and citizens are engaged in their community's decisions and activities
- pregnant women and new-borns will thrive
- infants and children thrive
- children are ready for school
- children succeed in school
- children live in stable, supported families
- youth choose healthy behaviours
- youth make successful transitions to adulthood; and
- families and individuals live in safe and supportive communities.

As well as exposing the interdependence of all agencies concerned with delivering outcomes for children, including the local community, this approach also sharpens the focus on 'what works'. In Hogan's view, communities must not only agree what outcomes they would like to achieve, they must also agree the best ways of delivering them (Hogan 1999).

In the UK the debate concerning what qualifies as 'evidence' of effectiveness in a social care context continues (Newman 1999; Macdonald

1999). For example, some commentators remain unconvinced of the evidence base in social care, arguing that most interventions, in the UK at least, remain untested by the 'gold standard' of randomised controlled trials and long-term evaluation studies (Macdonald 1999). Others argue that applying such standards to social care research undervalues the importance of other forms of evidence, not least the views of service users (Everitt and Hardiker 1996), and may diminish the importance of process issues, such as fairness, equity and respect (Sinclair 1998; Schorr 1998). Policy makers in Vermont have taken a rather more pragmatic approach. Rather than get bogged down in discussions about the nature of evidence, the focus has been on how to engage local communities in shaping local solutions attuned to local conditions (Murphey 2000).

In spite of disagreements about the nature of evidence, most commentators would agree that child welfare interventions should be based on the best *available* knowledge of good practice. The challenge is how to ensure that decision makers get ready access to this information, and put it to practical use. Some commentators have proposed a single clearing house for evidence-based social care research, modelled on, if not integrated into, similar initiatives in health, such as the Cochrane Collaboration, (www.cochrane.co.uk) and the NHS Centre for Reviews and Dissemination (Macdonald 1999; Davies *et al.* 1994).

Clearly, few English local authorities, or for that matter, public health departments, would claim to have the necessary skills, time or resources to mount large-scale evaluative research studies of childcare interventions. Hence, much local government and health authority research activity has tended to focus on describing trends in the volume and spread of presenting child health and social care problems, rather than on evaluating the impact of agency interventions. Nevertheless, this is a useful starting point for local and health authorities, assuming that reliable and consistent management information is routinely collected (Little and Mount 1999). Opportunities for small-scale evaluation exercises, comparative studies and before and after monitoring may also arise within local partnerships such as Sure Start, Health Action Zones and New Deal for Communities. Indeed, in those areas where such initiatives overlap, it might make sense to combine research resources for population needs assessment and programme evaluations (Utting 2001).

Various other solutions have been suggested for dealing with the messiness of needs. For example, a small number of local authorities have adopted an approach that starts from the position that the claims children make on the resources of the state are so strong that they must be treated as rights rather than needs; for instance the right to live free from abuse and exploitation, and the right to education and play. Typically, agencies have used the United Nations Convention on the Rights of the Child as the starting place for their planning frameworks (see Children's Rights Development Unit 1996). Since these rights are universal, the approach has proved particularly effective for framing plans aimed at all children living within an authority.

Categorising needs

Whilst health professionals might turn to the pages of the International Classification of Diseases (ICD) in order to help them describe, code, and categorise presenting problems into common disease groupings (as Sinclair and Little argue in Chapter 6) there is currently no standard system of classification that service planners can use to differentiate categories of children in need. Hence the enormous variation with which social services departments have approached this task, with well over 100 different definitions of children in need identified in one survey (Sinclair and Carr-Hill 1996). Attempts by the Department of Health to standardise information about children in need known to social services have led recently to the development of eight descriptive categories to be used in annual audits.

The first national census of children in need took place in February 2000. Its purpose was to identify how many children in need there are and what resources social services spend on them in a 'typical week'. Prior to this, centrally held information only covered looked after children and those on the child protection register. This meant that a significant but unknown quantity of social services activity and expenditure was regularly omitted from national statistical returns (Department of Health 2000b).

Recently published findings suggest that, in the census week, there were upwards of 381,500 'children in need' who required some form of social service provision, representing an average of 2500 per local authority department. The vast majority of these children were not looked after, but in receipt of home-based family support services. The average cost to each local authority was £175 per child; just over half the overall expenditure went on services to looked after children (www.doh.gov.uk/public/cinresults.htm).

Forrester (2000) suggests that this exercise will put the Department of Health in a stronger and better informed position in putting the social services case to the Treasury. At a local level the data also have potential for useful benchmarking exercises both within and between local authorities. Indeed, the data may well be a test for 'pragmatic cross-party co-operation' (Forrester 2000) as groupings of needs and resources by postcode and electoral ward become available to local politicians for the first time. Inter-agency co-operation might equally be tested were similar data available from partner agencies regarding their involvement with children in need.

Whilst such initiatives may improve the classification of those children in need who are known to social services departments, there is still the potential difficulty of identifying them in the population at large. If, as Hardiker and colleagues suggest in Chapter 3, local authorities need to develop plans which shift resources from the third level of intervention towards the primary and secondary levels, they will require an understanding of need at a community level. This will be particularly important if the build-up of preventative and early intervention services is dependent on external funding. Re-focusing initiatives resourced by the European Social Fund, Single Regeneration Fund, Sure Start programme and the Children's Fund all require evidence of need at a population level.

Work undertaken in a number of local authorities suggests that it is possible to reach a consensus between agencies, professionals and the community in order to construct a practical definition of children in need which may be employed at a local population level. For example, as Ward and Peel describe in Chapter 10, in North Lincolnshire the work of the Children and Families Assessment Project has resulted in a common framework and method for identifying acceptable standards of parenting, which can be used across all child welfare agencies in a given locality. The work of the British Communities that Care programme also demonstrates how local communities can be fully involved in both needs audits and evaluation exercises at a local community level (France 2001). Exploratory research conducted by Dartington Social Research Unit in one inner London authority has also shown that it is possible to arrive at an empirical definition of children in need, which can be applied at a population level (Axford, Little and Morpeth 2000).

The challenge now is to devise a national classificatory system which can be used consistently to monitor the impact of central government strategies on children in need in the population at large, in much the same way as the Compendium of Clinical and Health Indicators is used by health authorities to monitor their progress towards national targets for health improvements. As Chapter 6 demonstrates, work is currently underway on developing a taxonomy of need that, it is hoped, will make it easier for planners to describe the aggregate needs of their child populations and link this to information on the outcomes of their service interventions. In the meantime, Little and Mount (1999) suggest that local agencies could assist with this endeavour by ensuring that any new programmes collect reliable information about the children they are supporting and the particular problems they are trying to address.

Developing a framework for population needs assessment

Once a taxonomy has been agreed, the next question is how best to approach the task of collating and aggregating needs-based information. There is no simple answer as the choice of approach and methods will inevitably differ according to:

- the objectives of the needs assessment
- what is already known about local needs
- the availability of reliable routine information sources
- the accessibility of the population of children and/or families of interest
- the need for precision
- the resources available, including the time-frame for completion; and
- the personal and political perspectives of local commissioners.

(Bell *et al.* 1978; Stevens and Gillam 1998)

However, experience suggests that to be of maximum practical value, the process should draw on a variety of information types from a diverse range of sources of which the main elements are:

- statistical information, relating to known and prospective need, including local data on the prevalence of risk and protective factors in the population, service activity data and unit cost information, as well as incidence and prevalence data drawn from studies undertaken elsewhere

- the views of existing, past and prospective service users and the local community on felt need; and
- the perspectives of local professionals and other key informants on normative and comparative need, including local, national and international perspectives on the optimum level and range of services required to meet and satisfy local needs.

(Gough 1992; Percy-Smith and Sanderson 1992; Wright, Williams and Wilkinson 1998)

Involving service users

Both the Children Act 1989 and the NHS and Community Care Act 1990, together with the recent introduction of Best Value give local authorities and health agencies the responsibility for seeking out the views of service users as well as the wider community and engaging them in an ongoing role in the strategic planning and development of services. The requirement to engage in *regular* consultation with the wider community presents agencies with particular challenges, not least because in the context of children and family services many of the potential recipients, by virtue of their age and vulnerability, are frequently excluded from conventional consultation processes.

Thankfully, there is now a growing body of experience within local government and health authorities about how children and families can be involved in the planning process; therefore, much can be learnt from others who are currently engaged in this work. Approaches include: children's advocacy and rights services, school councils, youth forums, in-care and after-care groups, customer surveys, shadow committees, advisory groups, user panels and focus groups, annual conferences, peer-led research and monitoring and other participatory and empowerment techniques. Some of these processes are described more fully in Chapters 5 and 10.

Most children, whatever their age or ability, can express their opinions about services, although agencies may need to find new and multiple ways of engaging them in discussions about issues that are important to them and apply methods which optimise their participation (see Fajerman, Jarret and

Sutton 2000 for a useful summary). The messages from the user movement are clear:

- Agencies need to move away from consultation and research exercises that treat children and families as objects of investigation rather than as equal partners in the process of assessing service needs and outcomes. This means involving them, where possible, at each stage of the process, from setting the agenda to designing and testing data collection methods, collecting the data, analysing and interpreting the evidence, disseminating the messages and monitoring the impact of service interventions. At the very least this will mean working with a planning group of children and families right from the start.
- Making contact with vulnerable families and, particularly, vulnerable children, is likely to require assistance from those closely involved in their support and care. Clearly there is much to learn from those who are experienced in working with children and families. However the degree to which professionals may be willing to assist in such work may itself be determined by how committed they are to user participation and how far they feel that children and families may benefit from such involvement. Professionals can therefore be a key factor in either blocking or enhancing user involvement. Involving them in setting the agenda can help staff work through their fears.
- The culture of involvement starts in the workplace. There is much evidence that staff empowerment and job satisfaction are likely to be increased by user involvement. However some workers may need specialist training and support to enable children's voices to be heard. Joint training initiatives involving teachers, health professionals, voluntary workers and social workers may enhance those skills in communicating with children that should be regarded as a core element of any professional health, education or social work qualification.
- Consultation with users of child and family services, as with any other user group, can be costly and time-consuming. Indeed, users themselves may question its value, arguing instead that the monies could be channelled into better services. The costs of

engaging children and families in needs assessment should therefore be judged against the potential outcomes for service users (and value for money for the organisation). This might mean focusing, at least in the first instance, on specific practice-based issues of concern to children and families, rather than on the broader canvas of needs that may take longer and be more expensive to identify.

- Giving regular feedback is crucial if agencies want to be taken seriously and retain goodwill. It is also a way of making payment for participation.
- Any attempts to engage service users, the wider community and service providers in discussions are unlikely to reveal a single 'truth' about needs or how they may best be met. Indeed, they may reveal conflicting perspectives. Whilst there are no easy solutions to how differences might be reconciled, sustained participation is likely to promote better understanding between different interest groups and could lead to the development of new solutions.

Consulting with stakeholders

Local people and professionals who work in the statutory and voluntary sector will possess detailed knowledge about the needs of the community. Indeed, they often give very vivid examples of the impact that service gaps have on the lives of children and families. Our experience suggests that it is useful to consult with as wide a group as is practically possible. Not only does this offer a richer picture, but it can also lead to a greater sense of ownership of the results.

Whilst some might argue that consulting with providers potentially allows vested interests to influence the outcome of the needs analysis, it is our experience that the greater the degree of involvement of local providers, the more the impact on service planning and delivery. Indeed, one of the major criticisms of the separation of purchasing and provider functions is that provider interest in planning is dismissed as partisan, when in fact it is often providers who have the most direct understanding of service users' needs. It therefore makes sense to consult closely with them in any needs analysis. In recent years, planners have experimented with a variety of different methods for generating information from key informants about needs and unmet needs and arriving at a consensus about local priorities. These include traditional surveys, focus groups, consensus conferences, rapid appraisal, the Delphi technique, and the Matching Needs and Services method discussed in Chapter 5. The last three methods are particularly cheap and easy to use and are designed to enable practitioners as well as service users to work collaboratively to identify and prioritise local health and social care needs.

Statistical information

A number of local authorities have used needs-based data to assess what Davies (1978) refers to as 'territorial justice'. As 'Fair Access' is one of the key dimensions of Best Value, this is an area that is likely to receive increasing attention in the future. Local authorities have undertaken studies to:

- review the balance of resources between the rural and urban poor
- assess how Section 17 budgets are allocated between area teams (Gordon and Loughran 1997)
- develop a formula for the spatial allocation of resources, using data on referred need and surrogate indicators of need at the population level. (Carr-Hill, Rice and Smith 1999; Cubey 1999)

Over the past decade, the use of population data to inform the development of anti-poverty strategies has become well established (Alcock and Craig 1998). There is now growing interest in developing indicators that will allow agencies to monitor the impact of their collective efforts to reduce social exclusion (Hearn and Sinclair 1998). Using an approach based on a life-cycle model, Howarth and colleagues identified a set of 'key indicators' drawn from existing sources that could be used to monitor social exclusion at critical stages from birth to old age on an annual basis. The section on children includes the following nine indicators:

- children living in workless households
- children living in households with below half average income
- the percentage of low birthweight babies
- the number of accidental childhood deaths

- the number of young people gaining no GCSEs above grade D
- the number permanently excluded from school
- the number of children whose parents divorce
- the number of births to girls aged under 16 years; and
- the number of under 16s in young offender institutions.

(Howarth *et al.* 1998)

Although it has some limitations, the model demonstrates the feasibility of monitoring on a regular basis the government's progress on tackling social exclusion and poverty. Indeed, the authors have since produced their third annual report which plots trends in these indicators since New Labour took office. Such indicators may also provide a useful baseline or benchmark against which local authorities might assess the impact of their own attempts to improve the health and wellbeing of their local child population. A similar approach has been applied in the United States, where annual trend data on a range of indicators that affect the wellbeing of children for each state can be traced back to 1985 (www.aecf.org/kc).

In England, the Department for the Environment, Transport and the Regions' Index of Local Deprivation (2000) and the recent release of ward-based Neighbourhood Statistics (National Statistics 2001), in addition to the information requirements of recent government initiatives such as Sure Start, the Children's Fund and Connexions, present local and health authorities with the opportunity for monitoring the health and wellbeing of children and families at local authority and small area level. Recent Children's Fund guidance recommends that before applying for funds, local partnerships should map out those factors associated with poor outcomes for children in their areas as well as the strengths that exist within communities and families.

Population and activity-based information has also been used by some authorities to map out expenditure across each of the levels of intervention identified in Hardiker's Grid as described in Chapter 3. Such exercises present the promotional and protective duties of the local authority as complementary activities rather than competing ideologies. The mapping of need and spending across the Grid can also help local authorities explore how their balance of expenditure is spread across a broad range of possible preventative strategies.

There's data in them there hills...

In theory, the experiences of individual children in need should be a rich source of planning information. Ideally, aggregate data drawn from individual health, education and social work assessments should be used to inform the future commissioning of services. Used alongside population-based data, these can reveal, and in some cases explain, variations in outcomes.

In practice, there are several problems with this. Many agencies still hold information on individual assessments on paper-based files. These are often written in narrative form, under broad headings, making the aggregation of needs-based information possible only through time-consuming case-file studies. Even where the information required is specified in advance, and is capable of being held on computer, attempts at aggregation have been beset with problems of missing data, inconsistencies, software incompatibility, limited technical expertise and resources, different personal identifiers and restrictions on data sharing. Thus, potentially useful information about the needs of children often remains buried away in unwieldy databases held by a number of different agencies, making data extraction and analysis difficult and expensive. Indeed, much of the hardware and skills required for data manipulation and analysis have long been lost to social services departments as shrinking budgets have forced financial cuts on those activities which do not have a direct impact on services.

Hence, many local authorities have responded to the need for greater rationality in planning by choosing to invest their Quality Protects funding in improving their management information capacity. Although the additional funding is welcome, anecdotal evidence suggests that gaining access to the data from health and education necessary to monitor progress towards Quality Protects objectives has often been a major issue. The problems of data sharing are not restricted to children looked after:

> In one instance an injury surveillance system was developed that allowed the NHS Trust and the local authority to use geo-coded data to identify localities where child injuries were most frequent. Despite the reduction of child accidents being a specific priority within the National Priorities Guidance, the developers of the scheme were told that sharing data at anything below ward level contravened the Data Protection Act 1998.
>
> (Lyons, Sibert and McCabe 1999, p.373)

As the recent government document, *Information for Social Care*, acknowledged 'the push for joined-up government and seamless services potentially conflicts with the need to provide confidentiality on records and protect Human Rights' (Department of Health 2001f, Appendix 3, p.7).

Service utilisation data can be an important indicator of the general health of a particular service. However, these are often unavailable, of dubious quality or lacking in detail and thus their potential value as a source of information is lost (see Di Leonardi and Yuan 2000). For instance, Alexander (1999) comments on how the paucity of ethnically coded information contributes to our continued lack of knowledge of the service needs and preferences of Black, Asian and ethnic minority groups:

> It is not clear to what extent institutional racism and cultural language barriers impact on service utilisation rates. Such information is important to planning appropriate services and supporting broad-based community provision, including that offered by the independent sector. (p.34)

It is likely that some children in need and their families may be denied equal access to services because of language and cultural barriers, whilst others may be deterred from taking up services which are perceived as inappropriate or insensitive to their circumstances. The results of the recent Children in Need census suggests that ethnic monitoring of service users in local authorities is improving. The challenge is to ensure that this information is used to shape local services.

The requirement on local authorities under Best Value to assess their performance against that of other potential providers is leading to an increase in the use of comparative data. At a population level the Department for the Environment, Transport and the Regions data on child poverty provide one way in which local authorities can compare the number and proportions of potentially vulnerable children in their communities. These data, combined with information drawn from the Children in Need audit, should allow local authorities to undertake some basic statistical benchmarking on patterns of expenditure.

Recent developments in the Department of Health's Key Indicator Graphical (KIG) system have given local authorities access to comparative data on expenditure and service volume. This system can allow them to identify variations in the range, level and cost of services provided by authorities of similar socio-economic composition. In the absence of any other information about the optimum level of services required, such data can act as a starting point for a more detailed analysis of local service provision, particularly if striking differences between similar authorities are revealed.

A few local authorities have also now joined together to form benchmarking clubs to compare outcome-based data derived from the Looking After Children materials. Their experience suggests that although the comparison of aggregated data can be a useful exercise in itself, the real learning for local authorities rests on understanding the reasons for the difference. This makes benchmarking a far more complex undertaking, for in order to understand variations in outcome, they must also collect and compare data on needs and services (Ward, McDonald *et al.* forthcoming).

Geographical Information Systems (GIS)

One tool of proven value in capturing and analysing statistical information about children in need is the software application known as Geographical Information Systems (GIS) (Noble and Smith 1994). The use of GIS within a social care context is still relatively underdeveloped, both in the UK and in North America (Pinnock and Soper 1996; Queralt and Witte 1998). This is surprising since, with the assistance of GIS, much of the computerised information about service users that local authorities and NHS Trusts routinely collect, could be retrieved and analysed at neighbourhood level, allowing agencies to:

- assess whether services are reaching their intended populations and help target scarce resources more effectively
- integrate data from a number of different and disparate agency sources into a single picture, to present information on the scale and intensity of community problems
- manipulate and present data across different and potentially shifting organisational and community boundaries
- monitor trends and patterns in service take-up and service outputs
- forecast future need and plan service developments; and
- engage with stakeholders more effectively on needs and outcomes by presenting complex spatial data in map form.

GIS can also be a useful place to store information about resources that may require regular updating, such as the availability and occupancy of local day care services or the location of foster carers, thus giving front-line workers and, potentially, members of the public immediate access to information on local resources. In the authorities we work for, information presented in this form has been particularly useful in supporting judgements around the development and restructuring of family support services, particularly at a primary and secondary level (see Chapter 3). The access to free, high quality needs-based information has also been particularly welcomed by the voluntary sector which has used it extensively to support funding bids. By placing some of this key spatial information about needs and services on a web-site (www.ccnap.org.uk) we hope to improve further its accessibility to the local community.

However the spatial analysis of data can only take the analysis of needs so far. For example, whilst GIS may be able to identify where it would make sense to locate a family resource centre, based on the residences of actual and potential service users, it cannot suggest what shape such a service should take or who is best placed to deliver it. Hence the importance of consulting with users and other stakeholders.

Resourcing the needs assessment process

Many local authorities attribute their slow progress in population needs assessment to their limited access to technical expertise. Whilst most health authorities employ public health research teams with experience and skills in epidemiological enquiry, few local authorities can draw on dedicated research and information staff for assistance. Although needs assessment will at times require specialist research skills, it is important not to be paralysed by the complexity of the undertaking.

> Needs assessment is too easily seen as the arcane preserve of public health specialists. The technical skills required can be exaggerated. Basic numeracy and common sense are the most important prerequisites.
>
> (Stephens and Gillam 1998)

Similarly, whilst needs assessment at this level can be labour intensive, if health and social care agencies work together and pool skills and resources it may be possible to keep within existing budgets and avoid unnecessary duplication of effort. A joint approach should also help maintain standards within the needs assessment process and open up a dialogue with other agencies about 'joined up' solutions. Other options for resourcing needs assessment activity include forging partnerships with neighbouring authorities, national research bodies or local universities through the development of organisations such as Making Research Count and Research in Practice. Local authorities can also develop and enhance the resource base for needs assessment at population and service levels through the promotion of community-led and service user-led research and service monitoring. Indeed, such developments are becoming increasingly common as local authorities seek to secure agreement for the restructuring of existing services (Rickford 2001). This suggests that researchers and planners may have to develop their portfolio of skills in order to engage and support local communities in participatory approaches to population needs assessment (France 2001).

Clearly there are tensions to be resolved in gathering local evidence of needs and outcomes, as the resources at the disposal of local planning teams are often woefully inadequate for the sort of sophisticated and detailed statistical analyses demanded by some research purists (Ghate 2001). Staff are often acutely aware of trying to maintain the methodological integrity of the process on the one hand, whilst on the other, having to make pragmatic decisions about what is and is not possible within available resources. Indeed, Ghate suggests that the research community could perhaps do more to help local health and social care agencies develop 'good enough' rather than 'perfect' methodologies (examples are discussed in Chapters 5 and 10).

The actual process of needs assessment has intrinsic benefits – particularly at an inter-agency level. Simply defining the terms of reference can be a useful exercise in itself. Similarly, whilst some agencies may not always be able to share information, the process of negotiating access can lead to a better understanding of each other's information needs. It can also bring the obstacles to information sharing into sharper relief. Reports and documents should not therefore be seen as the only or indeed, the most important outputs of the process.

Needs into deeds

Having information is one thing – putting it to use is another. Some local authorities are now rich in the sort of information that they need in order to plan, but they lack the time to make sufficient use of it, thereby emphasising Simon's point (1997):

> In our enthusiasm for global networks of unlimited information, we sometimes lose sight of the fact that a new scarcity has been created: the scarcity of human time for attending to the information that flows in on us. (p.23)

As already indicated, although there is clear evidence that over the past ten years the idea of planning and shaping children's services has become routine in most local authority social services departments, very little is known about how information of the type described in this chapter is used within organisations or how far it influences decision making. As Baldwin (1996) has observed:

> ...to judge from the literature, very few researchers with interests in public sector management currently have strong interests in social services as such, and how, in general, they approach policy making, planning and management. I was quite taken aback by the paucity of research and writing – and specifically research-based writing – on these issues. (p.62)

As a result, the nomenclature of children's services planning has become confused. Shelves groan under the weight of strategic plans, management action plans, tactical plans, business plans, service plans, Best Value plans and so on. In each, the declared intentions are expressed in an array of goals, aims, objectives, values, missions and promises.

For our purposes, we believe it is useful to see the process of planning for children at three interactive levels:

- *Operational Planning* – making ongoing plans for individual children, young people and their families.
- *Service planning* – developing annual plans to shape specific service areas, such as the fostering service, or the youth offending team. These may be broken down further into individual unit plans.
- *Strategic planning* – constructing medium-term plans, which are usually held between agencies, stating broad goals, and which demonstrate how agencies are responding to political, environmental, social and technological change.

In the same way that agencies are seeking to construct an evidence base for social work, perhaps we should be aiming to develop an evidence base for planning itself by asking what sort of approach will most reliably produce better outcomes. In our experience, highly rational planning arrangements are resource hungry, stifle innovation, lack responsiveness and are unattractive to user representatives. Often they simply break down under the weight of their own ambition. We believe that the most important factors in developing an effective joint planning process are the skills and knowledge, maturity, and perseverance of the people involved. Often a little commitment goes a lot further than a diary full of dull committees!

Perhaps a more useful way of thinking about planning is to see it as a process of organisational learning (de Geus 1988). The idea of the learning organisation has become increasingly popular over the past ten years (Senge 1990). Indeed, the Chief Inspector of the Social Services Inspectorate has called for social services departments to face the challenges of change and improvement by seeing themselves as 'learning organisations' (Department of Health 1999e).

Organisational learning theory suggests that a key task in encouraging the necessary 'systems thinking' is the development of appropriate feedback arrangements (Senge 1990), a point also made by the SSI/Audit Commission (1999):

> ...the key message to authorities from this analysis of Joint Review findings is that, if councils are to succeed in meeting the needs of vulnerable children and their families, it is essential to pay attention to the whole system and to the interconnections between different aspects of the service. (p.37)

Such systems should allow agencies to use both quantitative and qualitative information to develop a deeper understanding about the relationship between needs, thresholds, services and outcomes. For example, we have seen how needs and outcome-based information can be used to support decision-making around:

- the distribution of resources
- the setting of inter-agency priorities
- improving the targeting of resources
- the design, pattern and level of services; and
- the commissioning and decommissioning of services.

As with all learning processes, knowledge is built up over time. In this sense, it is more useful to see the process of needs assessment as an ongoing dialogue between the agency, its planning partners and the community rather than just a one-off technical exercise to gather information for the 'next plan'.

Ten habits of good planners

Despite the difficulties of the undertaking, and the intractability of the problems they seek to address, local authorities and their planning partners are now being urged to develop plans that are more 'rational' both in formulation and content. This objective is often expressed in the need for more 'joined-up working' in the formulation of the plan and in greater 'transparency' in the plan itself.

While calls for greater rationality and co-ordination in planning are not new, the idea is now being claimed by a new generation of policy makers who can perhaps be forgiven for being unaware of the excesses that have been previously spawned in its name. There is now a danger that agencies feel compelled to invest time in maintaining the illusion of highly rational planning systems that in reality contribute very little to bringing about better outcomes for children and families (see Ward and Skuse 2001). In the past, commentators have been pessimistic about the possibility of improving the co-ordination of policy implementation between agencies (Hudson 1987; Challis *et al.* 1988). However we believe that the participants in the planning process can take action to improve its effectiveness. We offer the following as a checklist for 'good enough planning' (see also Department of Health 1999d):

- Are the aims of joint working clearly expressed in terms of client outcomes?
- Is the 'culture of joint planning' orientated towards the needs and preferences of the service users – in this case children in need and their families?
- Is the process of planning inclusive? For example, are existing and potential service users, their carers and their advocates playing an active part in shaping the output, at an early enough stage?

- How can staff members at different levels in the organisation contribute to the planning process?
- Does the process encourage participants to challenge existing policies and patterns of service delivery?
- Do agencies have an adequate capacity for undertaking analysis in sufficient depth and breadth?
- Are the decisions in joint planning supported by appropriate resource planning within agencies? This would include budget planning, human resource planning and capital programmes.
- Does the planning process ensure co-ordination of planning objectives at service interfaces? Examples are child protection and adult mental health, transitional planning for children and young people with a disability.
- Does the joint planning team consider evidence of effectiveness when making decisions about resource allocation?
- Are agencies able to monitor the progress of planning initiatives, evaluate their impact and feed back results into the planning process?

The factors described above are intended to represent an 'ideal model' of planning. Encouragingly, studies such as the Quality Protects national surveys do provide evidence of commitment from agencies towards creating an environment in which closer joint working can take place. For example, a number of local authorities have attempted to develop statements of shared values in order to set the 'living rules' within which joint working can be conducted. The actual process of negotiating and agreeing such statements can be an important stage in the development of trust and clarity of purpose and as such provide an important starting place from which to advance joint policies, plans and protocols. They may also form a shield to defend policy making and planning against the unwelcome intrusions of short-termism, ad-hocery and partisan interests.

Conclusion

Despite a slow start, there is growing evidence that local authorities have made efforts to identify the extent to which there are children in need living in their area and to use this information in their planning processes. The introduction of CSPs and MAPs have given added purpose to Schedule 2 of the Children Act 1989 and have virtually re-invented planning in services for children and families.

In this chapter we have sought to demonstrate how agencies might use aggregated data for planning purposes. In doing so we have highlighted a number of problem areas that, broadly speaking, fall into three main groups:

- Problems associated with the definition of needs and outcomes. It is said that the Innuit of Alaska have as many words to describe types of snow as the Bedouin of the Middle East have to describe types of camels. Sadly, the English language has been less generous to those involved in the planning and study of social care. Words like assessment, need and outcome have become overloaded and overused to the point where their lack of precision has become an obstacle in itself.
- Problems associated with the very idea of planning. Elegant planning frameworks and processes will not in themselves lead to better futures for children. There is a danger that we invest too much time striving to create the illusion of rationality, rather than spending our energies in activities that will lead to real change. Planning needs to be seen as a process of organisational learning.
- Problems associated with the co-ordination of policy implementation between agencies.

Despite these difficulties, our experience of trying to support and manage the process of needs assessment within a multi-agency setting leaves no doubt that this can play a part in improving the effectiveness of services – subject to the following conditions:

- The agencies involved must be committed to change and therefore prepared to use the evidence generated as a basis for planning and commissioning services.
- Needs assessment should be closely aligned with joint planning and commissioning functions, otherwise it will quickly fall into disrepute.

- The process of needs assessment must be transparent and agencies must be prepared to be held accountable for their response to the findings.
- Agencies should be prepared to accept that needs assessment is not an exact science; that the construction of needs is contentious and that their assessment and analysis is often messy and imperfect.
- Needs assessment should be an inclusive process and should be approached by agencies as a process of shared learning, not as a 'review' or 'investigation'.
- Needs assessment can provide a vehicle for beginning a dialogue between service planners and users, during which it is common for tensions and contradictions to surface and be reconciled. The process will thus be as important as any written output.
- The time, resources and skills required for needs and outcomes assessment can be costly. However there are economies of scale in sharing these across agencies.

The process of needs assessment can play an important part in helping children and families strengthen their claim on scarce local resources and in influencing the ways in which services are provided. We acknowledge that representing needs in the planning process is often a difficult and messy business. We also recognise that there is no great body of knowledge waiting on the library shelves marked 'needs-based children's planning'. Nor are there any procedure manuals or guidance and regulations to direct us through the practical and conceptual difficulties. Often we have to borrow and adapt approaches from a wide range of different disciplines and fields of study.

Given these factors, there is a danger that we simply become overawed by the complexity and impossibility of planning. Nevertheless, we believe that we should take heart from the advances that have clearly been made over the past ten years. However naive and clumsy our efforts may feel, however small a contribution they may seem against the enormity of the task, we must continue to develop and share our ideas on how the processes of planning can support our collective ambitions to bring better outcomes for children and young people.

CHAPTER FIVE

Matching Needs and Services

Emerging Themes from its Application in Different Social Care Settings

Jo Tunnard

Matching Needs and Services *is a practice tool designed to improve planning for children in need. It provides a quick and easy method of assessing the needs of children and families referred for services. Similar needs can then be clustered into discrete groups, to provide a framework for developing services appropriate to the different groups identified. The methodology has been tested by practitioners, managers and planners in a range of European and North American child welfare settings. Experience in the UK highlights the benefits of using the tool for joint work by health, education and social services, and of incorporating user perspectives at an early stage.*

Introduction

Agencies have to understand the needs of their local community before devising services that will be responsive to them. *Matching Needs and Services* is a practice tool designed to help local managers and practitioners with both these tasks. It provides agency staff with a methodology for auditing local needs and then designing and evaluating children and family services in response to the needs identified. The methodology relies on four linked concepts: need (for services), thresholds (of seriousness of need and priority for intervention), outcomes (thought achievable by professionals and actually achieved by the child), and services (that can meet the need and help achieve the outcomes identified).

This chapter traces the development of *Matching Needs and Services* and describes some early findings from a variety of different applications. These may be of value to local authorities, as they fulfil their duty under the Children Act 1989 to identify the nature and extent of need in their area, and to local neighbourhoods, as they engage in new ways of collecting data and planning services to improve the life chances of children and families (France and Crow 2001).

The development of Matching Needs and Services

Matching Needs and Services was developed originally as a way of identifying which looked after children would need residential care. This involved devising a method to assess the needs of all children being looked after in one year, in order to plan services (and so decide who should be in residence and what type of residence) in the next year. The method was applied in one authority and the approach refined by a working group of the Department of Health's Support Force for Children's Residential Care. The revised method was then tested in three local authorities and a report produced (Dartington Social Research Unit 1995) which explained how to use the approach. Over a third of English and Welsh local authorities have applied the methodology to cohorts of children looked after, initially under the auspices of a Department of Health initiative advising new unitary authorities on a strategic approach to this population.

It was clear from the results produced in the pilot sites that the method had relevance to a wider group of children than those who needed to be cared for away from home. As a result, the approach has since been developed for various purposes (Dartington Social Research Unit 1999a, 2001):

- It has been used to refocus children's services in the light of the findings of the Audit Commission (1994) and the Department of Health overview (1995b) of child protection research studies. Both publications highlighted the tendency in recent times to view the social worker's dilemma as having to choose between child protection and family support, when it might be more fruitful to decide how family support services could address the needs of different groups of children, including (where necessary) a need for protection. The method has been applied to some two thousand children newly referred to social services for child protection or other needs.

- Its potential for improving children's services planning has been explored – by encouraging health, education, social services, the police and voluntary agencies to conduct joint audits of local need and then plan services accordingly. The benefits of multi-agency audit work have led to the tool being used to develop action plans in Health Action Zones and in On Track, Sure Start and Children's Fund neighbourhoods.
- It has provided the framework for developing a comprehensive planning mechanism for children looked after in residential care. This involves using *Matching Needs and Services* to identify children in need of residence; *Structure, Culture and Outcome* (Dartington Social Research Unit 1999b) to organise residential placements to cater for the identified needs of children placed there; and *Looking After Children* (Department of Health 1995a) to monitor children's progress through homes and to assess the outcomes for children and units.
- It has been adapted for particular groups of service users. These include families of children with disabilities, families referred to family centres, children placed for adoption, those referred to Child and Adolescent Mental Health Services (CAMHS), and young people in contact with youth offending teams. It has been used in work for the Audit Commission on school exclusions and unauthorised absences. Voluntary agencies have used it to identify needs and service responses for vulnerable children transferring to secondary school, for people with special housing needs, and for mothers and children seeking refuge from domestic violence.
- An aspiration is to adapt it for whole population samples, using the *Matching Needs and Services* dimensions as the framework for a questionnaire completed with all families, to gauge patterns of need in local communities.
- An international project in Europe and North America is testing its applicability in different cultural contexts, initially in relation to children looked after away from home.

The common thread in all this work is the desire to start with the needs of the population under scrutiny, to aggregate those needs, and to search for better ways of responding to them.

How *Matching Needs and Services* works

The method has been adapted slightly for the varied uses described above. But the essence remains the same, with the approach resting on five key principles that have long underpinned research approaches to children:

- using a retrospective and consecutive sample of children who are representative of the agency's activity, rather than taking a static, snapshot view of children in receipt of services on a particular day
- taking a rounded view of children and families, rather than considering problems only
- concentrating on child and family needs, rather than services offered
- including the views of children and parents at an early stage
- clustering children and families according to the needs that emerge during an audit exercise, rather than fitting people into pre-ordained administrative groupings or categories of need.

An audit is conducted as a group exercise by local managers and practitioners. They transfer information from case files to a short audit form, a single A4 sheet with three vertical columns. In the first column, salient facts about the child and family situation are recorded under five dimensions: living situation, family and social relationships, social and antisocial behaviour, physical and psychological health, and education/employment. In the second column, the auditors record their own analysis of the needs of the child and family. In the third column, they describe the realistic outcome for the child if identified needs are addressed. The task is to use professional expertise and research knowledge to identify the child's needs and make a prediction about the child's future progress.

Aggregating into need groups

This next stage is the essence of the *Matching Needs and Services* method. Once forms are completed, the audit team identifies the patterns of need in the sample, working together until satisfied that they have clustered the cases in a meaningful way. It is akin to shuffling a pack of cards until they end up in the right suits. The team members take it in turns to read out the audit forms. They give background information (the child's age, gender, ethnicity, age at referral, who made the referral and why) and then describe the situation and needs of the child. The aim is to reach a consensus about what most needs to change for the child's difficulties to ease. As each case is discussed, the team builds up groups of children with similar needs. There are no right or wrong answers here, and no prescribed number of need groups. Each area produces its own set of discrete need groups, identified and owned by agency staff, that serves as a needs-led framework for local planning.

The need groups that emerge

The Dartington Social Research Unit has now assembled some three dozen sets of need groups from the range of audits described earlier. What follows is a fairly typical set of need groups from a local authority audit of children newly referred to social services. The order reflects the relative size of the need groups, starting with the largest. The number in brackets indicates the frequency with which each need group has occurred in the first 12 audits of new referrals.

- *Practical support* (11) – the primary need is for information, advice, advocacy and/or material help for adults or young people in relation to housing, day care, finances and debts, social isolation, and queries about childcare matters such as contact and adoption.
- *Confident parenting* (11) – the primary need is for parents to be helped to gain confidence in their ability to parent their children well. They need guidance, support or advice to help manage a temporary parenting difficulty or behaviour problem such as coping with a new baby, having a demanding toddler, settling children into routines, adjusting to becoming a new parent figure or being a very young parent, and dealing with low-level difficulties in adolescents.

- *Adult conflict* (11) – the primary need is for parents or other adult carers to resolve the conflict in their relationship and avoid involving the children in their difficulties. Adults need to understand the adverse impact of their disputes on the children. Children need insight into why the adults behave as they do, and reassurance about their future living situation and (where necessary) contact arrangements with parents, siblings and other relatives.
- *Much improved care* (10) – the primary need is for children to receive much better physical care and attention from parents. The children are at risk of suffering significant harm on account of a range of severe problems including personal and home hygiene, health, safety, delayed development and poor family relationships. Parents need to understand that their children should be cared for safely, whatever difficulties the family may be experiencing. Intensive support is likely to be needed over a long period.
- *Parent/child relationships* (9) – the primary need is to resolve tensions between children and parents. They need to listen to each other and learn ways of dealing with conflict in a non-violent and non-abusive manner. Help may be needed to control a young person's difficult behaviour, but poor relationships between children and parents need to be resolved before these other problems can be addressed.
- *Emotional/mental health issues* (7) – the primary need is to understand and address the mental health problems of parents or children. Parents need practical and emotional support to address difficulties which affect the life of the whole family and their ability to parent, resulting in behavioural problems for some children. The needs range from self-reported depression and reaction to life crises, to severe and enduring mental illness, treated or untreated. The needs of the children are for socialisation, routines and boundaries, safety, and relief from caring responsibilities. Young people with mental health problems need support to understand and address their difficulties and to be safe from harming themselves or others.

- *Physical health/disability* (7) – the primary need is for support, advice and practical help arising from a child or parent's illness or disability. The needs include equipment to increase mobility, fees for respite activities, practical help in the home or with transport, and help to come to terms with a diagnosis. There is a wide range of health conditions, from asthma to terminal illness, and including both physical and learning disabilities.
- *Improve child's behaviour* (8) – the primary need is to improve or control the child's behaviour because, even if it stems from relationship difficulties with parents, it is severe enough to warrant direct attention. Children need insight into their antisocial behaviour, and help in controlling it, to ease tensions at home and to improve school attendance and progress. Adults need to learn new ways of addressing difficult behaviour. A sub-group in some areas relates to young people in trouble with the police. They need to understand why they offend and the consequences of their antisocial behaviour, and they need help to reduce their offending and to cope with court action.
- *Loss or trauma* (12) – the primary need is for parents or children to understand and be able to cope better with past or current events, to reduce the impact of the trauma on their life. The needs stem from experiencing or witnessing physical or sexual abuse, or the loss of a parent or close relative through death or a difficult separation, or adoption breakdown, or racial conflict or war.
- *Immediate protection* (7) – the primary need is to ensure that the child is safe from harm, or to make enquiries to ascertain whether the child is suffering or is likely to suffer significant harm and, if so, to ensure the child's immediate protection. After that, the child will move into another need group (depending on the needs identified) or will be deemed to have no need for service.
- *Alcohol and drug misuse* (2) – the primary need is for parents to stop or reduce their problem drinking or drug use because it is interfering with their ability to parent well, or for older children

to do so, because of the adverse effect of the misuse on their health, behaviour and school attendance.

- *Asylum seekers* (1) – the primary need is to address the particular issues arising from the family's asylum status, especially isolation, poverty, housing and communication difficulties. Other needs may also be present, especially physical and emotional/mental health needs.

Comment

The apparent simplicity of the above list should not be taken to indicate that the compilation and description of need groups is a mechanistic or easy process. It requires intense concentration throughout one or two days, coupled with a willingness to be open to the different perspectives of colleagues. An audit group starts, not with a set of headings to which they allocate cases, but with an empty table on which they build up their own need groups as they discuss the circumstances and life events of children in the sample.

Nevertheless, there is something simplistic in the procedure described. It attracts criticism from some observers that families' needs are more complex than is conveyed in the description of need groups and that the need to protect children is lost in the process. In rebuttal, it is important to bear in mind that subsequent computer or manual analysis of the audit forms provides a detailed explanation of the full range of needs within each group, and that the tool is intended for strategic planning purposes, not for assessment and care planning for individual children. The growing national database of need groups reveals some interesting similarities and differences which merit closer analysis. Work is underway at Dartington to test the validity of the findings, and to understand the reasons for the differences between geographical areas.

Using need groups to plan services

The purpose of aggregating cases into need groups is to provide some evidence for predicting the likely future demand for services across the spectrum of needs presented, and to assist in the development of services that are more responsive to the needs identified. This part of the process involves taking each need group in turn, identifying desired outcomes for children and families in the group, and identifying services that will focus on the outcomes to be achieved.

Agencies have found it difficult to move beyond the stage of identifying need. In response to the practical difficulties encountered, a methodology for responding to the question, 'how do you create services?' has been developed and tested, in the same way that the audit tool itself was devised in response to the earlier question, 'how do you identify need?' This methodology provides a formula for moving logically through a series of discrete steps.

First is the importance of *setting the scene for service planning*. Those involved in the audit work disseminate their findings, to pave the way for common understanding and commitment to the process. They clarify the concepts (need, threshold, outcome and services) that have underpinned their work, and set out the need groups that have emerged and their likely size in future years.

A one-day seminar has proved useful here, ideally open to all agencies in the area, as well as to both horizontal and vertical groupings within social services, including elected members. The meeting provides a good opportunity to focus on the corporate responsibilities to children in need and to recruit enthusiasts to sign up for the next stage of the work. It can also help determine which need groups will be tackled first. Ideally, agencies work simultaneously on each need group, producing an overall plan that can be implemented gradually, as and when resources allow. More often, agencies have been more cautious, starting with planning for three or four of their need groups – perhaps the largest, or the ones more amenable to successful work across agencies, or those that the community would most like to see tackled.

The next step is to *review the composition of the need groups*. The principle here is that services should rest on evidence of need. The planning group for each need group must be clear about the circumstances and characteristics of the group as a whole and how it is distinguished from other groups. A quick perusal of the audit forms will be helpful here, together with any statistical analysis of the material collected. Any other local information on need should be included (such as that identified from the sources described by Pinnock and Garnett in Chapter 4), in order to have as complete a picture as possible of the available evidence about children and families in the group.

Next comes the move *from needs to desired outcomes*. The aim here is to draw on professional and managerial knowledge, as well as research findings, to establish a set of indicators that will show whether needs have been alleviated in one or more of the five dimensions used for assessment: living situation, relationships, behaviour, health, and education/ employment. Different indicators will apply to different need groups. For one group, a realistic outcome under education might be that children attend school regularly and achieve their potential. But this might be too idealistic for another need group where the realistic outcome might be that children are getting to school more often than not.

The next step is about moving *from outcomes to services*. The task here is to plan a service, looking for practical solutions to identified problems. It is the opportunity to think creatively, to reflect on services provided elsewhere, and – in light of available research evidence about 'what works' – to consider the service responses most likely to produce optimal outcomes for children in the need group. This work should clarify the exact nature of the response needed, who is the best person or agency to provide it, from where in the community the service will be offered, for how long, and for which family members (child, one or both parents, siblings, other adults).

Evidence is important here, too. There will be the information collected (on the back of each audit form) about the services that families in the selected need groups have actually received. What is also needed is information about the full range of current services in the area relevant to each need group. This will help ensure that time is not wasted designing something that already exists. Such a map of services is rarely available in local authorities, despite the requirement under the Children Act 1989 to publicise services. Some radically new service ideas may emerge. But, more likely, ideas will prove to be an enriching or reworking of existing services, with interventions more focused, time-limited and outcome-orientated, and so easier to evaluate. Either way, plans need to be as specific as possible; a good test might be whether a parent or young person who is told about the service would understand exactly what was on offer.

Ultimately, the test of success will be whether outcomes improve for children. Hence the next stage, *building in evaluation*, to determine how outcomes will be measured and the extent to which desired outcomes are achieved. This requires attention to thresholds, to help ensure that the right children receive the right services and that the correct procedures are followed prior to service intervention.

The aim here is to build up, over time, evidence that will increase our understanding and certainty about what works for which groups of children.

It has not been easy to get evaluations established, even where there is enthusiasm in principle for the task. There are various barriers to progress, including uncertainty about the purpose of evaluation, the methods to use, the costs involved, and the impact on busy professionals and service users. These dilemmas are not confined to *Matching Needs and Services* work; all feature in the current public debate about the principles and practice of evaluation in social care (Utting 2001).

The evaluations that are required for piloting new services are those that provide a reasonably robust test of whether the changes in service delivery are having the desired effect. The most rigorous test is through a randomised controlled trial, where cases are randomly allocated to two groups, with one group offered the new pilot service whilst the other group receives the normal service. Existing services would also benefit from such scrutiny, to help clarify which should continue or be extended and which should be withdrawn or revised. In view of the difficulties of evaluation, it is not surprising perhaps that the one area that has succeeded so far in setting up evaluations of new *Matching Needs and Services* designs has had research funding to co-ordinate the work.

Comment

The journey from need groups to new services is complex and fraught. Part of the dilemma is the vacuum around service planning (identified also in Chapter 4), characterised both by a lack of key personnel with particular expertise and a mechanism for doing the work. As a result, delay can set in while people who might be able to contribute are drawn into the exercise. They then need to be introduced to the *Matching Needs and Services* methodology but, not having been involved from the start, may find it difficult to focus firmly on the need groups arising out of the audit work. Another tension stems from the consistent finding that services in response to need groups need to be multi-agency at the point of delivery. This is more difficult to plan for if social services have conducted their audit without the help of health and education colleagues. Here, again, setbacks can occur as people struggle to get on board and up to speed.

The attempts so far to use evidence of need to create new services offer some pointers for the future. Generating a spirit of purpose and optimism seems to be important. The excitement of having to understand and plan for the needs of a community for the first time – as in a new unitary authority –

was, in one area, a stimulating challenge for staff at all levels, enabling them to think creatively about their new responsibilities and about possible allies in other agencies. Data collection was swiftly followed by the establishment of a forum which attracted the participation of all local agencies providing support at home for children in need. The aggregated data on need from the audit, together with the set of social services need groups of new referrals, formed the agenda for joint work. Service duplication and gaps in provision were identified for each group in turn, and several small developments – drawing on different combinations of agency skills – were put in place for the five largest need groups identified.

Another important factor is what might be described as 'clarity and clout'. The work is likely to founder unless it is owned by senior managers who have a vision about services for the area, and unless those key people in the local and health authority can drive through the changes needed for money and staff to be used differently. This will probably require a readiness to de-commission services, rather than simply add to what already exists. It may require the ability to enthuse agencies to set aside parochial self-interest in favour of pooled budgets and teams that include professionals from different disciplines. For example, discussion of audit findings in one area concluded that social workers and mental health specialists needed to work together, over the same period, to address the needs of children and their parents. It led to CAMHS staff and social workers from the family and adolescent team working alongside each other in a new way.

Change may be needed, too, within an individual agency. In another area, the audit has speeded the development of the social services day nurseries into family centres providing a range of specific services to address identified need groups, such as building up the social networks of isolated families and offering proactive support to young teenage parents. Each proposed new service must specify which need group it seeks to address, the outcomes wanted for children and parents, the evidence that the service is likely to deliver those outcomes, and plans for evaluating effectiveness. The audit has also helped re-focus the purchasing of services from the local voluntary sector. Again, the start point is achieving progress for children falling into the locality's identified need groups.

An overriding strength of the audit work in this area has been the creation of a structure to support and promote joint work, set out in a multi-agency plan that spells out links with other developments in the locality and with national priorities and initiatives for health, social services and education. Within this, the contribution of social services is acknowledged as small and specialist in comparison with the greater contact health and education have with children. Value is placed on providing social work services in community settings felt to be less stigmatising than traditional team offices, and there is a wish to enhance the contribution of professional skills across agency boundaries. The joint activity has left agencies well placed to draw on their contribution to need assessment and subsequent service planning in their response to various government initiatives such as Behaviour Support Plans, Early Years Development and Childcare Partnerships, and Best Value Reviews, and to the shift – via the NHS Plan – to joint budgets, lead commissioners and integrated provision by health and social care agencies.

A final lesson is that designing service specifications using audit material is a specialist task, and one for which local authorities at present seem ill-equipped. A great deal of time and energy has been invested in encouraging audit groups to develop ideas for new services that draw on the evidence collected about local needs and traditional responses to them. But progress has been slow, and at this stage the work in some agencies has ground to a halt. More progress has been achieved since agencies have been able to choose from a set of service designs drafted by Dartington for several of the common need groups, rather than having to do the design work themselves.

An example of a service design, arising out of an audit of children newly looked after, is set out below. Others can be found at www.dartington-i.org.

Service design for children whose parents have mental health needs

1. Need:

> The need is to acknowledge and address the mental health problems of parents. Parents need practical and emotional support to deal with difficulties that affect the life of the whole family and their ability to parent well. The health needs relate predominantly to self-reported depression and reaction to life crises, with a smaller number affected by severe and enduring mental illness, treated or untreated.
>
> The needs of the children are for socialisation, routines and boundaries, safety, and relief from caring responsibilities. Some appear unaffected by

parental behaviour, whilst others display emotional and behavioural difficulties. Some older adolescents are unwilling to continue living with their parents. In the past, the local authority has started looking after approximately 50 children in this category each year.

EVIDENCE OF NEED FROM THE *MATCHING NEEDS AND SERVICES* AUDIT

The incidence of both chronic and acute mental health problems in parents is twice as high as for the whole sample (all children newly looked after in the 12-month audit period). Stress is very high (50% vs. 12% for the full sample) and suicidal feelings also run high (29% vs. 7%). There are high levels of domestic violence (56% vs. 34%). Physical health problems are slightly higher than the norm, affecting just under a third of parents.

Children's relationships with their mother are similar to the full sample, with about a third described as having a poor relationship. The incidence of poor relationships with fathers is higher than the norm (39% vs. 29%). Physical harm by fathers is also high (36% vs. 14%). The children's experience of low warmth/high criticism is marked (27% vs. 4% for the sample). Children's behaviour at home is ordinary. At school, both statementing and truancy problems are lower than for the whole sample.

THE AUDIT IN CONTEXT

Parental mental health problems account for a third of the audit sample, making it the largest reason for children being accommodated in the local authority area. The group is a little larger than the next biggest need group – parents who misuse substances.

The children are of all ages, and about half are in sibling groups of between two and four children. One family is Indian, another Bangladeshi, the rest white UK. Just under half the parents are lone carers.

Initial placements have tended to be made in an emergency and have lasted for several months. A few older young people move directly to independence, and one or two babies are placed for adoption. The rest have returned home, mainly to parents, with a few being cared for long term by other relatives.

2. Outcomes:

TIME

Change (for parents with depression) or stability (for those with more enduring mental illness) will be sought within six months from the point of referral, with follow-up to monitor which developments are sustained at 18 months.

LIVING SITUATION

- that children remain with parents, other relatives or family friends, or live independently and in contact with parents, other relatives or family friends
- those not with parents remain in contact with them
- contributing factors to parental stress – such as housing and finances – are reduced.

FAMILY AND SOCIAL RELATIONSHIPS

- families recognise the impact of parental mental health needs on their children and can take early action to cope with recurrent onset of symptoms
- children remain safe from parental behaviour that stems from their mental health needs
- children have another source of support who assumes the role of significant adult.

SOCIAL AND ANTISOCIAL BEHAVIOUR

- parents are less isolated
- children have increased ability to make peer friendships
- children are less burdened by adult roles and responsibilities.

PHYSICAL AND PSYCHOLOGICAL HEALTH

- parental or child depression is reduced, or illness is being treated
- parent or child self esteem is increased.

EDUCATION AND EMPLOYMENT

- parents and children take up at least one educational or vocational opportunity that would not have been available had there not been a referral

the priority outcomes are parental and child health, family and social relationships, and behaviour.

3. Service:

TYPE

This is an intensive service to reduce the number of children looked after over a period of 18 months because of parental mental health needs.

BACKGROUND

The service will provide a consistent response – irrespective of the source of referral – that harnesses the skills of child and family workers, primary health workers and those engaged in adult mental health services. This will ensure that adults with mental health problems are seen as parents as well as individuals, and that services for adults and children take account of the impact on children's health and development of parental mental health difficulties.

The service will seek to engage positively with family members, stressing the normality of mental health needs and intervening at an early stage to increase people's competencies and to offer help with their health, childcare and social needs. Its proactive style will require professionals to speak with parents in a straightforward manner about their mental health needs and to provide an individual service that is responsive to their fears and concerns about their children's safety and wellbeing. Given the acknowledged risk of children in this need group developing mental health problems themselves, the service will seek to build up their resilience and boost their pro-social behaviour and educational achievements. Use of the Carers (Recognition and Services) Act 1995 will help make best use of the strengths in families, to support vulnerable adults and children.

SERVICE

Agencies will introduce parents to the project co-ordinator or, if that is not possible, alert parents that they will be invited to use the new service. Parents can identify a professional of their choice to act as their mentor and be their link person to the co-ordinator. A package of services will be agreed for individual families within two weeks of referral. This will address their health, child-related and social needs and will include some or all of the following:

HEALTH NEEDS

- information about, and the opportunity to discuss, the mental health difficulties (and, where relevant, substance dependency) that affect them, and their possible impact on children's development
- information about, and the opportunity to discuss, the range of mental health interventions and the best option for them
- a named health worker to provide ongoing health care
- practical help attending appointments, getting day or hospital treatment, and understanding/coping with any change in the help offered
- a creative alternative to hospitalisation, such as a safe house for parents and children together.

CHILD-RELATED NEEDS

- the identification of relatives, or a resource family, backed by financial support, to provide continuity in care such as occasional or planned respite periods of care during emergencies
- home-based attention to early anxiety experienced by new mothers in relation to a baby's feeding, sleeping and crying
- home-based individual cognitive behaviour therapy to address parenting and relationship difficulties with young children
- individual and family counselling to help parents and older children understand their difficulties and work for positive change

- practical help in the home, to reduce the burden on children of adult responsibilities
- a volunteer befriender for school-age children to take a special interest in their educational and recreational achievements
- for children, the opportunity to join a group of peers whose parents have a health problem (not necessarily mental health) in order to give them the chance to have time for themselves, discuss their fears, learn coping strategies for dealing with stigma and embarrassment, enjoy normal activities, and socialise.

SOCIAL NEEDS

- advice/advocacy on issues that trigger or exacerbate depression, such as housing, income, discrimination and significant life events
- a recreational activity to increase competency while having fun doing normal activities
- focused group work, to provide an opportunity to learn from and contribute to the coping strategies of others with mental health needs
- a co-ordinator who ensures that a proactive style of work is conducted in each case. This assertive outreach work will include follow-up visits if parents do not engage with the service initially, or miss appointments, or have returned home from a treatment programme.

Parents, and older children and other family members, will be given an emergency contact card which they can use to get 24-hour advice and support, including (where necessary) a link to a psychiatrist or self-referral for treatment. A named worker will respond without fail to telephone messages.

4. Thresholds:

LEVEL OF SERIOUSNESS

These are children whose impairment is significant or likely to become so without provision of a service. The impairment is emotional and social.

PROCESS 1 – ENSURING THE CHILD IS IN THIS NEED GROUP

Questions to be asked at referral to ensure the child is in the need group and so eligible for this service:

1. Is the child living at home (including those who have been cared for by relatives or friends in the past six weeks)? (yes).
2. Are parental mental health needs adversely affecting their parenting, or likely to do so? (yes).
3. Has the parent expressed some interest in providing better care for the child? (yes).
4. Do professionals judge there to be potential for the child to remain safely at home over an 18-month period (including spells of respite away)? (yes).

PROCESS 2 – ENSURING THE FAMILY GETS THE SERVICE

1. All referrals to meet each process threshold above.
2. Co-ordinator invites parent to use the service and, with help of mentor, clarifies outcomes to work on and services needed.

5. Evaluation:

By randomised controlled trial or, if that is not possible, by cases matched with similar families from another area or team who are getting a different service. Outcomes measured in terms of:

- reduced parental depression, or stabilisation of mental illness
- improved parent/child relationships
- improved parental and child self esteem.

Professional and user validation

Professional activity

The increasing use of the *Matching Needs and Services* methodology means that the audit data collected and aggregated by one team or authority can be compared with findings elsewhere. Some interesting results are emerging from this work. For example, within social services, audits of new referrals and looked after populations tend to produce a core of similar need groups which, in turn, resemble those that emerge from audits of children with disabilities and children referred to CAMHS. The same also holds true between agencies: similar need groups emerge when separate clustering exercises are completed by health, education, social services and police teams.

These common descriptions of need from different professional settings raise the prospect of validating the method so that there can be confidence that a researcher or professional applying the method in one place is talking about the same needs and need groups as their counterparts in other places. The Dartington Social Research Unit has begun to use its database of cases from a variety of samples as a national archive for validation exercises. Computer cluster analysis provides an opportunity to explore whether the qualitative needs clustering exercise completed by professionals and local managers is validated by independent statistical analysis. It is also intended that activity and outcomes for children in identified groups will be compared to actuarial or reference tables that set out the typical ranges of activity and outcomes for each need group.

Successful validation offers the prospect of developing a classification of children's needs that is meaningful for a range of professionals. It also offers the possibility of trying to understand more about the factors at play when audit groups seek to define needs. For example, people struggle at present to sort out whether they are classifying needs (such as to reduce adult conflict) or problems (such as parental domestic violence) or manifestations of need (such as self harm or substance misuse). These and other issues about emerging taxonomies are explored by Sinclair and Little in Chapter 6.

User involvement

So far no mention has been made of the children and families intended to benefit from *Matching Needs and Services* audits. How do they understand need? What impact do they have on the professional task? Would they recognise, and endorse, the identified need groups emerging from current samples?

The early piloting of the practice tool had tested new ways of incorporating the user perspective in research work, moving beyond interviews with children and parents, and seeking instead to ask user groups to comment on proposals for new services. But that work was itself limited, not least because it came so late in the process. As a result, the method now incorporates user perspectives from the start.

The current model proposes a shadow team of users – parents and young people – working in parallel with the professional audit team, compiling its own set of need groups from the data extracted from case files by the professionals. The results of the two clustering exercised are compared, with discussion of similarities and differences. So far, user need groups have closely resembled those created by professionals.

More telling differences emerge at the earlier stage, when cases are discussed and need groups created. Users find it easier than professionals to focus on needs without being distracted by budget or other service constraints, and they tend to have more discussion about the impact of sudden or prolonged poverty on parental ability to raise children with confidence. They are more openly critical of absent or non-caring fathers, and keen to bolster the men's parenting role. They are keen to see children removed from neglectful parents, but only as an interim measure whilst home conditions are improved. And their language about need is clear and jargon free, such as when they describe the need for the parent of a child with disabilities to have a 'break from caring' rather than 'shared care', or when parents need 'help to understand and cope with a child's behaviour' rather than 'parenting skills'.

The early validation by users in some areas has boosted the confidence of professionals to move on to the next stages of the work, and to involve users there too. As a result, users have spoken at local and national dissemination seminars, have struggled alongside professionals to determine outcomes for identified need groups, and have contributed to the detailed planning of new or revised services in response. They have clear views about the social work task they want to see preserved and promoted: early attention to problems to avoid more intrusive action later on; continued advocacy from social workers over health, housing, social security and education problems; and respite measures so that parents and children can get a break from one another or children can get temporary relief from neglectful parents or impoverished surroundings.

At a personal level, too, users have gained. They have felt affirmed by having their views valued and by seeing their family experiences used for the benefit of others. They have commented that being involved in the audit has enabled them to venture further from home than before, to meet others with similar or worse problems, and to become motivated to return to work.

The piloting of shadow user groups has also produced some lessons for future consultation exercises. These are about starting the planning early, establishing criteria for user selection, aiming for a representative group, having a staff link person, and perhaps using an external facilitator. Of equal importance is treating people as experts about themselves, paying them for their time and effort, and giving feedback on the use made of their work. Such issues have relevance beyond *Matching Needs and Services*, especially for departments keen to comply well with the consultation requirements in the Children Act 1989 and in Quality Protects.

Other implications for policy and practice

The main value of *Matching Needs and Services* audit work lies in its contribution to the strategic planning of services. But its varied use has also produced a range of helpful spin-offs for policy and practice development, some of which are discussed below.

Refocusing child protection services

The first local authority to apply the tool to a sample of new referrals to social services was a large county authority keen to achieve a better balance between its child protection and family support work. It saw in the method the potential for linking an assessment of the needs and experiences of individual children to the planning and organisation of services for children in need. The audit sample included the county's first 250 consecutive 'child protection' referrals and the first 250 consecutive 'other children in need' referrals from a common start date.

The aggregation exercise produced a set of need groups similar to those listed earlier in the chapter. How were the 'child protection' and 'in need' cases distributed amongst the need groups? Apart from the health need group, where all cases had been referred under the 'in need' procedure, the cases were spread fairly evenly across the rest of the need groups. The implication was clear: children and families have very similar needs, no matter how they come to the attention of social services, and no matter how their case is processed. Their needs cut across administrative boundaries about child protection and family support.

Similar findings have emerged when this exercise has been replicated in other local authority areas. The findings endorse the determination of departments to develop a service that is responsive to the identified needs of children and families and, where necessary, building protection into that response rather than focusing too narrowly on investigating particular incidents of abuse.

Increased impetus for multi-agency planning

Statistical analysis of data available from early audits provides information about the nature and extent of health and education issues for children newly referred to social services. At the time of referral, a third of the children in this type of audit (34%) had an identified health need. Problems around physical health and/or disability predominate, recorded for 19 per cent of children. Mental health problems come next (9%), with smaller numbers of children recorded as having developmental delay (4%) or needs arising from their misuse of alcohol or drugs (3%).

Professionals record more health problems for children's parents, with an overall incidence of 41 per cent. Here, mental health needs predominate, affecting 18 per cent of parents, and with noticeably higher levels recorded in authorities in inner London (41%) and the north-east of England (30%). Next comes substance misuse, at 9 per cent. Physical health needs are noted for 7 per cent of parents, and disability for 4 per cent.

In relation to education, almost half the school-age children (47%) had an identified need, classified under one of three headings: special education, truancy and exclusion, and behaviour causing concern. Poor behaviour in school is recorded for 17 per cent of children, whilst poor attendance and special needs each feature for 15 per cent of children.

There is nothing new in stating that social services, education and health have children in common. What the audits did, for the first time, was to quantify the extent of that overlap and help identify – for each need group – the likely demand on each agency in the following year. They also highlighted the importance of social services not working in isolation from other agencies. The first audit of new referrals triggered an invitation to key statutory and voluntary agencies to join forces with social services in developing services to respond to the identified need groups. Multi-agency planning groups, reporting to a joint commissioning strategy group, developed new service specifications for piloting in three areas, focusing on the county's largest need groups: about 'confident parenting', 'much improved care', and 'behaviour change in parents in conflict'.

Multi-agency audits of need

The acknowledged pitfalls of not including all agencies from the early stages of audit exercises have prompted the development of multi-agency audits of need within local authority or primary care group boundaries. Typically, social services include new referrals to each local duty team, education include children needing help over and above the normal classroom setting, health take referrals to family doctors that involve social care needs, and the police include all incidents involving children in the audit period.

Agencies start by conducting their own audit and agreeing their own need groups. They then work together to see whether they can composite any or all of the need groups, checking with the audit forms as they go, to ensure that any groups that get amalgamated do contain children with similar needs. The end product is a set of locality need groups that provides a framework for the joint planning of new services. An alternative approach is for a small group of representatives from each agency to work together on all the cases, teasing out the pattern of need across the different agencies.

Noticeable outcomes of such multi-agency work are a confidence amongst professionals that they are speaking the same language about need, and a strengthened resolve to work across and beyond agency boundaries. The energy generated by the audit work seems to smooth the way for the more onerous task ahead: that of creating service responses that are also multi-agency.

Management information

Experience points to the value of agencies using *Matching Needs and Services* on a routine basis to help inform their planning and development of children's services. The dimensions used in the audit to record family circumstances give a quick picture (as accurate as is recorded on case files) of the incidence of specific needs. Statistical analysis of this information provides aggregated data – by both need group and geographical area – about variables such as age, gender, household composition, ethnicity, domestic violence, family income and housing conditions, and (as indicated earlier) the incidence of health and education issues. For example, domestic violence is recorded on files in between 10 per cent and 16 per cent of cases, with an average incidence of 13 per cent. Whilst this is likely to be an under-recording, the similarity of incidence tends to support the robustness of the method as a means of collecting data about families. The figure is close to the incidence rate of 16 per cent in the *General Household Survey* 1997 (Office for National Statistics 1999).

The data collected from files can be grossed up to predict levels of need across all groups for a full year. For example, services in response to needs around substance misuse will be determined by the number and characteristics of parents and children in that group. But planning will also need to take account of other parents or children also misusing substances, but allocated to a different need group because of their other, more pressing, needs. Once all the groups are considered in this way, the agency will have a complete framework for future planning.

Another product of the *Matching Needs and Services* tool is management information about the impact of services on children and families. Herein lies the value of taking a retrospective sample, for if cases are included from a common start date several months before the beginning of the audit, the agency can build up a picture of its activity throughout that period. This activity is recorded on the back of the audit form. Information collected about outputs includes the way cases are processed, whether services are offered and taken up, and whether there are subsequent referrals; whilst information on outcomes indicates whether needs are met and whether children remain safe.

The data will also indicate where adjustments may be needed to services already provided. For instance, a consistent finding is the low take-up of services to deal with trauma or loss. Such information offers the opportunity to scrutinise both what is offered and how, and to create and test out approaches that might be seen as more helpful. There is the added advantage that cases used in the audit might provide a source of clients who can be consulted and involved in this work.

Audit data can also help underpin an authority's corporate response to needs. For instance, the pursuit of a joint strategy for prevention and support around domestic violence, including help for women and children to stay in their community, will benefit from the active involvement of the housing department. Similarly, aerobic sessions and other activities organised through the leisure department may be a welcome extra option for family doctors and other professionals wanting to boost the emotional wellbeing and mental health of parents under stress. At a more general level, aggregation exercises have been well received by elected members keen to supplement their detailed knowledge of their own electoral ward with an overview of needs and services across the whole local authority.

Finally, repeat audits will help planners keep track of changing needs and required responses. Is the pattern of need similar year on year, as the methodology assumes? The answer will be clear only if it is put to the test. It has proved harder than anticipated to get agencies to conduct repeat audits. An annual audit is probably over-ambitious. But some regular review needs to be in place, perhaps linked to the review of the Children's Services Plan or to the planned evaluation of new services.

Recording ethnicity

A sober finding in local authority audits is the generally poor level of recording of ethnicity. Practice is slightly better where the casework referral form requires practitioners to select from a menu of options rather than use free text to describe ethnicity. Even so, this important management information goes unrecorded in between 31 per cent and 78 per cent of cases. It points to the continuing need for rigorous attention to sound ethnic monitoring if local authorities are to comply fully with the requirement of the Children Act 1989 to take account of race, religion, language and culture. The shocking gap, echoing similar findings from over a decade ago (Rowe, Hundleby and Garnett 1989) also highlights the undoubted need for training to boost professional understanding and confidence about why and how to ask families about their ethnicity.

Assessment skills

On a more positive note, the direct involvement in audit work has boosted practitioner confidence in a needs-led approach to individual casework. In areas where audits have been conducted, managers have commented favourably on child protection reports which now contain a clear and specific focus on the needs of children and families. Some have used the audit form to help guide discussion in supervision sessions. Others have used it to conduct joint assessments with parents of needs and desired outcomes, and women's refuges across one local authority have piloted it as a self-assessment tool by mothers accessing the service.

Support for the social work task

Audit work has tended to affirm the positive contribution of professionals to vulnerable families. Analysis of audit forms reveals that the bulk of referrals still come from the general public. In response, there is a wider range of activity with children and families than is sometimes thought to be the case: the view that social workers have time only for complex and time-consuming child protection work does not seem supported by evidence from audits. But what is supported is the need for a more proactive approach to low-level needs, the earlier provision of family support services, greater clarity in describing the precise nature of the work done by social workers, and continued liaison with other agencies to ensure that families who are referred for specialist services succeed in getting them.

Audits have also prompted renewed discussion about the value of joint recording with families, of having agreed statements of needs and outcomes, and of specifying – in both discussion and writing – the research basis for pursuing one course of action rather than another.

Conclusion

Matching Needs and Services begins with a systematic assessment of children's needs. It then clusters cases into groups with similar characteristics and uses this information to consider what services are appropriate for the various groups identified. The methodology has been tried and tested for a variety of client groups and in a variety of single and multi-agency settings.

There is still much to be done to test the validity of the early findings described in this chapter, and to increase the early involvement of children and families in the methodology to help counter the predominantly professional perspective of the casework files used for audits. The long-term aim is for the methodology to lead to the development of new services, or the reshaping of existing services, designed on the basis of evidence about children's needs, and then evaluated against desired outcomes. Evidence so far suggests that the design and implementation of new services is a struggle for agencies, either alone or in partnership with others. Work underway in various local authority sites should help tease out more about the obstacles to progress as well as testing possible solutions.

In the meantime, there are encouraging developments. *Matching Needs and Services* offers a relatively quick and easy way of involving front-line staff as well as managers and planners in creating a robust framework and strategy for local planning which seek to improve the match between the services they provide and the needs of the communities they serve. It helps quantify the extent to which the needs of children and families cross agency boundaries. And it paves the way for planning that starts from a shared analysis and understanding of children's needs, and a consensus amongst professionals and users of the desired outcomes for vulnerable children and their families.

CHAPTER SIX

Developing a Taxonomy for Children in Need

Ruth Sinclair and Michael Little

This chapter explores the rationale for establishing a taxonomy that consolidates some of the frameworks so far developed for describing children's need and develops them into a dynamic classificatory system. The proposed taxonomy would be developed around five axes: manifestations of need; contextual factors; antecedents; severity of need; and positive factors. Its ultimate objective would be to provide a methodology that makes it possible to predict the likely trajectories of different groups of children, with or without service interventions.

Introduction

Before the needs of children can be understood they must first be described. This is true for professionals working with children in need, whether the task is assessment or deciding how best to meet identified needs. It is equally the case for those responsible for planning services on behalf of whole populations of children in need. The statement also holds for policy makers operating nationally.

Recent years have seen a growing interest in frameworks for describing the needs of individual children, in tools to record these and in mechanisms for aggregating the results to assist service planning. Many of these developments are the subject of chapters within this book. Is it possible to take this thinking further? Can we build upon existing knowledge and develop a comprehensive framework for describing the needs of children?

Can we then extend our thinking and consider how this framework can be used to develop a taxonomy for children in need? We believe the answers to these questions to be 'yes'. Our purpose in writing this chapter is to share some early thinking on developing such a taxonomy for children in need, a formulation that seeks to build upon and co-ordinate existing models for describing the needs of children.

The ideas represented here emerged from a series of meetings and seminars jointly organised by the National Children's Bureau and Dartington Social Research Unit and sponsored by the Department of Health. The participation in these gatherings represented wide-ranging interests, including professionals from health, education and social services, policy makers, researchers and practitioners. The discussions have been broad ranging and have borrowed ideas from economics, medicine and the natural sciences. A sobering conclusion from all this talk has been the realisation that nearly all other disciplines rely heavily on some form of taxonomy.

Taxonomy as a concept

A very general definition of taxonomy might be 'the science or practice of classification' (Collins English Dictionary). Scientists generally distinguish a taxonomy from a typology; the former resting on facts about actual objects or people, the latter emerging from some conceptual classification (Hair *et al.* 1998). Taxonomy, then, is more than a simple list of groupings. It is a way of applying a logical and comprehensive structure to describe characteristics and the way in which these are inter-related to form identifiable groups. Furthermore, this structure should be one that allows for differentiation, such that it is possible to assume that those entities placed in any one category have more in common with others in their group than those in any other group. The strength of any taxonomy depends on the extent to which it allows such differentiation.

Most branches of science depend upon some form of taxonomy; all established taxonomies are dynamic and subject to continuous empirical testing. Chemistry has its periodic table charting the structure of the elements and their relationship to each other; Linnaeus set out a taxonomy of plants, now subject to extensive revision in the light of new understanding about genetics. Medicine has several classifications (see below) that are also subject to radical revision brought about by research on the genetic structure of disease (Department of Health 1995d).

The nearest (although still distant) equivalent to services for children in need is the medical field. The World Health Organisation has produced several updates of the ICD (International Classification of Diseases) into which all known diseases are placed into groups in a systematic structure based on common characteristics. The current version is ICD-10 (World Health Organisation 1992). Similarly the DSM (Diagnostic and Statistical Manual) provides a grouping of psychiatric disorders (American Psychiatric Association 1994). There have been other attempts in the psychiatric field. Freud (1965) produced a developmental profile based on psycho-analytical concepts. The gradual evolution of the ICD and DSM classifications has depended on fierce arguments about the basis of the frameworks used (Cantwell and Rutter 1994; Feighner *et al.* 1972).

This is not the place for a full exposition of the nature of these arguments; this can be found in Cantwell and Rutter (1994). In essence, they revolve around: the basis of the taxonomy (should it reflect the cause of the disease, its symptoms or its trajectory?); whether to use a series of dimensions or categories (the former concentrating on the way of understanding the disease, the latter a more specific representation); what to include in the dimensions or categories (including the re-emergence of genetic factors); and how to validate any scheme produced (for example by statistical analysis, epidemiological data, trajectory or response to intervention).

The experience of developing the ICD and DSM (IV) suggests that the development of any new taxonomy will be an iterative process, an exploratory journey. It also suggests that the process itself, the discussions and arguments, are of great value in deepening understanding, both of the concept of taxonomy and of the characteristics it seeks to categorise. A similar experience would have much to offer to the field of children in need.

The resolution to such arguments depends on an answer to one question: 'what is the purpose of the taxonomy?' Some aim to be solely *descriptive* – they provide a logical structure to enable members of professions to describe better the similarities and differences in the characteristics of groups. Others may have *explanatory* properties – enabling users to explain the relationships between the different groups and other dimensions. For example, in medicine a taxonomy may help explain how one set of symptoms may be related to others or consider the effects of medical interventions on particular symptoms.

It is also possible for taxonomies to be *predictive.* If sufficient is known or has been proven about the differential effects of interventions or the relationship between different factors, then it may be possible to use a taxonomy to predict with greater accuracy the likely outcome from a specific intervention for people with different characteristics.

The study of children in need is some considerable way behind the other areas described here. Aspirations, therefore, should be modest. The ultimate aim of a taxonomy in this area might be to contribute to and underpin some general theory about the relationship between the needs of children, the services which best meet those needs and the likely outcomes for children in receipt of such services. Such an endeavour requires better science, which is looking to the future. A first step is the development of a framework that systematically describes the needs of children. This has the potential to lead to the second stage: grouping together children in working taxonomies that make sense to clinicians, administrators and researchers operating in different parts of children's services (health, education, social services) and in different cultural contexts.

Why a taxonomy for children in need?

In the first seminar that led to this chapter, considerable work was needed to clarify different aspects of taxonomy. A consensus was swiftly achieved to organise it around children in need. As previous chapters have already indicated, the Children Act 1989 requires local authorities to identify children in need, an exercise that should be empirically based and demands inter-agency co-operation to draw common thresholds of potential or actual impairment, harm and, therefore, intervention. The Act also places a duty on local authorities to safeguard and promote the welfare of children in their area who are in need. To support this work at a practitioner level, the Department of Health has issued guidance on the process and practice of assessing the needs of children and again has clearly focused on children in need (see Chapter 8) (Department of Health, Department for Education and Employment and Home Office 2000a). Taxonomy can, therefore, contribute to an exercise with which most local authorities are already struggling and, in the process, ally approaches to management information, practitioner evidence bases and research.

'Children in need' is a term widely accepted in children's services and increasingly taken up by other agencies working with vulnerable children. Current thinking about the planning of services for vulnerable children provides three other strong reasons why a taxonomy for children in need may be advantageous. It could depend on and, therefore, provide: a conceptual framework to underpin work to address the needs of children; the beginnings of a common language to improve communication; and a practical mechanism to link individual and collective childcare planning. These are discussed more fully below.

A conceptual framework

Given the great diversity in the circumstances of children and the range and complexity of their problems, it becomes impossible to assess their needs, either individually or collectively, without being able to impose some structure to assist understanding. This means it is necessary to synthesise or categorise children in some way. Although the particular constellation of need of any one child may be unique or specific to that individual, all children are more or less like other children. The similarities and differences between one child and another can be measured only with the help of a conceptual framework which includes the dimensions on which these similarities and differences can be calculated. This could be important for planning as well as practice and research.

The effective provision of welfare to children in need within any locality requires a conceptual understanding of the demands made on welfare services and of how professionals, practitioners and planners can best meet these. That in turn requires meaningful categories of children in need and that depends on a useful conceptual framework. The use of conceptual modelling has long been a tool in social policy to assist our understanding of complex social phenomena. In building a conceptual framework to link preventative work with models of welfare, Hardiker and colleagues (Chapter 3) draw on Titmuss, a major thinker on social policy. His view summarises what we see as the fundamental purpose of a conceptual framework:

> the purpose of model building is not to admire the architecture of the building, but to help us to see some order in all the disorder and confusion of facts, systems and choices concerning certain areas of economic and social life.
>
> (Titmuss 1974, p.30)

A common language

For practitioners, managers, policy makers and researchers to be able to hold useful conversations about the needs of children, both within and across agencies, a common language will be required. Malek (1993) has graphically described how children with very similar needs are sometimes found within specialist education, sometimes dealt with by the justice system or by social services or by child and adolescent mental health services. Within each service, such children will be described by a different label: as being educationally or behaviourally disturbed; as offenders; as beyond parental control; as having a conduct disorder. If professionals are to work better together, they require words to describe the needs of the children they collectively seek to help.

If this is true for practitioners and for managers, it is also true for researchers. A common system for categorising the needs of children would allow accurate comparison to be made between research studies and enable research findings to be built into a more substantial body of knowledge. This would increase the confidence with which such findings could be applied. It would also enable practitioners more easily to test the appropriateness of any research findings to their own particular situation. The requisite for researchers to have a common language is particularly strong in seeking to develop a more robust evidence-based link between outcomes for children from the services they receive to meet their assessed needs.

Preliminary work at the Dartington Social Research Unit (1998) is using concepts evolved in 30 years of its research work to produce tools that can see these ideas applied in practice and which together will produce empirically testable theory. This work is being tried in 12 sites in Europe and the United States. This is just one approach to a common language that, even if it fails to make significant headway, should encourage a wider pursuit of its ideals.

Linking different levels of care planning

A systematic way of describing the needs of all children is the necessary foundation of any framework for assessing the needs of individual children. Moving from the level of individual casework to that of the agency as a whole requires some concordance between the units of analysis. Policy makers and service planners need to operate at a more collective level, aggregating individual needs into demands for services. The collection of information on individuals and groups, whether for planning or research purposes, requires some synthesis.

If information relating to the needs of individual children can be regarded as the micro level, then the information needed to plan and commission services locally might be regarded as the mezzo level. There is also a third or macro level. Central government has to be able to make decisions about what resources should be allocated to achieve their objectives; to do this they require information that is manageable, meaningful and comparable across local authorities. This also requires some standardised form of describing and categorising the needs of children.

Focusing on a taxonomy for children in need will help develop a conceptual framework that is applicable at all these levels: a framework that is useful to a practitioner working at case level, to a local service planner and to a national strategic planner in central government.

Building on existing models

Although the concept of taxonomy may be new to some readers, attempts to classify or categorise children and their needs are not. For instance, social policy researchers have often devised groupings to explore and explain the relationships they were researching. Here one thinks of Packman, Randall and Jacques' (1985) classification of 'the victims, the volunteered and the villains' to explain differences in the main groups of children entering the care system; or the use of the terms 'long-term settled, long-term unsettled and teenage entrants' by Garnett (1992) to describe the different care paths of those leaving care. In the context of antisocial behaviour, the principal distinction has been between life-course-persistent and adolescence-limited offenders (Moffitt 1993).

The categorisations just described are not equivalent. The latter, produced by Moffitt, might be thought of as a true taxonomy in that it is firmly based on empirical data. The Moffitt taxonomy is, however, difficult to apply in practice mainly due to its concentration on offending which is often only one part of a professional's task. The former groupings have also emerged from data but they have not been firmly based on it. The categories are conceptual but produced by researchers (who are often also qualified practitioners) who are totally familiar with their data. As a consequence, the groupings they produce tend to be much more useful in practice.

Putting cases into groups is a preoccupation of planners as well as researchers. Central government has always sought, with limited success, to find a way of describing different administrative populations, such as juvenile delinquents, children looked after, children with special educational needs and so on. For example, the Department of Health's statistical collections record reasons for being looked after, the reason why children's names are placed on the protection register and the type of young people placed in local authority secure accommodation.

Some of this thinking has been taken up in the drive towards better management information in children's services in England. Operational and planning tools tend to be rooted in conceptual frameworks that require the needs of children to be categorised. For example both the Assessment and Action Records of the *Looking After Children* materials (Parker *et al.* 1991; Ward 1995; Department of Health 1995a) and *Matching Needs and Services* (Bullock, Little and Mount 1995; Little, Ryan and Tunnard 1999) provide complementary frameworks for describing or categorising the developmental needs of individual children.

These approaches have been further developed in the *Framework for the Assessment of Children in Need* (Department of Health, Department for Education and Employment, Home Office 2000a). This recognises that a child's needs cannot be fully described uni-dimensionally, but require more than one axis or domain. Hence the Framework adopts a triangular, or multi-axial, approach describing the needs of the child within three domains: the developmental needs of the child (as in *Looking After Children*); the capacity of parents or caregivers to respond appropriately; and wider family and environmental influences. Each of these three axes comprises several dimensions, which taken together have the potential to describe the children's needs arising from their current situation in a holistic way. The Framework is fully discussed in Chapter 8.

A different approach was used by the Department of Health (2000b) in its census on children in need (CIN), undertaken in February 2000 (www.doh.gov.uk/cin). Social services departments in England were asked to identify all their open cases, the characteristics of the child and the services they received. All cases were allocated to a 'need group'. These groups related to the cause of their need.

This is not an exhaustive list of approaches, but *Looking After Children, Matching Needs and Services* and the 'needs groups' of the CIN census are being widely used in local authorities in England, as well as in other countries. Each has been developed from a different starting point and, as such, they illuminate different and, only occasionally, contradictory aspects of our understanding of children's needs. For example, *Looking After Children* offers seven *dimensions* in which the complete developmental needs of children can be described. In contrast the 'causes of need' is categorical, in that each description stands as a separate category. Taken together, they represent a good way of considering the strengths and weaknesses of different ways of building a taxonomy.

Categorising children in need

In operationalising the concept of children in need as used in the Children Act 1989, many local authorities devised their own definitions of which children they regarded as having passed that threshold (see Chapter 7).

Table 6.1 Examples of local authority definitions of children in need

Nature or concept of need	Examples from local authorities
Causes of need	Child has physical, learning or sensory disability Children whose normal development is impaired due to social/cultural isolation
Manifestations of need	Child is in family where there is a risk of family breakdown Children whose behaviour is a danger to themselves and others
Service responses	Child receiving shared care Children receiving financial assistance under Section 17 of Children Act 1989
Social-economic factors	Child living in a family on low income Child in family with one parent
Statutory duties	Child in private fostering placement Child receiving support under Section 24 of Children Act 1989

Source: Adapted from Carr-Hill *et al.* 1997.

In 1995, as part of a wider study, a survey of these was undertaken in all local authorities in England (Carr-Hill *et al.* 1997). The result of this exercise was a list of over 108 different ways in which local authorities described children in need, excluding all obvious semantic variations.

It was clear from this list that several different conceptual approaches were being used. Some related to the causes of the child's need, some to presenting problems. Others focused more on the needs deriving from the child's community, such as environmental factors or socio-economic indicators. Others were more service-led and reflected local provision or local authority statutory duties. Although the concept of needs-led planning has almost universal acceptance now, much of the language used remains resource-led. Table 6.1 offers some examples derived from the local authority responses.

A list of 108 different definitions is evidence itself of the requirement for taxonomy, better conceptual frameworks and the common language argued for above. But by the same token, the definitions did not provide a workable schema. Further analysis by colleagues in the Department of Health was undertaken to group these definitions using a needs-led approach and within a single logical construct. One model which met these criteria and which encompassed most of the 108 different definitions emerged from the several that were tested. This model focused on the underlying causes of the child's need. A child could be described as a child in need as a result of one of seven antecedent factors as shown below (Sinclair and Carr-Hill 1996):

- physical condition, disability or developmental difficulties
- deprivation, poverty or social disadvantage
- parent or carer's disability, illness or addictions
- abuse or (wilful) neglect
- living in unstable or otherwise detrimental family
- breaking the law
- rejection from, estrangement from or collapse of family
- other reason.

This model for categorising children in need has now been applied in several different contexts (Sinclair and Carr-Hill 1996; Sinclair 1999; Tunstill and Aldgate 2000; Department of Health 2000b). This suggests that in broad terms this categorisation presents a meaningful structure for grouping children in need. The approach does, however, throw up questions about the extent to which the complexity of children's lives can be synthesised. Should categories be regarded as mutually exclusive or is it permissible to place a child in more than one? The answer depends on the purpose for which the information is being used. The multiplicity and complexity of a child's needs must be fully documented in individual assessment, but may be less relevant to service planning.

Table 6.2 Children in need

Children in need as result of:	Any mention		Main type	
	N	%	N	%
1. Physical condition, disability or development difficulties	145	32.3	56	13.9
2. Deprivation, poverty or social disadvantage	182	40.3	16	4.0
3. Parent or carers' disability, illness or addictions	172	38.3	65	16.1
4. Abuse or (wilful) neglect	154	34.3	59	14.6
5. Living in unstable or otherwise detrimental family	263	58.6	77	19.1
6. Breaking the law	97	21.6	58	14.4
7. Rejection from, estrangement from or collapse of family	168	37.4	57	14.1
8. Other reason	22	4.9	15	3.7

The application of this categorisation shows that most social workers generally perceive children's needs as resulting from a combination of factors and, given the option, select on average over three of the seven causes of need described above. But respondents were also readily able to select a main overriding cause for the child's current needs. For example, the results of the first study, presented in Table 6.2, which asked social workers to describe the causes of need of 424 children, demonstrates the perceived multi-faceted origins of need, but also an ability to prioritise one main cause of need (Sinclair and Carr-Hill 1996). When this exercise was repeated with social workers and the respondents were encouraged to discuss the process and the relevance of the categories, few expressed any difficulty in readily identifying one or more causes of need and also the main cause of need (Sinclair 1999).

Further successful piloting has led to the adoption of this framework (with modifications) for the CIN census in February 2000 and in the data required in Quality Protect*s* management action plans (Department of Health 1998b, 2000b). The need categories have a short title, a final definition and some guidance on inclusions. The results of the first census, as shown in Table 6.3, indicate that for open social services cases, abuse or neglect was the single most common main cause of need.

This is one model, based on an assessment of the possible causes of need, built up from service planners' descriptions. Other models are structured to describe children in need in terms of their presenting problems or the way in which their needs become manifest. Three pieces of scientific development work funded by the Department of Health have started from this premise: *Looking After Children, Matching Needs and Services* and the *Assessment Framework*, all of which have been described elsewhere in this book (see Chapters 5, 8 and 13). It is only possible in this chapter to summarise briefly how the approaches contrast and therefore complement one another in the search for a workable taxonomy.

Table 6.3 Causes of need categories

Short title	Definition	Results of census %
1. Abuse or neglect	Children in need as a result of, or at risk of, abuse or neglect	35
2. Disability	Children and their families whose main need for services arises out of the children's disabilities or intrinsic condition	13
3. Parental illness/disability	Children whose main need for services arises because the capacity of their parents or carers to care for them is impaired because of disability, illness, mental illness, or additions	6
4. Family in acute stress	Children whose needs arise from living in a family going through a crisis such that parenting capacity is diminished and some of the children's needs are not being adequately met	11
5. Family dysfunction	Children whose needs arise mainly out of their living in families where the parenting capacity is *chronically* inadequate	13
6. Socially unacceptable behaviour	Children and families whose need for services arises primarily out of the children's behaviour impacting detrimentally on the community	6
7. Low income	Children living in families or independently, whose needs arise mainly from being dependant on an income below the standard state entitlements	6
8. Absent parenting	Children whose need for services arises mainly from having no parents able to provide for them	3
9. Cases other than children in need	Casework that is required for legal and administrative reasons only and there is no child in the case who is in need	5

The two most widely used tools, *Looking After Children* and *Matching Needs and Services*, provide for different functions in children's services but each can be thought of as evolving towards the other. The former is a clinical tool to be used with individual children looked after, the results of which can be added to those on other children to produce an aggregate picture. The latter is a planning tool, which relies upon hastily assembled information on representative groups of children. A project to show how *Looking After Children* data can be aggregated (Ward and Skuse 1999; Skuse, Macdonald and Ward 2001; Ward *et al.* forthcoming) informs the development of the *Integrated Children's System* (see Chapter 14) which will eventually do away with the need to use *Matching Needs and Services* on some samples of children. A project to produce clinical instruments for health, education and social services professionals which dovetails with *Matching Needs and Services* promises to bring the strengths of *Looking After Children* to those children supported in the community (Dartington-i 2001).

Each approach collects information about the whole child, albeit in slightly different dimensions. *Looking After Children* collects data directly from children and families, whereas *Matching Needs and Services* relies on data gathered from case files. The clinical approach collects much information on a narrow population (children looked after for six or more months) whereas the planning tool collects just 300 bits of data, but extends to children in need supported by health, education and social services at home as well as away. *Looking After Children* assembles output and outcome data prospectively – which has enormous advantages in research terms – whereas *Matching Needs and Services* uses information retrospectively assembled.

Both projects should provide valuable information to test some of the proposals for a working taxonomy of children in need described below. A specific research programme is currently exploring how data from *Looking After Children* materials completed with 242 long-separated children in six local authorities can be aggregated and transformed into management information (Ward and Skuse 2001; Ward *et al.* forthcoming). Similar projects are being undertaken in Canada (Flynn and Biro 1998; Kufeldt, Vachon and Simard 2000). *Matching Needs and Services* has produced information on over 5000 children in need, mostly supported at home, including over 1000 cases in countries abroad.

The Assessment Framework adopts a similar approach to that of *Looking After Children*, but recognises that it is necessary to place the child's manifestations of need alongside the capacity of parents to meet these needs, together with any other positive or protective factors in the child's situation. The *Assessment Recording Forms* (Department of Health and Cleaver 2000), produced in order to help practitioners operationalise the Framework and currently being trialled in a large number of local authorities, will also become a rich source of data on need in these three domains.

From working models to a taxonomical framework

From this range of different ways of describing and categorising children's needs, how can we move forward to a framework for a taxonomy? Each of the approaches described so far is based on different premises to serve different purposes. Each has different strengths and weaknesses and none is on its own sufficient for the overall task.

For example, the Core Assessment Records, the tools being developed to support the Assessment Framework (see Chapter 12), offer a very detailed method by which to describe a child's situation. In their current form, they contain much less guidance on how elements of need relate to one another or how to translate the quantities of information into an assessment of type and level of need, or a categorisation of children in need.

By contrast the framework used in the CIN census is categorical, with a more logical structure in that each group is derived from a similar basis – the underlying antecedents to current problems. But here there is limited articulation of the criteria to be used in assigning a case to one 'need group'.

One conclusion of these comparisons is that we can only fully understand the needs of children when we describe them in several different ways with clearly defined criteria. For example to know which needs are being currently manifest may not be a reliable guide to an appropriate response. Far better to know something about the antecedents of the need, its origins and precipitating factors. Clearly, any judgement is going to have to take into account the severity of the need, or what Dartington's common language work calls a 'pure threshold' (Dartington Social Research Unit 1998). When a child has significant developmental needs, account should be taken of other protective or supporting factors in their life. All of this points towards some kind of multi-axial framework favoured by the pioneers of medicine, such as the concepts used in the development of psychiatric taxonomical models.

That selection of appropriate dimensions depends on the purpose of the taxonomy. The deliberations around the work already completed have made clear the ultimate objective of a taxonomy of children in need: it is to predict the trajectories of different groups of children in need, with and without service interventions. With that in mind, the following axes become manifestly important.

Axis 1: Manifestations of need

The principal axis records the presenting needs of the child. The dimensions for recording need include those used in the *Looking After Children, Matching Needs and Services* and *Core Assessment* models. The important principle here is that data are assembled about all aspects of the child's life, including those outside immediate presenting problems.

Axis 2: Contextual factors

This axis describes the context in which the child is living or to which they may return. It incorporates age, gender, ethnic origin, current living situation, some description of 'social class' and family structure. This immediately throws up difficulties of using a taxonomy with social variables. In some cases where the model has been tested, a situation can be described as a need whereas in another it would be thought of as context. Poverty and overcrowding are likely to be cases in point. Clear rules will have to be drawn for the taxonomy to work in practice.

Axis 3: Antecedents

This axis looks at the causes or the underlying factors that would seem to have led to the child being in need (although this is not being used in the scientific sense to imply a proven causal relationship). The classification was used by the Department of Health in its pilot exercises on expenditure collection and, as noted earlier, subject to minor amendment, forms the basis of the new 'children in need' statistical collection (Department of Health 2000b).

Axis 4: Severity of need

This provides for an assessment of the level of need in each area of the child's life. There may eventually be some connection here with the work on 'pure thresholds' being tested by Dartington and encouraging professionals from different standpoints to make consistent judgments about the severity of a child's need.

Axis 5: Positive factors

No assessment can be built on negative factors alone. The developing model demands some assessment about positive factors in either the child, the family situation or in the local environment that may ameliorate the needs of the child. Clearly, there is potential overlap here in the emerging thinking about protective factors that may lead to future adaptations in the model. There are also close parallels to the family and environmental dimension of the new Assessment Framework (Department of Health, Department for Education and Employment, Home Office 2000a).

These axes provide a possible framework for comprehensively describing children in need, as shown in Figure 6.1

From framework to taxonomy

The framework just described represents a first important step towards taxonomy. It is by no means finished. But it does provide a mechanism to describe comprehensively the needs of individual children and could be used by a wide range of professionals working with children in need. Before we know how it works in practice, much empirical testing and refinement will be required.

How do we progress from this framework to a taxonomy for children in need? How do we move from comprehensive descriptions of individual children to an accurate yet practical structural overview of all children in need? If information was collected on each of the axes on sufficient children, it would be possible to discover whether identifiable groups of children have different developmental trajectories.

Such a taxonomy would make it possible to move beyond describing the children in need population. The capability to impose meaningful structure facilitates further research and analysis of the services received by children and the likely outcomes for children from those interventions. This is an important goal if we are to serve the needs of children through policies and practices informed by a robust comprehensive knowledge or evidence base.

Contextual Factors	Antecedents: child is in need as a result of	Manifestations of need or development deficits	Severity of child's need	Positive Factors	Overall Severity of need
Age Sex Ethnic origin Current living situation Family structure Legal status Class	Child's physical condition Child's disability or developmental difficulties Deprivation, poverty, social disadvantage Parents' or carers' disability or illness Parents' or carers' mental health/ addiction Abuse or wilful neglect Living in unstable or detrimental family Adolescent malcontent or misbehaviour Rejection/ estrangement from or collapse of family Other reason	Living environment }	negligible moderate severe	**In the child** • positive self image • educational attainment • secure attachment **In the family** • authoritative discipline • warm continuous relationship • realistic expectations **In the environment** • wider social relationships • decent housing	negligible moderate severe
		Health }	negligible moderate severe		
		Education }	negligible moderate severe		
		Identity and social presentation }	negligible moderate severe		
		Family/social relationships }	negligible moderate severe		
		Emotional behavioural devp and self-care skills }	negligible moderate severe		

Figure 6.1 A comprehensive system for describing the needs of children

The framework presented here is one step towards this goal. In taking that step we aim to consolidate rather than oppose the frameworks that are already known within services for children in need. Not only has this model still to be tested, it will require considerable revision, not least to take into account other developments described in this book. It will also have to achieve a resonance with the way in which practitioners and planners seek to improve their understanding of the needs of children.

CHAPTER SEVEN

Evolution Not Revolution

Family Support Services and the Children Act 1989

Jane Aldgate

This chapter traces the implementation of family support services to children in need and their families under Section 17 of the Children Act 1989 England and Wales. The chapter is based on the work of Aldgate and Tunstill in two studies undertaken in the early years of implementation and five years later (Aldgate and Tunstill 1995; Tunstill and Aldgate 2000). It also draws on some of the other 22 research studies commissioned by the Department of Health to evaluate the implementation of the Children Act 1989 (see Department of Health 2001c).

Introduction

The Children Act 1989 (England and Wales) marked a radical change in the legislative framework for services for vulnerable children and their families. This has been particularly evident in the area of providing services to support children and families under Section 17 of the Act. The changes were succinctly spelt out by Rose in 1992. Chapter 1 has described the duties laid on local authorities by the Act to provide services for children in need and the criteria by which they might be identified. To reiterate, Section 17 places a general duty on local authorities to safeguard and promote the welfare of children in their area who are in need, and subject to that duty, to promote the upbringing of children by their families. This new emphasis is for local authorities to work with the family and child in the family home and for local authorities to work with or facilitate the work of others.

This is reinforced in Section 27, with the new duty on other agencies to assist local authorities in the performance of their duties. The new provisions of the Act enable a range of services such as accommodation to be seen not as a breakdown in preventive service, but as a positive measure of family support. They allow for the development of imaginative and flexible services in partnership and in support of families with users' views taken into account and services assessed against the welfare checklist of Section 1. Such developments have a relatively recent history (Rose 1992, pp.ix–x).

There was, therefore, within Section 17, a change from previous child welfare legislation in England and Wales in three areas:

- a move from concern about an undifferentiated group of vulnerable children to specific groups
- defining these specific groups in the context of children's development
- linking children in need to the provision of services.

Section 17 defined local authorities' responsibilities towards children more broadly than the definition of prevention in previous legislation. Disabled children were considered to be a special case in their own right. Their inclusion in Section 17 was made in recognition of their special developmental needs. The other two specified categories of need are children 'unlikely to achieve or maintain or to have the opportunity of achieving or maintaining a reasonable standard of health or development' and 'children whose health or development might be significantly impaired, or further impaired without the provision...of services'. Here, the intention of the Act was to move consciously from identification of risk of harm, including child maltreatment, to the assessment of the *impact* of that risk on a child's development and the consequences of offering *no service provision* on that child's health and development. This move embraced the idea of safeguarding and promoting children's welfare simultaneously and of going further than merely identifying the impact of harm to actively providing services to meet children's needs. Given the breadth of issues affecting children's development, it followed that a broad range of services would be necessary to respond to those needs. However, the character of services offered to children in need and their families would, in the end, depend very much on how 'in need' was interpreted by local authorities.

How local authorities responded to the definition of children in need

Setting the definition of children in need within the context of child development indicated clearly that negative impacts on children's health and development could arise from a variety of circumstances. Therefore, as the Guidance and Regulations accompanying the Act suggested, it would not be legal for the local authority to confine its services only to children at risk of maltreatment:

> The definition of need...is deliberately wide to reinforce the emphasis on preventive support to families. It has three categories: a reasonable standard of health or development; significant impairment of health or development; and disablement. It would not be acceptable for an authority to exclude any of these three – for example, by confining services to children at risk of significant harm which attracts the duty to investigate under Section 47.
>
> (Department of Health 1991a, para 2.4)

Research on early implementation of Section 17 (Aldgate and Tunstill 1995) showed that local authorities had difficulty in arriving at a definition of 'reasonable standard of health and development' and 'significant impairment'. Reaching a common definition was difficult without guidance from central government. Confusion also arose because of instructions to local authorities to take account of local circumstances in their identification of children in need.

It was the intention of the policy makers to encourage local interpretations of this definition of need in order to ensure that any predetermined groups of vulnerable children could be identified and thus be targeted for priority services. With hindsight this was a mistake. Many local authorities were not at a sufficient level of sophistication in their thinking to respond appropriately to this challenge. In the absence of clear guidance from central government, local authorities ploughed their own furrows, as Colton and his colleagues found in a study of the implementation of Section 17 services in Wales:

> the deliberately broad definition of need, means, in practice, that the services provided by any local authority to a particular child or to any

> category of children will depend almost entirely on how the authority defines and prioritises the concept of need. (Colton *et al.* 1995, p.56)

Given licence to offer local interpretations of 'in need', some strove very hard to narrow the developmental definition of children in need and create eligibility criteria based on groups of children clearly at risk of significant harm. One authority, for example, recommended children in need should be defined as those at risk of child abuse, at risk of criminal proceedings and those accommodated (Aldgate and Tunstill 1995).

A cynical view expressed in one Welsh authority was that the absence of a clear understanding of how the definition of children in need should be interpreted allowed a form of flexible gatekeeping, whereby access to services could be changed according to the resources available at any one time. More precise definitions would 'open the floodgates and we wouldn't be able to cope with demands on resources' (Colton *et al.* 1995 p.61).

There were a minority of authorities who embraced the principles of the Act and adopted a broad definition of need designed to reflect the range of adversity in their area, such as this example from a shire county:

> In general, the following categories of children will be regarded as children in need within the definition of the Children Act in this authority:
>
> 1. Children with disabilities.
> 2. Children at risk of abuse or neglect.
> 3. Children who are delinquent or at risk of becoming delinquent.
> 4. Children separated from their parents by reasons of divorce, hospitalisation, parent in prison, immigration restrictions, and so on.
> 5. Children with caring responsibilities (e.g. teenage parents, children of disabled parents).
> 6. Children whose home conditions are unsatisfactory, e.g. those who are homeless, in temporary or substandard accommodation or accommodation for homeless families.
> 7. Children who may broadly be defined as living in poverty and at high risk of family breakdown – e.g. children whose parents are on low wages or income support, in one-parents families, overcrowded conditions, families with limited support etc.
>
> (Aldgate and Tunstill 1995, p.14).

While the approach of this county could be challenged on the grounds of being too inclusive in assuming, for example, that having a lone parent automatically meant a child would be in need, nevertheless, the breadth of definition embraced both family and environmental factors which research had suggested were likely to affect children's health and development (see, for example, Bradshaw 1990; Kumar 1993), and predispose groups of children to the risk of coming into the care system (Bebbington and Miles 1989).

Setting about establishing who were children in need

Alongside defining which categories of children were in need, local authorities were asked to ascertain the extent of need in their area, as a basis for identifying priority groups of children for service provision in the context of this information and their statutory duties. From the phrasing of Section 17, it might have been expected that there would have been a wide range of predetermined groups of children in a local community who would be 'in need' such as disabled children, children with severe health problems, refugees, young children living in poverty, as well as children in accommodation, leaving care or those at risk of significant harm, for whom the local authority already had responsibility.

This is an exceedingly complex section of the Act which was clearly misunderstood by many local authorities. Some were concerned about the implications for resources if they were required to offer a broader range of services to children and families within a wide range of predetermined groups. Providing family support would be rather different from preventive services to 'diminish the need for reception into care'. Some social services, led by their councils, believed that keeping a tight rein on access to services would be essential. As need was linked to services, it might be best not to be too rigorous in finding out the extent of need. As a social services senior manager told one research study early in implementation: 'The extent of need was a political issue for our authority, members (who were involved in Children Act implementation) of the ruling group discouraged us from finding out the extent of need' (Aldgate and Tunstill 1995, p.16).

Such a view was, it must be said, not evidence-led. Indeed, some of the evidence that existed suggested that families were capable of rationing themselves when offered the opportunity (see Aldgate and Bradley 1999). Other local authorities were simply confused by being asked to do something rather different. As one local authority manager put it, 'We felt at the time that some workers would see the Act as re-negotiating the terms of existing legislation, and it would be difficult to encourage them to see the Act as a whole' (Aldgate and Tunstill 1995, p.12).

There were two further problems which obscured the process of establishing who were children in need locally. Ascertaining the extent of need in an area demanded a fairly sophisticated level of communication. As two early implementation studies show, it was, for some, a new experience for different departments to cross the organisational divide and even talk to each other at a planning level (Aldgate and Tunstill 1995; Colton *et al.* 1995). However there were exceptions. Ian White, the then Director of Oxfordshire Social Services, held one of the first inter-agency meetings between different children's services and local academics in order to decide how to map need in the area.

Even where communication was good, different departments were often faced with inadequate and incompatible information systems. There was evidence in the early stages of implementation of very localised systems of data collection, which seriously hampered any exercise to map children 'in need': 'We are split into 31 localities, each locality collects the kind of data they think they need...so it means that across the county there is a multiplicity of methods for data collection' (Aldgate and Tunstill 1995, p.16).

There were also some serious technical problems resulting from lack of appropriate software packages, variability in scale and scope of data collection resources and inadequate staffing. Often authorities had been sold unsuitable software. Instead of starting again, they had tried to get the firms who supplied the original data to amend their packages. This was often a long drawn-out process, which hindered that of ascertaining need. Some of these issues are discussed in greater detail in Chapter 4.

In spite of the difficulties, Aldgate and Tunstill (1995) reported that local authorities did manage to achieve some mapping of children in need in their areas, although at the early stage of implementing the Act, it is clear that this was not a totally reliable picture. Authorities drew on both predetermined groups and referrals to social services to ascertain who were children in need in their area, but the predetermined groups chosen tended to reflect the characteristics of referred children. Thus, within the predetermined groups, there was considerable discrepancy between those for whom social services already had some responsibility and those in the community experiencing a variety of circumstances of disadvantage. Around three-quarters of social services departments identified children at risk of significant harm or neglect or those looked after to be predetermined groups of children in need.

Surprisingly, only two-thirds of authorities said they would place disabled children into predetermined groups, in spite of the fact that these children in need commanded an arm of Section 17 in their own right. Less than one-quarter of authorities mentioned children with a mentally ill carer as a predetermined group and only slightly more, around one-third, suggested that children who were excluded from school or who lived in substandard housing or, more worryingly, whose families were homeless might also form predetermined groups. It might have been that local authorities believed they had none of these groups in their area. However, the pattern of identification was so consistent across different parts of England, and was confirmed by interviews with managers and policy documents, that a more likely explanation was that social services were struggling with an operational definition of need for all the reasons described earlier. The situation is summarised by Aldgate and Tunstill:

> For many social services departments, the move from services led to needs led planning constituted a huge step, with which many had struggled. Some had succeeded but others had resorted to defining predetermined groups based on traditional services and data from referrals rather than on accurate and substantial local and national evidence. (Aldgate and Tunstill 1995, p.22)

Setting priorities for services

As critics of the Act pointed out early on, the concept of family support linked to the definition of 'in need' created a paradox. Although a wide range of services might be available to many groups of children under the auspices of Section 17, access to services had been narrowed from previous legislation to those judged to be 'in need' (Tunstill 1992). As already suggested, the character of family support services would very much depend on how local authorities defined 'in need'.

There was a further complication. Having set the pattern for ascertaining the extent of need through predetermined groups and referrals, the *Guidance and Regulations* accompanying the Act required local authorities to set priorities for services:

> Local authorities are not expected to meet every individual need, but they are expected to identify the extent of need and then make decisions on the priorities for service provision in their area in the context of that information and their statutory duties. (Department of Health 1991a, para. 2.11)

Once again, as with the decisions about who were children in need, local authorities were given considerable latitude to decide the range of services to be offered and to which groups of children in need. Aldgate and Tunstill (1995) explored this prioritisation of children in their study by eliciting information about priority groups under two headings: groups for whom social services already had some responsibility and children in the community. Tables 7.1 and 7.2 show the findings from this study.

Table 7.1. High prioritised groups of children for whom social services already have some responsibility (n=82)

	Number of SSDs (of 82)	Percent of SSDs (of 82)
Children at risk of significant harm	64	78
Children at risk of neglect	61	74
Children in care	61	74
Children accommodated under S.20	60	73
Children on remand	57	70
Children previously in care/ accommodation	52	63
Children in hospital more than three months	25	30
Privately fostered children	23	28

Note

High priority groups are not mutually exclusive, so that there is the possibility of 100% response rate for each group.

Given the problems around interpreting the definition of children in need, it was hardly surprising, as the findings in Table 7.1 show, that priority groups for service provision were weighted towards groups for whom social services already had responsibility. This meant that children at risk of significant harm led the priority groups. Over three-quarters of authorities in England prioritised services where they considered children were at risk of suffering significant harm. Children looked after were also prioritised. Children in hospital long-term (a new responsibility) and children privately fostered were given a low priority.

Table 7.2. High prioritised groups of children in the community (n=82)

	Number of SSDs (of 82)	Percentage of SSDs (of 82)
Family stability issues:	10	12
Children with behaviour problems		
Parents with marital/relationship problems	8	10
Children with divorcing parents	5	6
Housing issues:		
Homeless families	20	24
Children in bed and breakfast accomodation	12	15
Children in substandard housing	10	12
Children living in homes with gas/electricity/water disconnected	10	12
Poverty issues:		
Children in low income families	8	10
Children in one-parent families	8	10
Children with unemployed parents	6	7

Disability/health issues: Children with disabilities	44	54
Children with special health needs	23	28
Children with special educational needs	20	24
Education issues:		
Children excluded from school	9	11
Children who truant	7	9
Children in independent schools	5	6
Ethnic/linguistic minorities:		
Ethnic minority/black children	8	10
Children with English as second language	2	2
Involvement in crime issues:		
At risk of involvement in crime	27	33
Young people in penal system	27	33
Other children:		
Children at risk of HIV/AIDS	25	30
Children under eight	13	16
Refugee children	9	11
Children in specific geographic areas	6	7

Note
High priority groups are not mutually exclusive, so that there is the possibility of 100% response rate for each group.
From: Aldgate, J. and Tunstill, J. (1992, pp.74–75)

Such highly prioritised groups compared favourably with children in the community, shown in Table 7.2. Low priority was accorded to children whose behaviour or living conditions only were a cause for concern. Just over one-tenth of authorities considered that children were priority cases for services when they were living in households with no gas, water or electricity. Factors which had traditionally placed children at risk of impairment, such as homelessness, truanting and substandard housing were all but ignored.

There was one major surprise. Only 54 per cent of authorities said they would identify disabled children as a predetermined group for high priority access to services. Interviews with senior managers in the same study identified the same disturbing trend: that local authorities would only prioritise disabled children when there was a risk of child maltreatment. This seemed to contradict both the letter and the spirit of the Act to identify disabled children as children in need in their own right, by virtue of their disabilities.

In summary, therefore, it was clear that few authorities were going to prioritise services for children unless they had clearly defined responsibilities for them, as in the case of children looked after. There was a continuation of the situation that existed before the Act: children were unlikely to be offered services unless they were at risk of serious child maltreatment.

The emphasis on child abuse investigation and a mistaken definition of statutory duties

The emphasis on priority services for children at risk of maltreatment needs some explanation in the context of the times. The Children Act 1989 was implemented at a time when services for children and families in many social services departments were led by formal child protection systems that had been evolved to respond to some of the tragic child deaths of the 1980s. In 1985, the Department of Health and Social Security's research overview, *Social Work Decisions in Child Care* (Department of Health and Social Security 1985) had pointed out that families were forced to construct an agenda of risk that would allow compulsory measures to be triggered in order to gain access to any services. Indeed, it was this overzealous use of compulsory measures that in part influenced the Children Act agenda to restore a more balanced approach to enabling access to services based on need. As shown earlier, local authorities found it very difficult to make this transition. Some simply resorted to using old definitions of risk to identify children in need in their area and prioritise services.

For many local authorities, the definitional problems of 'in need' linked to their local interpretation of 'statutory duties'. To some extent this depended on whether authorities saw the Act as an opportunity to develop childcare policy within a new philosophy or whether they saw it as a reformulation of existing duties with some additional ones imposed. Authorities also found it difficult to change their mindsets from identifying risk of commission of abuse or neglect to identifying the impact of that abuse or neglect on children's development. Many local authorities tried to retain old definitions and simply bolt on the Act, thus aiming to equate need with risk of child maltreatment, despite instructions from the Department of Health to the contrary, as shown earlier. At least half the managers interviewed by Aldgate and Tunstill (1995) said they defined statutory duties under the Act as only those concerned with child protection. Duties to identify other children in need under Section 17 were mistakenly seen as an optional extra, as the following examples from the study show. A team leader said:

> As far as I can see we have a very clear boundary between services we have to offer and those that are optional. Obviously, we have to deal with child abuse referrals but if a mother comes in to ask for help with her marital problems we are not interested. We simply haven't the time. It's a great shame...

Another said:

> We are just police. It's no wonder the public doesn't like social workers. I can see the need to follow up families after investigation but we are not allowed to do so. It's all statutory work. (Aldgate and Tunstill 1995, pp.35–36)

The Children Act research studies (Department of Health 1995b; Department of Health 2001c) reveal just how difficult it was for authorities to shift their views from this limited and mistaken interpretation of statutory duties. Consequently, in well over half the authorities in England, in the first four years of the Act, child protection concerns continued to be the main trigger by which families could gain access to services (Brandon *et al.* 1999). Social workers and families were still trying to get round narrow, illegal eligibility criteria set by individual social services departments.

Significantly, it was *only* if there was evidence of potential significant harm that access to family support services could be gained in many authorities. This was directly against the intentions of Part III of the Act, which were that services were to be needs-led within the definition of

Section 17. The provision of services was never intended to be dependent on formal Section 47 enquiries to ascertain whether a child was a risk of significant harm. Section 17 and Section 47 can both be gateways to Part III services. Without clear recognition or acknowledgement of this relationship, the strong ethos of identifying and combating child abuse continued after the Act was implemented, to the detriment of other children in need (Department of Health 2001c).

In their study on family support in cases of abuse and neglect, Thoburn, Wilding and Watson (2000) suggested an exclusive focus on identification of whether maltreatment has occurred can be 'deleterious to child welfare, by allowing needs to go unnoticed, allowing problems to recur, or by dealing with cases via a Section 47 investigation that do not warrant it' (Thoburn *et al.* 2000, p.7).

The refocusing debate

The move towards a more balanced vision of children in need and family support services was not to take place until 1994. That shift, which became known as the refocusing debate (Department of Health 1996a), was inspired by cumulative evidence from a variety of sources, particularly research findings from the arena of the child protection system. It was not until the evaluation of this system, reported and disseminated widely through the Department of Health's overview, *Child Protection – Messages from Research* (Department of Health 1995b) suggested that resources might be refocused, that the balance intended by the Children Act began to be restored.

The child protection research overview concluded:

> A more balanced service for vulnerable children would encourage professionals to take a wider view. There would be efforts to work alongside families rather than disempower them, to raise their self esteem rather than reproach families, to promote family relationships where children have their needs met, rather than leave untreated families with an unsatisfactory parenting style. The focus would be on the overall needs of the child rather than a narrow concentration on the alleged incident.
>
> An approach based on the process of Section 47 enquiries and the provision of Section 17 services (including those for children looked after away from home), might well shift the emphasis in child protection work more towards family support. This, in turn, might encourage local authorities to review the type of Section 17 services provided and to

> consider how well these are matched to their priority cases. (Department of Health 1995b, p.55)

Family support services eight years after implementation

The later studies evaluating the Children Act, which looked at the period after 1995, showed that improvements in the operational definition of need and careful prioritising of a wide range of services were beginning to take place in some areas (Tunstill and Aldgate 2000; Thoburn *et al.* 2000). Further, spurred on by the introduction of Children's Services Plans in 1996 (Department of Health and Department for Education and Employment 1996), social services departments were beginning to work with other agencies towards a common interpretation of in need, although considerable variation between authorities remained (Tunstill and Aldgate 2000).

In Tunstill and Aldgate's study on services for children in need in seven local authorities, carried out in the latter part of the 1990s, there was some evidence of a response to the refocusing initiative, although preoccupation with risk still dominated intervention at the point of access. In the initial screening of families, identification of risk, rather than the impact of risk on the children's development, was the key criterion for accessing services. But at the point of a fuller assessment, social workers shared parents' concerns about their children's development. This is a positive finding and suggests that social workers are taking seriously the twin aims of safeguarding and promoting the welfare of the child (Tunstill and Aldgate 2000, p.143).

These same authorities had widened their prioritised groups of children in need from the time of the first study on Section 17 (Aldgate and Tunstill 1995) to include families under stress and those with child behaviour problems at home and at school. Once they had gained access to the assessment process, many families, right across a range of needs categories, which now included problems intrinsic to the child, parental ill health, family stress, children's offending behaviour and social deprivation, received positive help from social services. Benefits included: 'relief of stress, help with child development, the alleviation of practical problems and improved family relationships' (Tunstill and Aldgate 2000, p.141).

Families who had gained access to services were generally satisfied with them and reported that social services would be an agency of first choice to which they could turn for help. Frustrations still remained, however, in finding out what services were on offer and getting through the door.

Access to services

One of the aims of the Children Act was to make access to services easier for families. Under Schedule 2, social services have a duty to publish services available to families with children in need. Volume 2 of *Guidance and Regulations* states: 'Authorities should take such steps as are reasonably practicable to ensure that those who might benefit from services receive the information' (Department of Health 1991a, para. 2.35).

Authorities are advised that special attention should be given in publicity to take account of the cultural and language needs of minority ethnic families and to be sensitive to those with sensory disabilities: 'as far as possible, the relevant publicity should encourage parents to seek help if it is needed' (Department of Health 1991a, para. 2.36).

The Department of Health's research overview on the implementation of the Children Act (Department of Health 2001c) suggests that such aspirations had not been met. Families who were seeking help from social services for the first time found it hard to locate which office to go to. Initial phone calls could be frostily received and there was an aura of 'deterrent prevention' which faced those referring themselves for help (Tunstill and Aldgate 2000). There was little available publicity about family support services, although the importance of publicity and helping families learn about specific social services was recognised by some workers.

As suggested earlier, one justification for such a controlled approach was that publicising services would open the floodgates to families turning to social services for help. Such an approach, it was argued, would strain to the limit already stretched resources. There was little evidence that such fears were justified. Families in Aldgate and Bradley's (1999) study of family support and short-term fostering fully appreciated the need for rationing services.

A consistent needs-led approach to the provision of services

While access to family support services was clearly inhibited by deliberately obscuring what might be on offer, there was another issue in accessing services: the absence of a consistent approach in the assessment of children in need. Similar children were being treated very differently in different authorities (Department of Health 2001c). Some children were sent down a 'child protection route' while other children in similar circumstances were assessed under Section 17 as being in need of Part III services. With the legacy of child maltreatment concerns still lingering on, in spite of the refocusing debate, some social workers deliberately manipulated the system to ensure children they judged to be in need were provided with services:

> We haven't very clear statements of policy anywhere. Sometimes it (the child protection route) is the only way to get a detailed assessment. It is not using the system appropriately, but out of sheer desperation with children who have huge needs but are not necessarily at risk… If you are a good salesman you can sell anything as a CP [child protection] issue or as a child in need. It's a case of how you present it. (Thoburn *et al.* 2000, p.128)

The research shows that decisions about who might access services were not transparent and were likely to vary from agency to agency, according to the individual judgements of workers processing requests for services available on the day, and departmental guidelines which listed priorities for the receipt of services. Parents who were disabled or whose children were disabled were especially disadvantaged and resented the fact that only families who maltreated their children seemed to get help (Thoburn *et al.* 2000; Tunstill and Aldgate 2000). Additionally, the combination of poverty and the high costs of caring for disabled children caused much distress and placed children in need of services:

> My husband lost his job. I asked if they could help with a playgroup as we are struggling with money. I didn't think I was asking for much. I would have paid for one day if they would pay for the other. How do you find out what you are entitled to? You shouldn't have to lie or beg or grovel. (Thoburn *et al.* 2000, p.132)

Consequently, families were confused about what services they might ask for and it was equally unclear why some were offered services and others in similar situations were refused. Families had more chance of gaining a single practical service such as day care but, even here, the grounds on which such a service might be offered were rarely revealed to families in any written family support plan. It is of interest that the researchers in Thoburn *et al.*'s study (2000) took leaflets with them to explain Part III services. This information was warmly received.

A more transparent approach to accessing services was evident in family centres and other resource centres which acted both as a resource in their own right, but also gave easy access to more specialist services (Department of Health 2001c). Where authorities had adopted an open access policy and had encouraged families to seek help through these open door centres, this seemed to work well and allowed both families and workers to assess the need for services efficiently and effectively (Aldgate and Bradley 1999). This 'one stop shop' approach, which had been recommended for family support services by the Audit Commission (1994), enhanced accessibility and was cost-effective in terms of swift and appropriate responses to families, including referral to specialist sources of help or agreeing that a service was inappropriate. It was also advocated as a way of providing cost-effective support and non-stigmatised services to those needing them for longer periods, thus avoiding the 'revolving door' type of processing whereby cases were closed as rapidly as possible, only to be opened again soon after (Thoburn *et al.* 2000).

Needs-led or service-led family support services

Unfortunately, the easily accessed gateway to Section 17 services was a minority resource for children and families. The more common route has been a haphazard pattern of access to services with little matching of needs to the services likely to be most effective in addressing a particular problem. Provision has been led much more by available services rather than by needs. This was not what the Children Act had intended and went against the rationale for ascertaining need and prioritising services as a result of information about need. At least three studies in the Children Act overview drew attention to the deficiencies of such a service-led approach, where families were offered services inappropriately drawn from an existing pool which did not meet their needs, rather than providing services based on a careful assessment of their needs (Department of Health 2001c).

Overall, the service-led approach has prevailed, as the Children Act overview reported:

> the more normal pattern was what might be called a 'sticking plaster' approach to assessment, based on what services might be in the medicine box. Families with complex problems were not assessed fully but were offered single services, which happened to be available, too late when problems had become entrenched and required a more sophisticated response. Not surprisingly, brief interventions were not effective at this stage. It is much harder to help children when they have been harmed over a long period. The research evidence suggests the needs of these

> families cannot be ameliorated by short-term intervention or a single service (Brandon *et al.* 1999; Tunstill and Aldgate 2000). Longer term complex intervention, in excess of twelve months, co-ordinated by social workers and delivered by skilled professionals from a range of agencies, is likely to be more effective. (Department of Health 2001c)

There were exceptions to this service-led approach. One was the provision of short-term fostering where there was an attempt to match need to service. Here, gatekeeping did take place but was based on assessments of families' capacities to use the service. These careful assessments led to successful outcomes in terms of relieving stress, improving children's quality of life and behaviour and helping parents feel more in control of their lives (Aldgate and Bradley 1999).

It was also evident, in spite of the lottery of services, that families who were offered practical services such as day care, attendance at family centres or brief social casework, at an early stage, responded well (Department of Health 2001c; Thoburn *et al.* 2000; Tunstill and Aldgate 2000). The importance of social casework as the foundation for Section 17 services was stressed by the studies, as exemplified by this view from Tunstill and Aldgate:

> It was clear that families in the study viewed social workers very positively and valued their social work skills in responding to family distress by means of a casework approach. Casework, contrary to common misperception, includes highly developed skills of assessment, purposeful counselling and acting the role of facilitator and advocate. Without this social work intervention, many families were clear that their circumstance would have deteriorated to the point of family breakdown. The role and contribution of social work should, therefore, represent a central component of current policy initiatives in respect of children, young people and families.
>
> (Tunstill and Aldgate 2000, p.156)

The first years of implementing Section 17 services: a summary

The conclusions from the research which has evaluated the implementation of Section 17 over the first eight or so years suggest that progress has not been straightforward. The Children Act was implemented at a time when investigation of child abuse dominated practice. The concept of identifying children in need based on the impact of impairment or harm was some distance away from an approach which was focusing on identifying risk and the commission of abuse or neglect. With hindsight, the aim of allowing social services and other agencies to identify children in need and set local priorities for service provision was too complex for the primitive technical infrastructure of the time. It was also difficult to shift the attitudes of local authorities to the broader perspective of family support.

The refocusing initiative in the mid-1990s, inspired by a powerful body of cumulative research which showed that families investigated for abuse might still be in need after the investigation, helped to change practice to some extent. There remained fears about the resource implications of opening services to a wider group of children. The evidence also pointed to a lottery of opaque service provision nationally which acted as a deterrent to matching needs to services consistently and, in spite of efforts to broaden provision, a lingering reluctance to assess children on any basis other than factors related to child maltreatment.

In spite of these flaws, there was evidence that families turned to social services as the agency of first choice and in some instances, if they were lucky, secured positive and effective family support services. It is perhaps therefore fitting to end this chapter on a note of optimism. Since the Children Act research was undertaken, the Department of Health has developed a *Framework for the Assessment of Children in Need and their Families* (Department of Health *et al.* 2000a) (see Chapter 8). The Framework takes the broad approach to identifying children in need that the Children Act intended. Once it is implemented, it should make a significant difference to identifying the children who are in need of services and responding effectively to those needs. Additionally, the breaking down of barriers to sharing fundings between agencies (Department of Health 1998c) will enable more resources to be used collaboratively. These two factors will provide a better infrastructure for implementing family support services. It will then be up to the planners, managers, workers and the children and families who need the services, to work together to ensure that provision of Section 17 services both safeguard and promote the welfare of children in need.

Part Two

Assessing the Needs of Individual Children

CHAPTER EIGHT

National Policy on the Assessment of Children in Need and their Families

Jenny Gray

This chapter discusses the recently launched government Guidance: the Framework for the Assessment of Children in Need and their Families *(Department of Health* et al. *2000). The Guidance expects that, in undertaking assessments, practitioners will focus on the inter-relationship of three domains: the developmental needs of the child, the capacity of parents or caregivers to respond appropriately to those needs and the impact of wider family and environmental factors on the two other domains. The substantial implications of these requirements for inter-agency working and for social work training are explored. New procedures introduced by the Guidance – to differentiate between initial and core assessments, to undertake the work within specified timescales and to record and review plans for all children in need – are also examined.*

Introduction

Securing the wellbeing of children, protecting them from all forms of harm and ensuring their developmental needs are responded to appropriately are primary aims of current government legislation and policy. A leading role in carrying out such responsibilities has been given to children's social services since the Children Act 1948. This has included 'the clear duty of protecting the child in his own home by enquiry into allegations of neglect or cruel treatment' (Pugh 1968, p.12), set out in the Children and Young Person's (Amendment) Act 1952, Section 2.

Although enquiry in this respect clearly meant that an assessment had to be made as to whether a child was in need of care and protection, the term 'assessment' was then generally only used in relation to children in care. The creation of predominantly residential observation and assessment centres in the 1970s reinforced the limited view of assessment as determining the most suitable accommodation for children being admitted to the care system (Sinclair, Garnett and Berridge 1995). A government working party on observation and assessment, established in 1978, conducted a wide-ranging review of assessment services. Unable to find any clear or concise definition, it opted to define assessment as 'a continuous process whereby problems are identified and appropriate responses decided upon' (Department of Health and Social Security 1981, p.2). It concluded with some far-sighted recommendations, urging the move away from institutional to community-based, inter-agency services and promoting a broad view of the assessment of children 'brought to notice as requiring special help'. (para. 112, p.29)

The first government practice guidance on assessment was issued to assist social workers undertaking comprehensive assessments for long-term planning where child protection issues had been identified (Department of Health 1988). In this publication, assessment was now firmly seen by policy makers as an essential component of the social work process of assessment, planning, intervention and review. Impetus for the guidance had come from a number of sources, including concerns from much publicised child abuse inquiries (Department of Health 1991b) and inspection findings (Social Services Inspectorate 1986) about social work preoccupation with procedures and formal systems at the expense of attention to practice, as well as the absence of a structured, focused approach to assessment. Known as the 'Orange Book', for over a decade it was regarded as a valuable handbook. However research studies and inspections later found that it was being used mechanistically and as a checklist, that practice in assessment was widely variable and that too often child protection plans had not been informed by comprehensive assessments (Katz 1997). There was also cumulative evidence that a significant proportion of children and their families, inappropriately referred with child protection concerns, were being filtered out by the child protection system when they could have benefited from services (Department of Health 1995b; Social Services Inspectorate 1997).

The government's response was to promote a new strategy for refocusing children's services, underpinned by the principle that services should be needs-led. The then Minister with responsibility for Social Services, Simon Burns, announced that good assessment would be the key and that social services would need to have in place procedures for assessing the needs for services and support of children and families referred to them, irrespective of whether 'they subsequently become the subject of a Section 47 enquiry' as a result of child protection concerns (Armstrong 1997, p.8). The New Labour government in 1997 set up the Quality Protects programme and published the *Government's Objectives for Children's Social Services* (Department of Health 1999a). Assessment of children in need and their families was one of the key areas to be addressed in the Quality Protects programme and improved assessment was one of the objectives set by the Government for children's social services.

As Chapter 1 has explained, under the Children Act 1989, social services departments in England and Wales, working with other local authority departments and health authorities, have a duty to safeguard and promote the welfare of children in their area who are in need and to promote the upbringing of such children by their families, wherever possible, by providing an appropriate range of services. The first part of this book has explored ways in which social services departments and other child welfare agencies assess need at an aggregate level and plan services accordingly. However a fundamental task for child welfare professionals is to ascertain with each child and family referred to social services whether a child is 'in need' under the terms of the Act and how that child and family might best be helped. The accuracy with which a child's needs are assessed will be key to the potential impact of subsequent actions and services and, ultimately, to the outcomes for the child. The second part of this book begins by setting out the recent government Guidance on the assessment of children in need and their families, and then explores both the rationale behind it and some of its implications before introducing a number of specific initiatives designed to help practitioners identify and assess children in need, plan appropriate interventions and monitor their outcomes.

ıment Guidance on the assessment of need

'ework for the Assessment of Children in Need and their Families* (the Assessment Framework), developed by the Government and implemented in England from 1 April 2001, provides a systematic way of analysing, understanding and recording what is happening to children and young people both within their families and the wider context of the community in which they live (Department of Health *et al.* 2000a). From such an understanding of what are inevitably complex issues and inter-relationships, clear professional judgements can be made. These judgements include whether the child being assessed is in need, whether the child is suffering or likely to suffer significant harm, what actions must be taken and which services would best meet the needs of this particular child and family. The evidence-based knowledge which informed the development of the Assessment Framework has been drawn from a wide range of research studies and theories across a number of disciplines and from the accumulated experience of policy and practice.

The Assessment Framework is not written as a practice manual setting out step-by-step procedures to be followed; rather, it offers a conceptual framework which can be adapted and used to suit individual circumstances, for it was intended that the Guidance would be flexible enough to respond to the huge diversity of child and family situations requiring assessment. The Guidance was issued under Section 7 of the Local Authority Social Services Act 1970, which requires local authorities in their social services functions to act under the general guidance of the Secretary of State. As such it does not have the full force of statute, but should be complied with unless local circumstances indicate exceptional reasons which justify a variation.

Who is the Guidance for?

The Guidance was produced primarily for the use of professionals and other staff who are involved in undertaking assessments of children in need and their families under the Children Act 1989. Social services departments have been given lead responsibility for assessments of children in need, including those who may be or are suffering significant harm, but, under Section 27 of the Act, other local authority departments and health authorities have a duty to assist social services in carrying out this function. Thus all agencies working with children and families, and with adults who have parenting responsibilities, are expected to be aware of the Assessment Framework and to understand what it might mean for them.

Many agencies have contact with and responsibility for children and young people under a range of legislation. The Guidance has, therefore, been framed in such a way that it is also relevant to assessments concerned with the welfare of children in a number of contexts. The Assessment Framework has been incorporated into the following other Government guidance:

- *Working Together to Safeguard Children* (Department of Health, Home Office, Department for Education and Employment 1999a)
- *Safeguarding Children Involved in Prostitution* (Department of Health, Department for Education and Employment, Home Office 2000b)
- *Carers and Disabled Children Act 2000: Policy and Practice Guidance* (Department of Health 2001g)
- *Children (Leaving Care) Act 2000: Regulations and Guidance* (Department of Health 2001d)
- *Provision of Therapy for Child Witnesses Prior to a Criminal Trial: Practice Guidance* (Department of Health 2001h)
- *Safeguarding Children in whom Illness is Fabricated and Induced by Carers with Parenting Responsibilities* (Consultation Document) (Department of Health 2001i)
- *Achieving Best Evidence in Criminal Proceedings: Guidance for Vulnerable or Intimidated Witnesses including Children* (Department of Health forthcoming)
- *Fair Access to Care Services: Policy Guidance* (Department of Health 2001j)
- *Special Educational Needs: Practice Guidance* (Department for Education and Skills 2001).

Government policy

Since 1997, Government policy has been directed to ending child poverty, tackling social exclusion and promoting the welfare of all children so that they can thrive and have the opportunity to fulfil their potential as citizens throughout their lives. To this end, a number of programmes have been introduced, such as Sure Start, Connexions, On Track and Quality Protects, as well as a range of policies to support families, promote educational attainment, reduce truancy and school exclusion and secure a future for all young people in education, employment or training. Many of these initiatives have been explored further in Chapter 2; all aim to ensure that children and families most at risk of social exclusion have every opportunity to build successful, independent lives.

At the same time, the New Labour government is committed to improving the quality and management of those services responsible for supporting children and families, particularly through the modernisation of social services, through the promotion of co-operation between all statutory agencies and through building effective partnerships with voluntary and private agencies.

Early intervention to support children and families before problems escalate into crisis or abuse is considered essential. Good joint working practices and understanding at a local level are seen as vital to the success of the early intervention agenda. Local agencies, including schools and education support services, social services departments, youth offending teams, primary and more specialist health care services and voluntary agencies are being exhorted to work together to establish agreed referral protocols which will help to ensure that early indications of a child being at risk of social exclusion receives appropriate attention. One of these initiatives is explored further in Chapter 10. The development of the *Framework for the Assessment of Children in Need and their Families* is a contribution to this integrated working.

Quality Protects initiative

The development of the Assessment Framework was announced by the Secretary of State for Health in September 1998 as part of the Government's broad aim to improve outcomes for children in need. The Guidance is regarded as a key element of the Department of Health's work to support local authorities in implementing Quality Protects, the Government's five year programme for transforming the management and delivery of children's social services. Quality Protects, which commenced in 1998, aims to deliver better life chances to the most vulnerable and disadvantaged children. Good assessment is seen as lying at the heart of this initiative.

The Assessment Framework has also been designed to assist local authority departments and health authorities to meet one of the Government's objectives for children's social services (Department of Health 1999): to ensure that referral and assessment processes discriminate effectively between different types and levels of need, and produce a timely service response.

The numbers of children in need in England

It was estimated that there were approximately eleven million children in England at the time the Assessment Framework was developed (1999), and of these, over four million were living in families with less than half the average household income. These four million children were defined as vulnerable on the grounds that they would benefit from extra help from public agencies in order to make the best of their life chances.

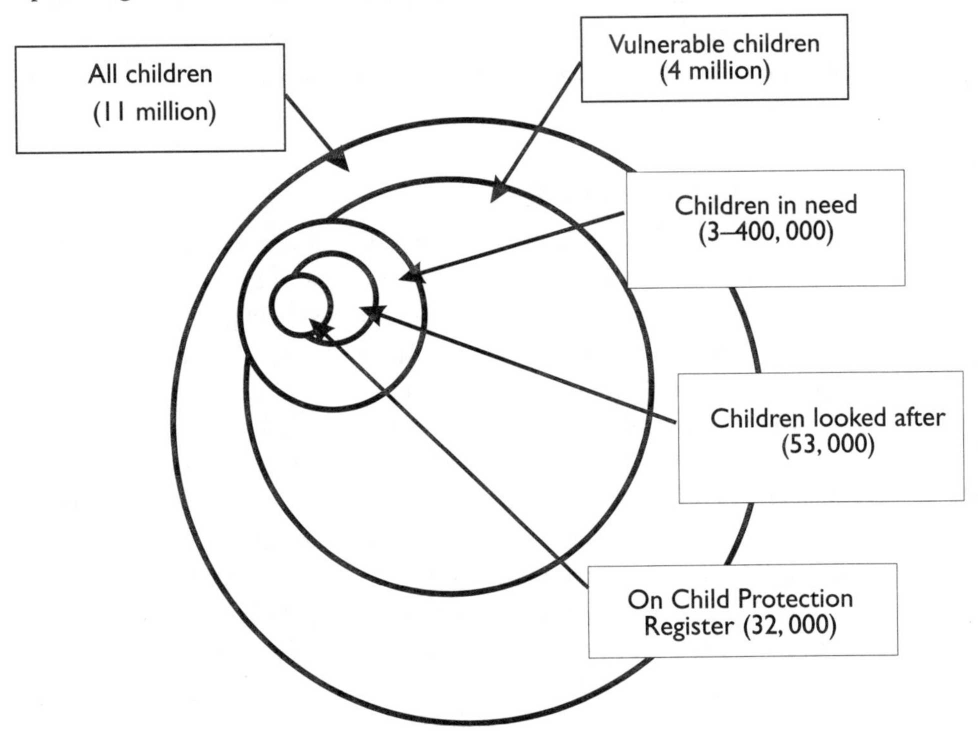

Figure 8.1 Representation of extent of children in need in England in 1999

'e 8.1 shows the extent of children in need within the context of vulnerable and all children in 1999. About 53,000 children were looked after in public care (Department of Health 1999f); this figure excludes those disabled children receiving respite care. Approximately 32,000 children's names were on the Child Protection Register because they required a child protection plan (Department of Health 1998d). Information on how many children were known to social services was not available nationally, but the Department of Health estimated that the numbers were between 300,000 and 400,000, a figure later confirmed by the Children in Need census (Department of Health 2000b).

As is evident from Chapters 3 and 10, professionals from a number of agencies, but in particular health and education, are a key source of referral to social services departments of children who are, or who may be, in need. They have a major role in assisting social services departments to carry out their assessment functions under the Children Act 1989, and in the provision of services to families where children are in need. Their awareness of and contribution to assessments within the Assessment Framework will facilitate communication between agencies and with children and families. This will also assist the process of referral from one agency to another, increasing the likelihood of acceptance of previous assessments, thereby reducing unnecessary duplication and strengthening local confidence in inter-agency work.

Assessing children in need

The *Framework for the Assessment of Children in Need and their Families* was developed on the understanding that assessing whether a child is in need and identifying the nature of this need requires a systematic approach which uses the same framework or conceptual map to gather and analyse information about all children and their families, but discriminates effectively between different types and levels of need.

Part III of the Children Act 1989 identifies the circumstances under which children are defined as being 'in need' and sets out the obligations of the state to assist their families in promoting their wellbeing. The detail of the legislation and the rationale behind it have been further explored in Chapter 1. The Assessment Framework was developed from this legislative foundation, from a set of principles described below, and from an extensive research and practice knowledge which is outlined in the practice guidance (Department of Health 2000c).

The principles that underpin the *Framework for the Assessment of Children in Need and their Families* rest on an acknowledgement that all assessments of this nature should be child-centred and therefore rooted in an understanding of child development. Other principles are that assessments of children in need should be designed to ensure equality of opportunity, and be ecological in their approach. Assessments should carry an assumption of close inter-agency working, both in their approach and in the provision of services. They should be viewed as a continuing process, not a single event, and should be carried out in parallel with other actions, including the provision of services. The expectation is that they will be grounded in evidence-based knowledge, will involve direct working with children and families and will build on strengths, as well as identifying difficulties.

Domains and dimensions of the Assessment Framework

Practitioners engaged in implementing the Assessment Framework require a substantial knowledge base, for they will be expected to demonstrate a thorough understanding of three inter-related systems or domains: the developmental needs of children, the capacity of parents or caregivers to respond appropriately to those needs, and the impact of wider family and environmental factors on parenting capacity and children's developmental progress.

Each of these three domains has a number of critical dimensions (Figure 8.2). The interaction of these dimensions requires careful exploration during assessment, with the ultimate aim being to understand how they affect the child or children in the family. It is expected that the resulting analysis of the child's situation will inform planning and action to secure the best outcomes for the child.

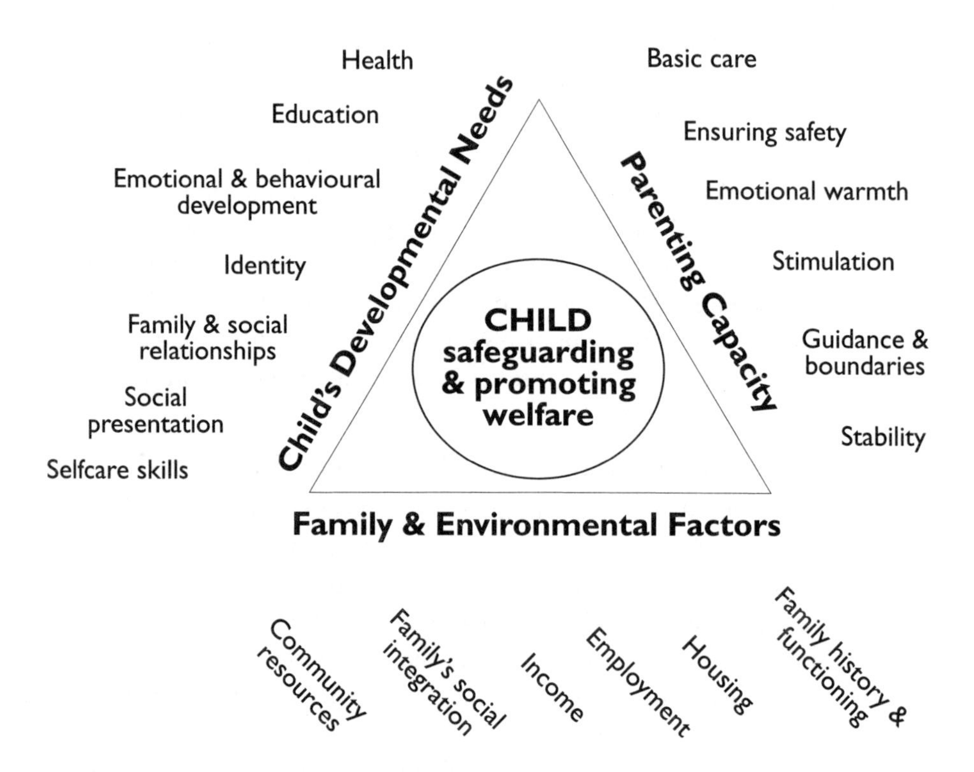

Figure 8.2 Assessment Framework

Child's developmental needs

The development of the Assessment Framework built on earlier work undertaken by the Department of Health to devise a methodology for assessing outcomes for children looked after by the State (Department of Health 1995a). A working party of academics and practitioners, commissioned by the Department of Health, identified the following seven dimensions as being those along which all children need to progress if they are to achieve long-term wellbeing in adulthood: health; education; identity; family and social relationships; social presentation; emotional and behavioural development; self care skills.

These dimensions provided the key areas for assessing outcomes for children in the Looking After Children system. The continuing research programme underpinning this work is explored further in Chapter 13. The developmental dimensions have been found to be universal for all children (Ward 1995) and were incorporated, therefore, into the Assessment Framework.

Although the Guidance gives a detailed, illustrative description of each of the developmental dimensions (Department of Health *et al.* 2000a, p.19), practitioners are expected to use their judgement about how to use them when working with a child and his or her family. The view that all assessment activity and subsequent planning and provision of services must focus on ensuring that the child's welfare is safeguarded and promoted is emphasised. Practitioners undertaking assessments are expected to examine each aspect of a child's developmental progress, in the context of his or her age and stage of development. The Guidance stresses that account must be taken of any particular vulnerabilities, such as learning disabilities or a physically disabling condition, and the impact these have on progress in any of the developmental dimensions. When assessing a child, practitioners are also asked to give consideration to the socially and environmentally disadvantaging factors which have an impact on development, such as limited access for those who are disabled, and discrimination. Those undertaking the assessment are expected to have a clear understanding of what the particular child needs to achieve successfully at each stage of development, in order to ensure that he or she has the opportunity to reach his or her full potential.

Parenting capacity

The Assessment Framework development team also considered the areas in which it is known that adults who have parenting responsibilities must function well in order to help their children negotiate the various developmental stages as they grow up. It is also known that the ability of parents or caregivers to ensure that the child's developmental needs are being appropriately and adequately responded to, and to adapt to them as they change over time, is critically important to a child's health and development. The agreed dimensions of the parenting capacity domain are: basic care; ensuring safety; emotional warmth; stimulation; guidance and boundaries; stability.

The Guidance gives detailed descriptions of each of these parenting tasks (Department of Health *et al.* 2000a, p.21) but these are illustrative rather than comprehensive. Practitioners are advised that the parenting tasks undertaken by fathers or father figures should be addressed alongside those of mothers or mother figures. In families where a parent is not living in the same household as the child, practitioners should be aware of the importance of identifying what role the absent parent has in the child's life and the significance to the child of the relationship with him or her. They are reminded that they cannot assume that parents who live apart are estranged, for the arrangement may be by mutual agreement.

In some families, a single parent may be performing most or all of the parenting tasks. In others, there may be a number of important caregivers in a child's life, each playing a different part, and this may have positive or negative consequences. A distinction has to be made between the contribution of each parent or caregiver to a child's wellbeing and development. In family situations where there is cause for concern about what is happening to a child, it becomes even more important to gather information about how the various tasks are being carried out by each parent or caregiver. Where a child has suffered significant harm, it is particularly necessary to distinguish between the different capabilities of the abusing and the potentially protective parent.

Children looked after may have a number of adults who are involved in parenting them and these may include foster carers and residential childcare staff. In some circumstances, children who have a number of caregivers may be more vulnerable to being maltreated. Practitioners are reminded that the needs of disabled children who experience multiple caregivers as part of their regular routine should receive special attention (Marchant *et al.* 1999).

When assessing parenting capacity, practitioners are advised of the importance of understanding the impact the parents' relationship with each other may have on their respective capacities to respond appropriately to their child's needs. Observation of interactions is as critically important as the way they are described by the adults involved.

Family and environmental factors

Finally, in developing the Assessment Framework consideration was also given to those areas, both in the wider family and in the community, which have a direct impact on children's development and on parents' abilities to carry out their roles effectively. The development team was very mindful that the care and upbringing of children does not take place in a vacuum. A wide range of environmental factors can either help or hinder the family's functioning. All family members are influenced both positively and negatively by the wider family, the neighbourhood and the social networks in which they live.

Practitioners are advised that the history of the family and of individual family members may have a significant impact on the child and parents. Some family members, for example, may have grown up in a very different environment to that of the child, some may have had to leave their country of origin because of war or other adverse conditions, and others may have experienced abuse and neglect as children. The narration and impact of family histories and experiences can play an important part in understanding what is happening currently to a family. An adult's capacity to parent may be crucially related to his or her childhood experiences of family life and past adult experiences prior to the current difficulties.

The Guidance emphasises that an understanding of how the family usually functions, and how it functions when under stress, can be very helpful in identifying what factors may assist parents in carrying out their roles. Of particular importance is the quality and nature of the relationship between the parents and how this affects the child. For example, sustained conflict between parents is detrimental to children's welfare. Relationships between siblings may also be of major significance. Account must be taken of the diversity of family styles and structures, particularly including who counts as family and who is important to the child.

The dimensions making up the third domain, wider family and environmental factors, are: family history and functioning; wider family; housing; employment; income; family's social integration; community resources. The Guidance gives a detailed, illustrative description of each family and environmental factor (Department of Health *et al.* 2000a, p.23) but, once again, these are not comprehensive.

The Assessment Framework domains and dimensions were developed by a process of discussion and consultation (Department of Health 1999g), drawing on the collective experience, wisdom and knowledge of people from many disciplines. They were also the subject of piloting with children and families. Importantly, a consensus was reached between children, parents and professionals that the dimensions described appropriately the areas to be addressed during any child and family assessment.

Interaction between the three domains

The interactions between the different factors in a child's life are often not straightforward. This is why the Assessment Framework Guidance (Department of Health *et al.* 2000a, para. 2.2.3) emphasises the importance of:

- gathering information and recording systematically with care and precision
- checking information and discussing it with parents and, where appropriate, with the child
- clearly recording differences in views about information and its importance
- assessing and understanding the strengths and difficulties within families
- examining the vulnerabilities and protective factors in the child's world
- clearly identifying the impact on the child of what is happening.

The Assessment Framework is, therefore, a conceptual map which can be used to understand what is happening to all children in whatever circumstances they may be growing up.

The Guidance points out that the response from social services departments to an initial contact or a referral requesting help is critically important. At that point the foundation is laid for future work with the child or family. Children and families may have contact with social services staff in a wide range of settings. These may be as diverse as a family or day centre, a social services office, an accident and emergency, adult or paediatric unit in a hospital, an education setting, an adolescent drop-in service or specialist services for adults. Not all staff in these settings will be professionals or qualified in work with children and families. This will be particularly true of those who work predominantly with adults. Whoever has first contact with a child or family member, however, has a vital role in influencing the course of future work. It is clear from research that the quality of the early or initial contact affects later working relationships with professionals. Furthermore, recording of information about the initial contact or referral contributes to the first phase of assessment. Therefore, all staff responding to families or to referrers are advised of the importance of becoming familiar with the principles which underpin the Assessment Framework and being aware of the value of the information collected and recorded at this stage (Department of Health and Cleaver 2000).

Common language

The Guidance makes it clear that effective collaborative work between staff from different disciplines and agencies who assess children in need and their families, requires a common language to understand the needs of children, shared values about what is in children's best interests and a joint commitment to improving outcomes. The Assessment Framework is designed to provide that common language, based on explicit values about children, knowledge about what they need to ensure their successful development, and the factors in their lives which may positively or negatively influence their upbringing. Such a language will increase the likelihood of parents and children experiencing consistency between professionals and themselves about what will be important for children's wellbeing and healthy development.

Prior to social services departments becoming involved with a child and family, a number of other agencies and community-based groups may have had contact. For some children, assessments will have already been carried out for purposes other than determining whether they are a child in need. In particular, health and education will have undertaken routine assessments as part of monitoring children's developmental progress. The familiarity of other agencies with the Assessment Framework should be of assistance in making a referral to a social services department or contributing to an assessment of a child in need, thereby facilitating a common understanding of the child's needs within their family context.

Principles underpinning inter-agency, interdisciplinary work

A key principle of the Assessment Framework is that children's needs and their families' circumstances will require inter-agency collaboration to ensure full understanding of what is happening and to provoke an effective service response. The Guidance demonstrates that inter-agency, interdisciplinary assessment practice requires an additional set of knowledge and skills to that required for working within a single agency or independently. All staff will need to understand the roles and responsibilities of other professionals working in contexts different from their own. As Chapter 10 demonstrates, having an understanding of the perspectives, language and culture of other professionals can inform how communication is conducted and prevent practitioners from misunderstanding one another because they use different terminology to describe similar concepts or because they are influenced by stereotypical perceptions of other disciplines. The Assessment Framework is intended to provide a language which is common to children and their family members, as well as to professionals and other staff.

The Assessment Framework sets out the following principles to guide inter-agency, interdisciplinary work with children in need. It states that it is essential to be clear about:

- the purpose and anticipated outputs from the assessment
- the legislative basis
- the protocols and procedures to be followed
- which agency, team or professional has lead responsibility
- how the child and family members will be involved in the assessment process
- which professional has lead responsibility for analysing the findings and constructing a plan
- the respective roles of each professional involved
- the way in which information will be shared across professional boundaries and within agencies, and be recorded
- which professional will have responsibility for taking forward the plan when it is agreed (Department of Health *et al.* 2000a, p.7 para. 1.23).

Practitioners are expected to undertake all phases of the assessment process in partnership with key family members and with their agreement. This includes finalising the plan of action. There will, however, be exceptions when there are concerns that a child is suffering or may be suffering significant harm, and here practitioners are advised to follow the Guidance set out in another Government publication: *Working Together to Safeguard Children* (Department of Health *et al.* 1999).

In the past, children and families have reported being unclear both about what was required of them during an assessment and the role of the professionals involved, as well as the process. Service users, in particular parents of disabled children, report that assessments are often repetitive and uninformed by previous work. At the beginning of all involvement, practitioners are reminded that it is important to agree an assessment programme with the child and family, so that all parties understand who is doing what, when, and how the various assessments will be used to inform overall judgements about a child's needs and subsequent planning. When joint assessments are being undertaken, they are advised to clarify whether this means that one professional will undertake an assessment on behalf of the team or whether several types of assessment are to be undertaken in parallel. In the latter situation, they are reminded of the importance of organising these in such a way as to avoid duplication. Managers are advised that the agreed process should be based on what is appropriate for the needs of the particular child and family, taking account of the purpose of the assessment, rather than what fits best with professional systems. Agreed protocols and procedures should be flexible enough to accommodate different ways of undertaking assessments within the overall Assessment Framework.

Provision of services

Having established that a child is a child in need, a purpose of the assessment is to determine what services should be provided by whom, within what timescales. Services may include those provided by local authority children's services, local authority adult services or other agencies, on a single agency, inter-agency or multi-agency basis. Services may be provided on a one-off or episodic basis or over a longer period of time as determined by a child in need plan, a child protection plan or a care plan to safeguard a child's welfare. Managers are reminded that it is the function of strategic planning for children and young people and their families to make sure this continuum of services is in place.

In determining what services should be provided to a particular child and his family, social services departments are not charged with the same duty as the courts that the child's welfare shall be the 'paramount consideration' (Children Act 1989 Section 1.1.) Rather they have a broader duty to promote children's welfare in order to achieve the best possible outcomes for each particular child. The Guidance stresses that, in assessing whether a child is in need, social services also have to take into consideration other children in the household and the general circumstances of the family. Their task is to identify the impact on the child of what is happening and also the likely impact of any intervention on that child and on other family members.

Assessment requires careful consideration of the repercussions or consequences of providing specific types of services and the extent to which they will both safeguard and promote a particular child's welfare and development. This may be a complex equation which requires a high level of skill and professional judgement, involving all the agency partners. Knowledge of effective intervention will be key to deciding which services to provide and how to work with children and families. To this end, the Department of Health has published a number of texts which summarise research findings and present them in an accessible manner for use by practitioners, managers and policy makers when assessing children and families and deciding which types of intervention are effective in a particular family situation (Department of Health and Social Security 1985, Department of Health 1991c, 1995b, 1996b, 1998e, 1999h, 2001c).

Timescales for completing an assessment

A timely response to a child's needs means that the process of assessment cannot continue unchecked over a prolonged period without an analysis being made of what is happening and what action is needed, however difficult or complex the child's circumstances. Prior to the publication of the Government's *Objectives for Children's Social Services* (Department of Health 1999a), no timescales had been set for completing assessments of children in need, although there had been timescales for action to be taken to protect children where there were concerns that they were suffering or likely to suffer significant harm.

The Assessment Framework sets out clear timescales for the assessment process and identifies three key points along this scale: there is an expectation that *within one working day* of a referral being received or new information coming to or from within a social services department about an open case, there will be a decision about what response is required.

A decision to gather more information triggers an *initial assessment,* defined as a brief assessment of each child referred to social services with a request for services to be provided. There is an expectation that initial assessments will be undertaken *within a maximum of seven working days.* Practitioners completing initial assessments are expected to address the dimensions of the Assessment Framework, determining whether the child is in need, the nature of any services required, from where and within what timescales, and whether a further, more detailed core assessment should be undertaken. An initial assessment is deemed to have commenced at the point of referral to the social services department or when new information on an open case indicates that an earlier assessment should be repeated.

A core assessment is defined as an in-depth assessment which addresses the central or most important aspects of the needs of a child and the capacity of his or her parents or caregivers to respond appropriately to these needs within the wider family and community context. While this assessment is led by social services, it will invariably involve professionals from other disciplines, who will either provide information they hold about the child or parents, contributing specialist knowledge or advice to social services, or undertake specialist assessments. At the conclusion of this phase of assessment, there should be an analysis of the findings which provides an understanding of the child's circumstances and informs planning, case objectives and the nature of service provision. The timescale for completion of the core assessment is a *maximum of 35 working days.* A core assessment is deemed to have commenced either at the point the initial assessment ended, or when a strategy discussion decides to initiate enquiries under Section 47 of the Children Act 1989 (see below), or when new information obtained on an open case indicates that one should be undertaken.

Practitioners are advised that these are maximum timescales and that the needs of some children, in particular those who require emergency intervention, may mean that the initial assessment stage is brief and that the core assessment is undertaken more rapidly.

Children suffering or likely to suffer significant harm

Some children are in need because they are suffering or are likely to suffer significant harm. Concerns about maltreatment may be the reason for referral of a family to social services or they may arise during the course of providing services to a family. In such circumstances, the local authority is obliged to consider initiating enquiries to find out what is happening and whether action is required to protect a child. This obligation is set out in Part V of the Children Act 1989:

> Where a local authority are informed that a child who lives, or is found in their area –
>
> i) is the subject of an emergency protection order; or
>
> ii) is in police protection; or
>
> iii) have reasonable cause to suspect that a child who lives, or is found in their area is suffering, or is likely to suffer, significant harm,
>
> the authority shall make, or cause to be made, such enquiries as they consider necessary to enable them to decide whether they should take any action to safeguard or promote the child's welfare. (Children Act 1989, s.47.1)

Practitioners are advised that, should there at any stage be suspicions or allegations about child maltreatment and concern that the child may be or is likely to suffer significant harm, they must follow the arrangements set out in the complementary Government guidance: *Working Together to Safeguard Children* (Department of Health *et al.* 1999). However the Assessment Framework is incorporated into this document, so that the processes of referral, initial and core assessment, described above, should also be followed when undertaking assessments where there are concerns that a child is or may be suffering significant harm. In cases where the police are also involved, the core assessment should also be planned and undertaken in such a way that it does not jeopardise any criminal investigations. Assessments undertaken within the structure provided by the Assessment Framework dimensions will provide information about whether a child's health or development is being impaired and if so, the extent to which this impairment is due to lack of parental capacity to respond appropriately to the child's needs within the family and wider environmental context. The assessment will thus provide the necessary evidence to inform judgements about the child's welfare and to make future decisions about how best to safeguard and promote it.

Practitioners are advised that where there is a concern that a child is suffering or is likely to suffer significant harm, the assessment should concentrate on the harm that has occurred or is likely to occur to the child as a result of maltreatment, in order to inform future plans and the nature of services required. There is substantial research evidence to suggest that the health and development of children, including their educational attainment, may be severely affected if they have been subjected to maltreatment (Varma 1993; Adcock and White 1998; Jones and Ramchandani 1999). The duty both to safeguard and promote the child's welfare continues throughout the process of finding out whether there are child protection concerns and deciding what action should be taken, so that some services may be provided under Part III of the Act, while enquiries are still being carried out.

The assessment process

The Guidance points out that many families who approach or are referred to social services departments are clear about their problems but may not be sure where to turn or how to obtain services. They may require nothing more of a social services department than sufficient advice and information to enable them to take appropriate action. An assessment is necessary where it appears that a child may be in need and therefore requires services. For some families, the process of assessment is in itself a therapeutic intervention. Being able to look at problems in a constructive manner with a professional who is willing to listen and who helps family members to reflect on what is happening, is enough to help them find solutions. During the assessment process, it may emerge that a family will best be helped by agencies other than social services. Armed with this information, some families may wish to seek solutions themselves; others may wish to have help in gaining access to other agencies or practical services.

However a significant proportion of families who seek help from social services are unable to resolve stresses or problems solely from within their own emotional or practical resources or from their own support network. It is for these families that assessment may be important in identifying the nature of their children's needs and, simultaneously, in becoming the first stage in a longer process of positive intervention. The practitioner is reminded that in most situations, meeting children's needs will involve responding also to the needs of family members. The two are closely connected and it is rarely possible to promote the welfare of children without also promoting the welfare of significant adults in their lives. Where consideration is being given to meeting parents' needs, as part of the plan of intervention, this must be on the grounds that this is in the best interests of the child and will assist in securing better child welfare outcomes. In some cases, meeting children's needs may mean giving others parental responsibility, either for short periods or on a longer term basis.

As stated earlier in this chapter, the social services department has lead responsibility for undertaking the assessment of children in need, and analysing the information gathered during the process. It can not, however, do this on its own. The knowledge of other professionals together with the views of the child and family members will all contribute to this process. The Guidance takes the practitioner through the process of assessment: gathering and analysing information, making judgements and decisions and making and reviewing plans. Attention is particularly drawn to the importance of analysing as well as gathering information: the Department of Health has developed assessment recording forms to assist practitioners and their managers in this phase of work (Department of Health and Cleaver 2000).

It is evident that for practitioners to understand the complex inter-relationships between the child, the family and the environment, they will have to draw on knowledge from research and practice combined with an understanding of the child's needs within his or her family. In making judgements concerning appropriate actions to secure the child's wellbeing and safety, they will also have to be able to assess both the likelihood of change and, at a later date, to review whether such change is being achieved.

The Department of Health has commissioned a number of studies designed to help practitioners and managers develop the knowledge base upon which they will draw when making assessments. The Open University is producing materials which will assist practitioners and their managers to update their knowledge of the ways in which children need to achieve certain tasks at particular ages and stages of their development (Department of Health and Open University forthcoming). There is a considerable literature to assist professionals when making a judgement about a parent's capacity and assessing what is a reasonable standard of care (Jones 2001; Cleaver, Unell and Aldgate 1999) 'even though [research] cannot provide the kind of numerical accuracy which is often sought' (Jones 2001, p.256). Some of these findings were summarised in the reader *The Child's World: Assessing Children in Need*, produced as part of the training and development materials which accompanied the Assessment Framework (Horwath 2001). Other studies, summarising research findings in specific areas, cover issues such as child sexual abuse (Jones and Ramchandani 1999); communicating with children who may have been traumatised or maltreated (Jones in preparation); the impact of parental mental illness, problem alcohol and drug use and domestic violence on children's development (Cleaver *et al.* 1999); and working with fathers (Ryan 2000). The practice guidance which accompanied the Assessment Framework has chapters on work with black and minority ethnic families, and on working with disabled children and their families (Department of Health 2000c).

The work currently being undertaken by the Open University, referred to above, will also draw practitioners' attention to information about those types of interventions which are likely to be the most effective in addressing the identified needs of a given child. The Guidance stresses that, in drawing up a plan of intervention, practitioners will have to take account of a number of issues, specific to each child's circumstances. These will not only include identifying those interventions which are known to have the best outcomes for the particular circumstances of the child, but also deciding what the child and family can cope with without being overwhelmed, determining how the necessary resources can be mobilised within the family's network and within professional agencies including social services, and identifying what alternative interventions are available if the resources of choice cannot be secured. Practitioners are reminded of the importance of ensuring that interventions achieve early success and have a beneficial impact, for the self esteem of children and parents is critical to the outcome of longer term service provision. Good experiences are important when many other aspects of family life may be in chaos, or problems feel insurmountable. There may, therefore, be an optimal hierarchy of interventions which distinguishes between what is achievable in the short term, what will have maximum impact on the child and family's wellbeing and what are the long-term goals. They will also need to identify what the child regards as the highest priority; for example, learning to ride a bicycle may be far higher on his or her list of wants than therapy. Taking account of such practical wishes may result in changes which will enable the child to make better use of more complex interventions such as therapeutic help at a later stage.

Children in need plans

The Guidance stresses the importance of following a robust planning process and keeping the child at its centre. Practitioners are advised that the content and timing of the plan must be informed by three actions which will have an impact on the child's health and development: ensuring the child's safety, keeping the child learning, and following a timescale that takes account of the fact that children cannot wait indefinitely.

The Guidance makes it clear that there are some parents who will not be able to change sufficiently within the appropriate timescales in order to ensure their children do not continue to suffer significant harm. In these situations, decisions may have to be made to separate child and parent on a permanent basis. Decisions about the nature and form of any contact will also be required, in the light of all that is known about the child and the family, and reviewed throughout childhood. Key in these considerations is an understanding of what is in the child's best interests, informed by the child's views (Cleaver 2000).

However most parents are capable of change, and are eventually able to provide a safe family context for their child. At times, children may have to be separated temporarily from their parent or parents in order to allow change to take place while the child is living away from home in a safe environment. During this time, practitioners are reminded of the importance of addressing the changes required in the parent as well as of meeting any therapeutic needs of the child and other family members by active programmes of intervention, appropriate deployment of resources and careful review of progress.

The details of the plan are benchmarks against which the progress of the family and the commitment of workers are measured, and therefore it is important that they should be realistic and not vague statements of good intent (Department of Health 1995b). The Guidance identifies some general principles about plans for working with children and families, whatever the circumstances in which they have been drawn up. First, wherever possible, practitioners are advised to draw up plans in agreement with the child or young person and key family members and secure their commitment to their content. They are also asked to bear in mind two caveats which, if ignored, can be damaging to families and jeopardise the overall aim of securing the child's wellbeing: objectives should be reasonable and timescales not too short or unachievable, and plans should not be dependent on resources which are known to be scarce or unavailable. They are also reminded that the plan must maintain a focus on the child, even though it may recommend the provision of services to a number of family members. As Jones (1987) writes: 'It is never acceptable to sacrifice the interests of the child for the therapeutic benefit of the parents'.

Reviewing plans

Developing written plans for all children in need is a new concept introduced by the Guidance, as is the recommendation that there should also be a clear recorded statement on the plan about when and how it will be reviewed. The timescales and procedures for reviewing plans for children on child protection registers, looked after and leaving care are already prescribed in *Working Together to Safeguard Children* (Department of Health *et al.* 1999), *The Children Act 1989 Guidance and Regulations Vol 3* (Department of Health 1991d) and the *Children (Leaving Care Act) Guidance and Regulations* (Department of Health 2001d) respectively. However reviewing the child's progress and the effectiveness of services and other interventions is a continuous part of the process of work with children and families. Where work is being undertaken to support children and families in the community under Section 17 of the Children Act 1989, the Guidance recommends that it is good practice to review the plan with family members at least every six months, and to formally record it. The child, their parents or carers and key professionals should also be involved in the review process and in constructing the revised plan.

Future policy developments

The Guidance to the Assessment Framework specifies how information gained in the course of an assessment of a child in need can be analysed and used as a basis for planning effective interventions that can later be reviewed. The *Looking After Children* materials (Department of Health 1995a) have offered a similar process for gathering information, making plans and reviewing the progress of children who are looked after by local authorities. Currently the Department of Health is leading work to bring together the Assessment Framework and the *Looking After Children* System into one Integrated Children's System which will provide an assessment, planning, intervention and reviewing model for all children in need (see Chapter 14).

Conclusion

The *Framework for the Assessment of Children in Need and their Families* provides, for the first time in England, a national framework within which all assessments of children in need are undertaken. It also provides a common language for all those working with children in need and their families. This language seems to have international acceptance with families and professionals alike, as is evidenced by its applicability in countries such as Sweden, Malta, Russia, Romania, Kenya and Australia. The Assessment Framework dimensions also seem applicable within legal jurisdictions which have markedly different cultural and legal traditions. Inter-country collaborative projects as well as research commissioned by the Department of Health to examine its implementation in England (Cleaver, Meadows and Walker forthcoming) will all make important contributions to the refinement of the Assessment Framework and the development of the Integrated Children's System.

CHAPTER NINE

Underpinning Theories for the Assessment of Children's Needs

Janet Seden

The Children Act 1989, the Looking After Children *materials and the* Framework for the Assessment of Children in Need and their Families *provide the policy environment for a developmental approach to the provision of children's services. This chapter considers the underpinning theories available to practitioners undertaking assessments within a developmental framework. The chapter analyses research findings on child development, parental capacities and social conditions that should be taken into account when undertaking a holistic assessment of a child's needs. Attachment theory, protective mechanisms, resilience, vulnerabilities, critical periods of development, family styles, family strengths and parental empathy are considered as critical components of assessment. Ecosystems theory is discussed for contextualising and organising these determinants in order to plan interventions.*

Introduction

Child development is a complex interaction of the individual, the adults who determine the child's upbringing and the social environment. Any holistic assessment of need must consider the interplay between these factors. It must also consider the meaning which they have for the particular child, family and community. As Chapter 8 has illustrated, action as an outcome of assessment depends not upon the crude collection of data but on careful analysis and judgement about the interactive dynamics of these three key constituents. The developmentally based 'in need' definition provided by the Children Act 1989 means that practitioners can utilise researched and evidenced psychological and ecological writing to inform professional understanding and action.

The relevance of a developmental framework must be considered in the context of debates about children's rights and adult responsibilities. Three strands of thinking make such consideration of the assessment of need and the underpinning theories highly topical. These are the Children Act 1989, the UN Convention on the Rights of the Child 1989, the Human Rights Act 2000 and government policy emphasising a broader approach to children's services. The philosophies of the Children Act 1989 mean that parental responsibility and the minimum necessary state intervention into family life are emphasised. International thinking on children's rights as encapsulated in the UN Convention leads to fundamental re-questioning about reciprocity in the child, adult, state equation, with a concentration on parental responsibility and the duties of parents to meet children's needs.

The refocusing debate in children's services, which followed the publication of *Child Protection: Messages from Research* (Department of Health 1995b) and the Quality Protects agenda (Department of Health 1998a, 1998b), points the way for serious rethinking about how best to safeguard and promote the welfare of vulnerable children. Research shows that many children are not receiving services at the appropriate times by suitable means either in the community or when accommodated (Department of Health 1995a; Ward and Skuse 1999; Skuse, Macdonald and Ward 2001). This has important implications for everyone involved with promoting the welfare of children.

When children and families request or are referred for help, the assessment of need becomes the first mechanism for the state to support parents to fulfil their responsibilities towards their children. Early intervention aims to avoid the long-term consequences of family breakdown, and to ensure that each child receives opportunities to develop normally alongside peers and contemporaries in a safe community. Assessment is the means by which professionals reach a view about whether a child's development is progressing satisfactorily.

Several theoretical concepts underpin our understanding of what is meant by a child's needs. Doyal and Gough's (1991) minimum level of provision for general populations lists: clean water; adequate nutrition; adequate protection and housing; a non-hazardous work environment; appropriate health care; security in childhood; significant primary relationships; physical security; appropriate education; safer birth control and child-bearing. Bradshaw (1972) suggests the definition of need might be more complex than minimum standards, and outlines four dimensions: normative needs (needs that most experts define for populations); felt needs (what people say they need); expressed needs (what people demand by their actions); comparative needs (needs established by comparing one group with another). Such underpinning theories are essential for conceptualising children's needs and devising the best responses. Eligibility criteria are only useful in determining which agency or person(s) are responsible in relation to specific provision. Normative needs might be guaranteed by the state. To avoid social exclusion, consideration has to be given to who should be meeting other categories of need. Decision making is likely to be contextual, subject to debate and brokered by professional assessment.

The basis for defining need under the Children Act 1989 (s.17. 10) is clearly developmental, grounded in psychological literature and related to research into what is expected to contribute to a child's successful growth from infancy, through childhood and adolescence to maturity. The dimensions stated in the legislation are broadly: physical; intellectual; social; behavioural and educational. These are developed in the *Looking After Children* dimensions to health; education; identity; family and social relationships; emotional and behavioural development; social presentation; and self care skills (Department of Health 1995a). As Chapter 8 has specified, the Guidance, contained in the *Framework for the Assessment of Children in Need and their Families* (Department of Health *et al.* 2000a) provides a 'systematic way of understanding, analysing and recording what is happening to children and young people within their families and the wider context of the community within which they live' (p.viii). The principles on which it is constructed are that assessments are: child-centred; rooted in child development; ecological in their approach; ensure equality of opportunity; require work with children and their families; build on strengths as well as identifying difficulties; are inter-agency in their approach to assessment and the provision of services; are a continuing process not a single event; are carried out in parallel with other action and providing services; are grounded in evidence-based knowledge (Department of Health *et al.* 2000a, p.10).

In using this framework to assess the way in which children's needs are met, social workers and practitioners from the associated caring professions can rely on a range of well researched theoretical perspectives.

Developmental psychology offers a wealth of information about emotional, psychological, educational, moral, spiritual, cognitive and relational aspects (Department of Health 2000d). This can relate to the needs of the individual child, the capacities of people who provide care and also to understanding the community in which the child lives.

Children's needs

Individual needs are documented by various commentators. Maslow's (1968) hierarchy is, in summary: physiological (food, warmth, shelter); security (protection from danger and deprivation); social (companionship, communal activities); egotistical (self esteem, sense of achievement); psychological (self-actualisation). Kelmer Pringle's (1980, p.34) categorisation remains key: love and security; new experiences; praise and recognition; responsibility. Black (1990) cites: physical care; affection; security; stimulation; innate potential; guidance and control; responsibility; independence. She quotes Cooper (1995) for a list of deficits: death; damage; deprivation; disturbance in development; distorted perceptions; demanding behaviour; delinquency; detachment (p.47).

These helpful dimensions are relevant to all children and supplemented by detailed developmental literature (Sheridan 1997; Bee 1995). They rely heavily on psychological research findings which help practitioners understand what appears universal to all children's development, what are individual differences and their meaning, the contextual nature of behaviour, the influences of culture and backgrounds and the social environment. Such knowledge can enable practitioners to balance genetic and environmental factors in assessments and to consider the interaction between biological and environmental variables.

Parental capacity and care-giving

Similarly the capacities of good parenting are well documented. Campion (1995) provides criteria based on observable functions which can be concretely described and measured: the provision of physical care; health care; protection from danger; education; adequate nutrition; opportunities for development; preparation for adulthood and independence; development of self esteem; opportunity for spirituality; identity; affection and trust; social and cognitive skills; stability in close relationships; economic support; moral guidance; modelling of adult behaviour; self regulation (p.255). Developmental theory since Bowlby has clarified that assessment of the needs of children is about the interaction between child, caretaker and environment. Jones (1997) considers that 'parental qualities include the following list of essential activities:

1. provision of adequate food and shelter
2. obtainment of necessary medical care
3. protection from harm (abuse and neglect)
4. security of affective relationships
5. responsiveness to the child's emotional needs
6. discipline and guidance of behaviour
7. inculcation of moral values
8. provision of new experiences
9. assisting a child in problem-solving' (p.536).

A recent analysis of developmental research relating to children and their families by Guralnick (1997) confirms these three salient features as the focus of assessment:

1. the quality of parent child interaction
2. the extent to which the family provides the child with diverse and appropriate experiences within the surrounding social and physical environment
3. the way in which the family ensures the child's health and safety (p.5).

The environment

Recent writing has summarised the components of necessary interaction between child and caregivers to meet need, but also emphasises that the social structure and environment must fully play a part. For example are local health services or a suitable school available? Moss and Petrie (1996) argue that the welfare of children cannot be separated from that of their families and neighbours or from the 'health and vitality of the communities that surround them' (Nelson 1996). Assessment therefore needs to pay attention to the interaction between child, family and the environment. An ecological approach to assessment ensures that this happens.

Attachment theory

Bowlby's work on attachment (1988) has been central in underpinning the professional activity of social work with people's concerns, losses and potential. For children, the weight of research into attachments and their significance is the bedrock of good practice, informing understanding of the baby's earliest development, the child's socialisation and the impact of transitions and losses for children who change carers, home, country or family culture.

Contemporary research developments confirm that attachment to a responsive other remains (as Bowlby identified) as important as food and shelter. A child needs secure, reliable, emotional nurture and relationships to develop well on a range of cognitive, emotional, physical and social dimensions. In the context of their relationships with adults, children learn, explore, relate to peers, self-regulate and socialise (Masten and Coatsworth 1998). Refinements in research have delineated the consequences of insecure attachment more precisely, and the significance of peers, siblings and environment. It remains fundamental that secure, warm early attachments are a predictor for good developmental outcomes on emotional, cognitive and behavioural measures. This reinforces the importance of providing compensatory mechanisms where this crucial element is weak or absent. 'The attachment system operates and functions as a security maintenance system. Most specifically attachment behaviour will be most intensely activated in situations where the infant is alarmed and anxious' (Morton and Browne 1998, p.1094). A secure internalised attachment system enables the growing child to cope with threats from the external world. Maltreated children may display less attachment behaviour but are, paradoxically, potentially less well equipped to cope with anxiety. Recent studies on attachment, as well as exploring complexity, are confirming that:

> Children with secure attachments are also likely to be more empathic, compliant, unconflicted and generally competent in their relationships with adults and peers. Children with insecure attachments tend to have trouble relating to other people because their behaviour is often either hostile and distant or overly dependent… These tendencies may extend into adolescence and adulthood, influencing significant social relationships as well as basic attitudes to life. (Fowler 1996, p.25)

Morton and Browne (1998), reviewing research studies which consider attachment and child maltreatment, confirm that the quality of infant attachment remains dependent on the sensitivity of the first caregiver, usually the mother. They conclude 'not surprisingly, on average maltreated children are less attached to their mothers than non-maltreated children' (p.1093). Very early relationships are a 'prototype' for the future, including later relationships with own children. Early intervention to support primary caregivers in forming sensitive attachments to children seems universally important. It is also possible that such models of caregiving are intergenerationally transmitted (Fonagy *et al.* 1994, p.233). There appears to be substantial evidence that the securely attached child relates better to peers, teachers and significant others. The internalised mental map in securely attached infants promotes strengths that enable them to cope with anxiety and threat throughout the lifespan (Howe 1995; Howe *et al.* 1999).

Developmental researchers have also explored particular facets of attachment theory such as resilience, protective factors, vulnerability and critical periods of development. These elements are now considered in more detail.

Resilience and protective mechanisms

It has been suggested that the search for resilience criteria in children in poor environments is a response to knowledge about the failings of state care and lack of resource provision for children, but this is too cynical. It is pertinent to ask what makes a child resilient and strong if that is viewed not as a way of reducing services, but as a positive tool in making assessments, providing interventions and judging potential outcomes of actions or non-actions in relation to individual children. Fonagy and colleagues (1994) assert 'the current interest in resilient children is part of a shift of focus to primary protection driven by economic necessity as well as by a desire for social justice' (p.234).

Some literature links resilience to notions of competence and strength, and it is important to note that, as Rutter (1999, p.120) stresses, 'the concept of resilience is necessarily broad...[it] requires attention to a range of possible psychological outcomes and not just a focus on an unusually positive one'. There is no single source of vulnerability or resilience; many components are relevant, such as genetic predisposition, temperament, personality, intelligence, social skills and self esteem. These are shaped by the environment, significant relationships, social and employment opportunities and social learning (Kinard 1998). Turning points in a person's life are important (Rutter 1993; Fowler 1996). For example, although patterns of antisocial or criminal behaviour have been found to persist from childhood through to adult life, if the individual enters a satisfying occupation or enriching personal relationships in early adulthood, such factors decrease the chance that deviant behaviour will continue. Intervention programmes are needed which provide a practical response to antisocial behaviour, built from this knowledge base.

Resilience has been variously defined, notably by Garmezy (1993):

> The central element in the study of resilience lies in the power of recovery and in the ability to return once again to those patterns of adaptation and competence that characterised the individual prior to the pre-stress period ...'to spring back' does not suggest that one is incapable of being wounded or injured. Metaphorically it is descriptively appropriate to consider that under adversity, a (resilient) individual can bend yet subsequently recover. (p.129)

Resilience has also been described as manifest competence in the context of significant challenges to adaptation or development (Masten and Coatsworth 1998), and as 'trait' and 'process' (Jacelon 1997). The understanding of resilience can be approached in four ways: the characteristics of resilient children; resilience as a process; the relationship between resilience and protective factors; the complexity of resilience conceptualisation and the variables which are involved in a holistic assessment.

The characteristics of resilient children

Much academic endeavour has been devoted to establishing the characteristics of resilient children. Masten and Coatsworth (1998) define resilience factors in competent children as a means of looking at strategies which might promote resilience in less competent individuals. A table of characteristics of the resilient child in relation to self, family and environment, is drawn from a thorough overview of critical research findings.

Table 9.1. Characteristics of resilent children and adolescents

Source	Characteristic
Individual	Good intellectual functioning Appealing, sociable easy-going disposition Self-efficacy, self confidence, high self esteem Talents Faith
Family	Close relationship to caring parent figure Authoritative parenting: warmth, structure, high expectations Socio-economic advantages Connections to extended supportive family networks
Extra-familial context	Bonds to pro-social adults outside the family Connections to pro-social organisations Attending effective schools

From Masten and Coatsworth 1998, p.212

Table 9.1 shows factors which predispose a child to resilience. A child possessing such individual resilience and family and community protection is unlikely to be in need of intervention. This offers a framework for both resilience and protective factors (sometimes called buffers against adversity) against which to measure children and families subject to assessments.

Fonagy and colleagues (1994, p.232) write that, 'the indicators of resilience which emerge from studies have a reassuring predictability about them'. They are:

1. higher SES (socio-economic status)
2. female gender if pre-pubescent, male gender after that
3. the absence of organic deficits
4. easy temperament
5. younger age at the time of trauma
6. absence of early separations or losses.

The 'specific features of a child's immediate circumstances which may play a part in protecting them from adversity' are identified as:

1. competent parenting
2. a good (warm) relationship with at least one carer
3. the availability of close social support
4. a better network of informal relationships
5. better educational experience
6. involvement with organised religious activity and faith.

The characteristics of psychological functioning which appear to protect children from stress include:

1. high IQ and good problem solving abilities
2. superior coping styles
3. task related self-efficacy
4. autonomy or internal locus of control
5. a higher sense of self worth
6. interpersonal awareness and empathy
7. willingness and capacity to plan
8. sense of humour. (p.232)

Fonagy *et al.* evidence these characteristics from a review of research studies. Traits associated with resilience cluster around ideas about: conduct and self-regulation; peer relations; social competence; attachment; relationships with caring adults; individual identity; socially appropriate conduct in a supportive cultural context.

Two clear critical factors in the promotion of resilience in adverse circumstances are relationships with caring pro-social adults and good intellectual functioning. The first derives from coping mechanisms built through sound, consistent attachments and has implications for the way in which young people are offered professional support. Developmental understandings about continuities and pro-social adult support for children would indicate that continuity is desirable, rather than the discontinuity that is often experienced. The second, good intellectual functioning, is the ability to problem solve. Recent research has shown that personality patterns can change for the better under certain circumstances (e.g. Rutter 1993; Fowler 1996). Associated with this is the ability to conceptualise. In studies of abuse it has been shown that 'the abused girl who can rationalise, explain and comprehend what has happened to her, and what she can do about it, may thereby be able to maintain her feelings of competence. She may even take steps to end the abuse' (Fowler 1996, p.23). Good intellectual functioning promotes resilience because of the derivative ability to problem solve. Education can thus be a major factor in the promotion of resilience.

Resilience as a process

Rutter (1987; 1990; 1993) provides the main theoretical framework, suggesting that resilience is the 'indicator of a process which characterises a complex social system at a moment in time' which may be the outcome of 'normal development under difficult conditions'. Resilience therefore needs to be seen as part of 'preceding and succeeding circumstances' (1993, p.627). There are some essential considerations in this view of resilience: the importance of potential turning points in people's lives; the way in which success in one arena can provide for self esteem which transfers elsewhere; the extent to which individual responses depend on previous experiences; the importance of temperamental attributes; the interplay between people and environments. Thus resilience is contextual. It changes according to the person's history, context and personal characteristics (Rutter 1993).

Resilience and protective factors

Rutter unpacks this concept, describing resilience and protective mechanisms as 'the positive role of individual difference in people's response to stress and adversity' (1987, p.318). That is, protective mechanisms are the means by which risk for one individual may not be risk for another. Risk changes with circumstances. Adoption, for example, 'probably carries with it an increased psychiatric risk for children from advantageous backgrounds but it may be protective for those born to deviant parents living in discord or deprivation' (Rutter 1987, p.318). Protection from adverse circumstances comes from: personality features; family cohesion and lack of discord; availability of external systems to support coping; the adaptive changes that follow successful coping. Individuals who have developed coping strategies already are able to re-deploy them as needed. Successful coping mechanisms may be built up so that adversity itself may even build resilience.

Rutter suggests that four main processes are important: the reduction of risk impact; the reduction of negative chain reactions; establishment and maintenance of self esteem; the opening up of opportunities (1987, p.325). Protective strategies that can reduce risk include: rehearsing children for situations such as hospital admission or change of placement; the creation of experiences of self esteem and self-efficacy; the focus on support at turning points such as leaving care. These are all ways in which protective processes can be begun. 'Particular attention needs to be paid to the mechanisms operating at key turning points in people's lives where a risk trajectory may be re-directed on a more adaptive path' (Rutter 1993, p.629). Thus people vary in the way they respond to adversity. Active planning can make a difference: 'it appears that resilience may be fostered by steps that make it more likely that people will feel in control of their lives and become effective in shaping what happens to them' (Rutter 1993, p.628). Resilience may therefore be promoted and built within individuals.

The variables involved and the complexity of resilience concepts

Resilience, while identifiable within traits and processes, cannot be reduced to a predictive checklist. What contributes to resilience at one point in time may not be present at another. Children have different needs at different ages. Gender, culture, ability and social circumstances are all closely related and important factors. Most researchers agree that 'resilience is a complex phenomenon that cannot be captured by a single indicator' (Kinard 1998, p.676). Three factors in relation to resilience are now considered: age, gender and culture.

Age-related development

Early resilience is a combination of temperament, secure early attachment, good social environment and experiences of competence, i.e. love and security; new experiences; praise and recognition; and responsibility (Kelmer Pringle 1980). Self esteem develops early, and while changing over time, harsh self-evaluation (low self esteem) remains a major cause of subsequent depression. In the earliest years, secure attachment is a legitimate goal of intervention, giving as it does a foundation for coping with later adversity. Security in the early years predicts many other attributes such as: social behaviour; affect regulation; endurance at tasks; orientation to social resources; and cognitive functioning (Sylva and Lunt 1982). Before children reach school, differences exist which may persist. As Masten and Coatsworth (1998) suggest:

> Children who enter school with few resources, cognitive difficulties and self-regulatory problems often have academic problems, get into trouble with teachers and are more likely to be rejected by peers and are at risk of disengaging from normative school and peer contexts, which sets them up for considerable difficulty in the transition to adolescence. (p.216)

Resilience and competence vary depending on circumstances and experiences, as children move from one developmental stage to another. While a child may seem resilient at one point, this may not continue over long periods, especially if cumulative stressors arise. Competence in children is judged by developmental milestones, often constructed by society, and including indicators of attainment, based on physical, cognitive and behavioural measures. (Sylva and Lunt 1982; Sugarman 1986; Rutter and Hay 1996; Jacobs 1998). Childhood is usually constructed in three stages for this purpose: the early years, middle childhood and adolescence.

EARLY CHILDHOOD

Early childhood is a key stage where the strengthening of skills and feelings of self worth are important for later adaptation. In terms of resilience this age is the foundation for: good attachment; development of the brain; critical periods for the development of certain skills such as language; the foundation of self esteem through success in play and interactions with others. The social environment, when positive and firm, allows the internalisation of self-regulatory behaviour and self-efficacy. Infants are consistently identified as the most vulnerable childhood group.

MIDDLE CHILDHOOD

Middle childhood is usually spent in education with peers as much as in the home. Peer relations and the adjustment to rules and behavioural expectations become key components in children's experiences of competence and self worth. Building and maintaining friendships is a protective mechanism. Actions which enhance peer activities are important; friends fulfil a protective function when things go wrong. Parental interest, expectation of achievement and encouragement of educational success are very influential. Targeting parental involvement in school and associated activities is an effective strategy. Extra-curricular activities offer new experiences and opportunities for success and competence.

ADOLESCENCE

Adolescence is a normal crisis of development characterised by physical changes and growing cognitive and emotional capacity (Rutter, Taylor and Hersov 1995; Department of Health 1996b; Jacobs 1998). There are new vulnerabilities: 'crime, depressive disorders, suicide and para-suicide, anorexia nervosa, and drug misuse all become much more common during adolescence' (Rutter 1992, p.453). Adolescents experiment and engage in more risk behaviours than adults. They are inclined to underestimate risk, having a heightened confidence (Quadrel, Fischhoff and Davis 1993). Adolescence is also a time to reappraise capacity, try new skills and revisit developmental opportunities. Experiences such as those found in the workplace and through peer activities are crucial for building efficacy and self confidence. Adolescence is a turning point where the life trajectory may be improved. Interventions which build on the plasticity and energy of the age group to create opportunity for growth are crucial.

Gender

The biological and social determinants of gender difference are well described in the literature (Archer and Lloyd 1995). However it is important to appraise those research findings which record resilience and vulnerability associated with gender in relation to certain ages and circumstances. For example the impact of family discord on boys might be different in its outcomes from the impact on girls. Research in education shows the benefits of single gender teaching groups for girls with consequent improved performance. Research into peer relations shows differential behaviour according to gender (Erwin 1993, pp.154–176). Age and gender-related issues require careful consideration for each individual in a family, as these may significantly affect resilience in certain circumstances.

Culture and discrimination

Research findings suggest that while 'ethnicity per se bears no natural relation to one's self esteem, psychological factors associated with the experience of a particular ethnic or cultural group will influence self esteem' (Fowler 1996, p.27). The building blocks of self esteem are abilities in activities, social support and approval of significant others, but sensitivity to the impact of racism or other discrimination is important. Judgements about competence have to take account of the cultural and community context (Quinton 1996). This includes awareness in assessment of where the child's community may be different from the larger society in which it exists, and especially what this means for the particular child and family. Religious affiliation, for example, may make a child's cultural context different but can be potentially protective and pro-resilience. Children who live in communities with high levels of antisocial peer behaviour may require parents to develop focused and proactive strategies about their friendships. The parenting attributes required in these circumstances may therefore be different from those for parenting in low-risk environments.

Vulnerability

Research into resilience in maltreated children offers important messages for practitioners about vulnerability. Maltreated children are more likely to score low on overall levels of competence. Measures are usually designed for: cognition; maturity; self esteem; ego-resilience and ego-control (Cichetti *et al.* 1993). Although some maltreated children appear to maintain their resilience, a review of 13 American studies considered it would be important to discern the mechanisms that either contribute to ongoing resilience and adaptation or that prevent such functioning (Morton and Browne 1998). At the time of the research, some children were showing measures of resilience, but there was no mechanism in place for measuring long-term outcomes.

Caution is needed about studies into the apparent resilience of maltreated children because the measures designed to consider competent social functioning and adaptation are not necessarily indicators of mental health or the absence of underlying depression. Behavioural outcomes are not the only important indicator (Luthar and Zigler 1991; Spaccarelli and Kim 1995). Another strand of research regarding maltreated children is that which considers their neurological functioning (Belsky 1993; Widom 1996). These studies indicate that for maltreated children, neurological functioning can be impaired in ways which may well resist repair or compensation.

Resilience measures alone do not necessarily signify emotional health. While the research shows some children who demonstrate resilience (i.e. competent functioning; recovery from trauma or other positive outcomes despite high-risk environments), care needs to be taken not to overstate the case. However given that some children do appear to show competence in the face of maltreatment, it is important to study and quantify what has enabled this to happen, in order to use such learning for finding ways to help other children achieve their optimal outcomes (Kinard 1998; Masten and Coatsworth 1998). Poor outcomes from certain risk situations are by no means inevitable.

Taken together, all these research findings reinforce the argument for early intervention to prevent maltreatment, together with the case for developing protective and supportive strategies in communities to promote resilience and enhance children's coping mechanisms. The presence of pro-social adults (e.g. community leaders, teachers, relatives and friends) as a feature of enhancing and promoting resilience is particularly relevant to social welfare programmes and initiatives.

Risk, stress and coping

It is useful to consider what is stressful for children. For Garmezy (1993) risk of stress can be defined as 'circumstances that increase the likelihood that a child will develop an emotional or behavioural disorder compared with children from the normal population' (p.134). Smith and Carlson (1997) identify acute stressors, chronic stressors and hassles. Acute stressors include: loss of parent; parental separation or divorce; moving home; serious accident or injury; illness of parent or sibling. Chronic stressors include: abuse and neglect; discrimination; homelessness; exposure to violence; disabilities; deprivation. Hassles include: starting school; changing school; family wrangles; peer difficulties (pp.232–233). Such factors need to be evaluated in context, especially at adolescence and other critical periods where hassles cannot be underestimated, and should be placed in the context of what is known of individual resilience and coping mechanisms which may moderate the relationship between the stress and the risk.

Research concerned with life events assists in considering adjustment and the relationship between vulnerability, risk, protective mechanisms and resilience. However, as Luthar and Zigler (1991) caution:

> building upon the existing knowledge base, future empirical endeavours can help to develop the theoretical models that are increasingly complex, and that incorporate the effects of multiple forces operating at the levels of

stress, competence and the moderating processes involved in resilience. (p.19)

It remains of central importance to continue the process of evaluating research findings, while recognising the value and practical usefulness of many of the theoretical perspectives discussed so far.

Critical periods of development

In assessing children, the raft of theory about critical periods for certain developmental tasks is useful. Attention can be paid to areas where delay in intervention and support might leave long-term deficits. The early years, for example, are critical for physical and speech development. Murray and Cooper (1997) give some support to the idea that there is a sensitive early developmental period in respect of cognitive functioning, although there is little known yet of the precise parameters involved. Conversely, trauma and stressful experiences are being considered as factors which possibly permanently change responses in maltreated individuals and are difficult to remedy (Perry 1993). This implies that effective intervention which addresses need at the appropriate time is crucial. It is therefore critical for practitioners to consider the relevance of timing in their interventions in children's lives. American studies argue that an approach to children's services which supports the optimum nurture and wellbeing of children within an ecological multi-dimensional framework is most likely to produce good outcomes (Belsky 1993; Puttnam 1998). Guralnick (1997) evidences the importance of effective early intervention for disabled children.

Family styles and family function

Resilience research stresses the importance of families in building the child's self esteem and competence. The roles learned within the family affect individual development and group functioning. Families are the first formative social experience. Satir (1972, p.4) suggests four recurring elements in families who seek help: feelings and ideas about the self (self worth); ways people work to make meaning with each other (communication); rules people use for how they should feel and act (the family system); ways people relate to other people and institutions outside the family (the link to society). Troubled families show: low self worth; indirect, vague communication; rigid, inhuman, non-negotiable, everlasting rules; fearful, placating and blaming links to society. More untroubled and nurturing families have: high self worth; direct, clear, specific and honest communication; flexible, human, appropriate rules; open and positive links to society.

Authoritative parents model nurturing styles, building strengths in their children which carry into school and peer relations (Masten and Coatsworth 1998). Their children demonstrate: feelings of self worth and confidence; high self esteem; good communication styles; effective rules of behaving and positive ways of relating to others. Styles in families which make for poor functioning are: placating; avoiding; blaming and preaching. These have a detrimental effect on self esteem, self-efficacy, positive relationships and problem solving abilities in children.

Families of all shapes and sizes are key environmental determinants of personality. Each child has a unique relationship with parent(s) and siblings. Warm, structured families with consistent rules and expectations for behaviour produce competent children. Antisocial children often have a history of harsh, rejecting and inconsistent parenting. Parents are not always consistent and sometimes are unable to provide as good an environment for one child as for another. Rutter (1987) comments that: 'children with adverse temperamental features (a composite of low regularity, low malleability, negative mood and fastidiousness) were more likely than other children to be the target of parental hostility, criticism and irritability' (p.321).

Miller *et al.* (1994), Hamilton and Orme (1990), and Gaudin *et al.* (1996) have studied dimensions of functioning in neglectful families and those who are in treatment following identified deficits in parenting. The indicators (or functioning categories) appear well tested and can establish dimensions for complex assessment. Gaudin *et al.* (1996) identify differences between neglectful families and argue for the necessity of differential individual family assessments across the key dimensions of: problem solving abilities; communication patterns; roles; affective communication; affective involvement and behaviour control. These are identified as areas for interventions which promote child welfare and authoritative parenting.

Resilient children are good at finding substitute families and nurture (Werner 1996). This finding relates to the importance of community networks and affiliations. Children who develop resilience in the early years will make the most of school and also of the inputs and relationships from wider kin, other community figures and respite care. Wider networks, if built, validated and supported, may effectively buffer children and sustain them when aspects of their immediate family life are vulnerable (for instance parent illness, temporary absences and times of hardship or change). Professional carers can become temporary pro-social role models.

Parental empathy

Rosenstein (1995), Murray and Cooper (1997), and Cameron (1997) link high levels of parental empathy with better outcomes for children. Parental empathy promotes positive child self-identity. Such parents are more likely to understand and respond to individual need. Knight (1995), a court welfare officer and mother, shows how empathy with her son was beneficial when his birth father made contact unexpectedly after several years of total absence:

> It happened suddenly and unexpectedly. James did not suffer in any way but over the months following the discovery of his father his confidence grew beyond measure and he began at last to make progress at school. It was really obvious he felt good about himself. He was a boy with a father and a family history unique to himself... I still write reports in cases where many parents argue that the absent parent is a stranger and any introduction may damage the child. Isn't the truth rather that the most likely cause of damage is the resident parent who has created a monster whom the child fears and who will be found out if contact takes place? The difference between my child and others in a similar situation is that I had unwittingly done the preparation during the seven years of silence from the child's father... How different things might have been if I had angrily destroyed the photographs and told the child that his father had cared nothing for him and had gone away leaving me to cope alone... I chose to tell him some of the truth...that his father had been a nice man who would love him if he knew him. (pp.158–159)

Empathic ability to view James' need for his absent father as valid meant he had the self esteem and resilience to benefit from his father's renewed contact. Parental ability to envisage the child as a separate human being with intentions, individual feelings and needs is essential in the construction of self-efficacy.

Family strengths approaches

In order to safeguard children through strengthening families, professionals need to recognise and build on existing abilities. The strengths approach is a perspective based on a set of values and is helpful in the context of undertaking assessments of need. The perspective shows how the practitioner can work positively towards partnership. Saleeby (1997) describes the values as: distributive justice; equality; respect for the individual; inclusiveness and diversity; autonomy placed back with individuals: and helping in terms of utilising the empowering elements in the environment. The relevant strengths are: what people have learned about themselves and the world; personal qualities, traits and virtues that people possess; what people know about their environment; the talents that people have; cultural and personal stories; and pride (pp.231–244).

Practitioners who adopt this approach build on what parents already possess and conduct interviews on solution focused and problem solving ideas. Key elements are:

- giving pre-eminence to the client's understanding of the facts
- believing the client
- discovering what the client wants
- moving towards personal and environmental strengths
- assessing in a multi-dimensional way
- discovering uniqueness
- using understandable language
- making assessment a shared activity
- reaching a mutual agreement
- avoiding blaming
- avoiding cause and effect thinking
- assessing not diagnosing.

(from Saleeby 1997, pp.3–17)

An ecological and systems approach

The ecosystems approach balances individual, family and environmental components of assessment in a way that is consistent with a strengths perspective that looks to the whole community as a resource. It sustains an approach to child welfare which sees protection through supporting families in their environments as the best safeguard from harm. Ecological perspectives are well established in literature (Siporin 1975; Maluccio 1981; Garbarino 1982). Key concepts are that:

- the person-environment relationship is continuous
- person, behaviour and environment are mutually interdependent
- systems theory is useful to analyse the ecology of the person in the situation
- behaviour is site specific
- assessment and evaluation are through direct observation of the person-environment system
- behaviour is the outcome of transactions between the person and the environment; and
- behavioural science should seek to understand and analyse these interactions.

(Allen-Meares and Lane 1987, p.518)

The systems approach, as described by Compton and Galaway (1989, pp.123–137), offers a helpful way of organising and studying information in order to make decisions about where and how to intervene and what services might be utilised. The benefits of the applications of systems theory to social work are to be found in: facilitating the worker's understanding of the employing system (roles and responsibilities); understanding the relationships between the employing agency and others; and understanding the client system in order to work in partnership, make assessments, solve problems and achieve change.

Genograms and eco-maps are tools for analysing the person and their situation holistically, linking individual and environmental factors such as family, community, hospitals or schools. Dynamic interactions can be observed between the constituent parts, with some relationships in the system more crucial than others. It is important in making an assessment to understand the complex interactions between the child and various levels of the social system in order to facilitate the best responses. This framework enables the practitioner to consider the impact of proposed change in one part of the system on another. This is crucial in looking for positive intended outcomes which will not produce unintended unhelpful consequences elsewhere.

Holism in needs assessment

A holistic assessment, therefore, requires consideration of the interaction of child, family and outside world. Risk, resilience, vulnerabilities and protective factors have to be weighed from an informed theoretical knowledge base because the child is a 'living system embedded within many other systems such as family and schools' (Masten and Coatsworth 1998, p.206). Accurate assessments reflect this complexity and utilise the underpinning theories relating to each of the three components. For example, 'understanding the pathways to resilience and adaptation in children facing stress such as maltreatment will make important contributions to the development of intervention strategies designed to maximise competence' (Kinard 1998, p.677).

To conclude, holistic assessments draw on a wide range of underpinning theories and a comprehensive body of research findings from many disciplines. To be effective, assessments consider strengths, resilience, vulnerabilities and protective mechanisms in conjunction with thoughtful, participative involvement with children, carers and communities. The focus should be on the impact that experiences have on children's lives and whether these factors protect or impair a child's development (Gilligan 2001). Intervention is needed to promote positive change at life's turning points. The purpose of children's services is to support families in meeting children's changing needs as they grow towards adulthood, with the aim of promoting their satisfactory development. In Kinard's words, 'the goal is to apply knowledge about how children successfully cope with stress and adversity to prevention and intervention efforts in order to maximise competence and adaptation' (1998, p.676).

CHAPTER TEN

An Inter-Agency Approach to Needs Assessment

Harriet Ward and Mark Peel

While there are immense advantages if child welfare agencies within a given locality can adopt commonly agreed standards for the identification of need, these are often frustrated by difficulties in developing robust inter-agency working practices. This chapter explores the construction and adoption of a common methodology now used by all child welfare agencies in one locality in undertaking assessments of need at the pre-referral stage. It relates the relative success of the enterprise to the extent to which five recognised elements of successful collaborative working were present: an identified purpose, consensus, choice, reciprocity and trust.

Introduction

The diversity of agencies in Britain that provide services designed to promote the welfare of children illustrates the point that 'it takes a whole village to raise a child'. If we place the child's home in the middle of the village, and his or her immediate family within that home, the 'next door neighbours' will be the relatives, friends, and acquaintances who make up the child's community. However the task of child rearing in Western societies is of such complexity that individuals cannot sustain it without support from professional providers of child welfare services. In the heart of the metaphorical village, and accessible to all children, one might place providers of universal services such as general practitioners, health visitors, midwives, dentists, teachers, the police and the staff of leisure centres. At a greater distance one might place those providers of more specialist services such as paediatricians, psychologists, special needs teachers, education welfare officers, social workers and youth offending teams. Their services are required by only a relatively small number of children, but these are likely to be more vulnerable than their peers, and a proportion of them will be 'children in need' within the meaning of the Children Act 1989. On the periphery one might, perhaps, place providers of services to significant adults, such as parents and other relatives, for the work of professionals such as adult psychiatrists, the staff of the benefit agency, probation officers and housing managers will undoubtedly affect the wellbeing of the dependent children of service users.

With so many professionals working in an extensive range of agencies, and fulfilling very disparate roles in respect of children and families with an immense diversity of need, there are obvious difficulties in co-ordinating services in such a way that they promote the wellbeing of the children and young people with whom they are concerned. Nearly a quarter of a century ago, in one of the few detailed analyses of the complexity of inter-agency working, Hallett and Stevenson (1978) identified a number of issues that are still apparent today. Differences in social class, in standards of education and training and in levels of accountability serve to compound the reluctance felt by many professionals to trust in one another's skills. Poor understanding of one another's respective roles and lack of confidence in the judgement of colleagues can mean that some areas of work are unnecessarily duplicated while others are neglected. Where the need is so great that there is a possibility that children may be at risk of significant harm, these difficulties may be compounded, as was shown in an analysis of the work of the early child protection case conferences (Hallett and Stevenson 1978).

Other authors, looking at the later Area Child Protection Committees (ACPCs), found that some members, particularly general practitioners and paediatricians, may lose interest in participating owing to the amount of time taken in reaching decisions and lack of communication as to their outcomes. Other members, such as the police or social services, may feel bound by their own professional accountability to take action without reference to the views of the wider group, thus destroying its initial cohesion (Lupton *et al.* 1997). Without mutual trust and co-operation between agencies, joint resourcing and the provision of a complementary service is impossible: in the long run, it is the children and families for whom the services are designed who lose out. This chapter explores one, relatively small-scale, initiative intended to address some of these issues. The Children and Families Assessment Project aims to identify common standards by which child welfare professionals within a given locality can co-ordinate their efforts in a specific area: the identification and assessment of children in need.

Who is in need?

Part III of the Children Act 1989 identifies the criteria by which children are defined as being in need and sets out local authorities' responsibilities to provide them with appropriate services. The legal specifications and the rationale behind them have been discussed in some detail in Chapter 1. Led primarily by their social services departments, local authorities exercise a duty to safeguard and promote the welfare of children in their area who are in need by providing appropriate services (Children Act 1989, s.17) and to make enquiries if they have reason to believe that a child in their area is suffering, or is likely to suffer, significant harm (Children Act 1989, s.47). However they are not necessarily in the best position to identify who these children are, for social services are not universal providers in the manner of health authorities or education departments, with whom all children will almost inevitably come in contact.

In Chapter 3 of this book, Hardiker *et al.* demonstrate a conceptual framework that identifies how children's services can be regarded as a sequence of incremental levels of intervention. At the base level are the universal services, available to all. Beyond them, at the first level of intervention, programmes such as Sure Start, that target vulnerable groups, serve to divert families from more intrusive services and enable them to make better use of universal provision. The second level covers supportive services to children in need and their families, designed to address early stresses through short-term interventions by social services and other agencies, with the aim of restoring personal and social functioning. At the third level are protective services, aimed at meeting serious stresses, including the risks of significant harm and family breakdown, and at restoring family functioning and 'good enough' parenting. Fourth level interventions 'cover a diverse group of issues: social breakdown, children looked after, children abused within the care system'.

As Hardiker *et al.* also point out, 'social services departments typically prioritise their direct services at second and subsequent levels of intervention'. Their role in the provision of universal services and first level interventions may be limited to such activities as funding voluntary organisations like Home Start to provide parenting support to families under stress, but at more intrusive levels it increases exponentially. The involvement of other statutory and voluntary child welfare agencies may be required in second, third and fourth level interventions, but social services increasingly take the lead responsibility, particularly for assessing need and for co-ordinating appropriate services.

This responsibility derives from the legal duties vested in the local authority under the Children Act 1989. It is the local authority, acting through its social services department, albeit in partnership with other public agencies, that has a duty to establish and ensure the effective functioning of the ACPC, to make enquiries if there is reason to suspect that a child in its area is suffering or likely to suffer significant harm (s.47); to co-ordinate assessments of need and subsequent inter-agency plans and, where necessary, to apply to the courts for an Emergency Protection Order or a Care Order (s.31, s.46) (Department of Health, Home Office, Department for Education and Employment 1999).

It is, perhaps, inevitable that, if social services departments have lead responsibilities for children in need, they will also encounter the greatest opprobrium when things go wrong. A series of well-publicised scandals in which child welfare agencies have failed to protect children from abuse within their own families (or indeed from abusers amongst their own staff) has almost invariably led to stringent criticism of the social services department involved, even when other agencies have been equally well placed to detect and prevent maltreatment (Hallett and Stevenson 1978). Inevitably, social services themselves have also become sensitised to the need to guard against accusations of negligence as well as to protect from possible harm the children for whom they are responsible (Department of Health 1995a). At the same time, a heightened public awareness of the prevalence of child abuse has led to greatly increased referral rates to social services departments not only from the community, but also from other agencies, concerned lest they be held accountable for failing to alert social services to what are perceived to be the latter's responsibilities. The emphasis on child protection referrals is also increased by a widespread understanding that, given current priorities in social services departments, families whose difficulties are perceived in these terms are most likely to receive a service (Aldgate and Tunstill 1995; Tunstill and Aldgate 2000).

There is no doubt that some children are at risk of permanent, significant and, in some cases, fatal harm if immediate action is not taken to protect them. Social services departments need to be able to respond to such cases urgently and effectively. However by no means all concerns about significant harm are of this extreme nature; indeed, the evidence suggests that the emphasis on investigating possible abuse has often been misplaced. Research completed in the early 1990s showed that of the 120,000 child protection investigations undertaken each year, 80,000 (67%) led to no further action, while only 40,000 (33%) led to child protection conferences, 24,500 (20%) to registration and a subsequent child protection plan and 6000 (5%) eventually resulted in a child being placed away from home (Department of Health 1995b). Moreover unnecessary child protection investigations not only take up scarce resources, but are also frequently detrimental to the wellbeing of the families concerned. There is little evidence that they result in the provision of family support services. Indeed, the process of such investigations often leaves children who do not require protection but nevertheless have extensive unmet needs unsupported and their parents reluctant to ask for assistance (Cleaver and Freeman 1995).

The Children Act 1989 lays on local authorities an equal duty to promote the wellbeing of children in need and to prevent their development from being significantly impaired. These can be seen as opposite sides of the same coin, for there is a continuum along which failure to promote children's welfare shades into a failure to protect them from harm. However the prominence given to abuse cases has meant that these two elements of welfare promotion and child protection are often regarded as unrelated, and the overemphasis on child protection work has resulted in an imbalance of services which has been detrimental to initiatives to promote the wellbeing of all children in need (Department of Health 1995a).

Refocusing services

The current debate revolves around the question of how, given the situation described above, resources can be shifted from their over-concentration on child protection investigations and used to improve services for all children in need. Hardiker, Exton and Barker (1991b) suggest that 'the question asked at initial enquiry should be reframed from 'has this child been abused?' to 'what are the needs of this child (including child protection) which cannot be met without the provision of services?' The refocusing initiative aims to move the concentration of service provision from the more to the less intrusive levels of intervention (from Hardiker's levels three and four to levels one and two). The hypothesis is that if more weight is given to early interventions, designed to promote children's welfare, there will be less need for the more intrusive services required to protect them from harm.

However while social services departments will generally lead more intrusive interventions, families whose needs are only beginning to emerge are likely to come to the attention of a wide variety of other agencies well before they are known to social workers. Similarly, services at these levels are provided by numerous agencies, such as health authorities, education or housing departments, the police and voluntary organisations, as well as by social services departments. If the focus is genuinely to broaden out from a narrow concentration on child protection issues towards the provision of services for all children in need, it is clearly necessary to meet three considerable challenges. These are: first, to devise a methodology whereby such a disparate group of professionals can reach a common agreement as to the standards to be employed in assessing whether, and to what extent, families require additional support; second, to find some means by which the professionals involved develop sufficient trust in one another's judgement to subscribe to whatever common standard is agreed; and third, to ensure that the adoption of a broader perspective does not result in a failure to identify those children who genuinely require protection.

The Children and Families Assessment Project

The Children and Families Assessment Project is a response to these challenges. Between 1997 and 2000 a consortium of key staff in the child welfare agencies based in a particular local authority worked with a team of researchers in order to explore how far all agencies with responsibilities for children who may potentially be in need could reach agreement about responses to the following questions:

- What does and what does not constitute good enough parenting?
- What are the key indicators that show that additional services are required to enable a child to reach or maintain a reasonable standard of health or development?

- How can these be distinguished from other indicators of concern where additional services may not be warranted either through lack of resources or because they are regarded as intrusive?
- How can responses to these questions be translated into a methodology that can be used to assist any worker to identify which children are – and which are not – in need?
- Is it possible for all child welfare agencies within the locality to agree to a common standard for the identification of need and to use a standard methodology for making initial assessments?

It was felt that a positive response to the final question would demonstrate that the programme had produced not only a viable methodology for needs assessment, but also a clearer understanding of the factors to be confronted if inter-agency work is to be successful. These latter issues have already been explored by Hudson *et al.* (1999) who argue that it is not enough for successive governments to exhort agencies to work together in order to improve practice, nor even to provide funds to facilitate the enterprise. For collaborative working to be successful, five elements are essential: an identified purpose, consensus, choice, reciprocity and trust. The success or failure of the Children and Families Assessment Project would depend on the extent to which these elements were present.

Choice and a common purpose

Although the initiative under discussion eventually represented a close collaboration between child welfare agencies and a university research team, within the authority, considerable work had been undertaken before the researchers were approached. Key representatives from the health authority, the education department, the police, the major children's voluntary organisations and the social services department had already agreed and identified a common objective: to develop and implement an inter-agency screening tool that helps workers identify whether a child is in need. The ultimate aim was to develop tools that could be used by any front line professional, and which were, as far as possible, acceptable to service users.

Although the research was commissioned by one agency, others had been party to the decision to take on this initiative, and an inter-agency steering group had already been identified to see it through. Preparing the ground in this way proved to be an extremely important element in this type of work. A number of other local authorities have since tried to replicate the Assessment Project under the aegis of their own ACPCs. The success or failure of the venture appears to have been closely related to the extent to which representatives from the various agencies concerned agreed to the objective and considered that they had been included in the decision to participate.

Choice played an important part in this process, for the experience from other authorities showed that, where agencies regarded themselves as having freely decided to subscribe to the programme, the initiative was far more successful than where they considered themselves to have been co-opted into it. However choice can only be freely exercised in setting up a programme such as this. Once an agreement has been made to engage in this type of work, it becomes increasingly difficult for agencies to withdraw without disrupting the whole venture. As the programme progresses from its current developmental, pilot stage towards full implementation, we anticipate that group pressure will increasingly be perceived as replacing the original element of choice, and that skilful negotiation will be necessary to retain the support of all those involved.

Identifying indicators of concern

Once the common objective had been identified, the first major step in the research programme was to work towards the establishment of agreed indicators of need and accepted thresholds of severity. The purpose was to establish and articulate a standard of 'good enough parenting' that reflected a consensus view from all those concerned in needs assessment within the locality: representatives from health, education, social services, voluntary organisations and other agencies, together with parents and children themselves.

The first task was to undertake a brief review of the available literature. Four areas were explored: demographic trends, normal parenting behaviour, successful and unsuccessful parenting styles and the relationship between parenting standards, children's developmental needs and outcomes (Peel and Ward 1997). Professionals from a range of disciplines were asked to nominate key texts that should be included, in order to ensure that the parenting standards that emerged would be experienced as relevant to as wide a constituency as possible.

There already exists an extensive body of research in psychology, sociology and social anthropology which can be used to begin to identify commonly agreed indicators of need. Moreover the *Looking After Children* Assessment and Action Records (Department of Health 1995a), which draw extensively on this research, are currently used by many social services departments to assess how far one group of children, those looked after away from home, are receiving good enough parenting. In each of seven dimensions of development (health, education, identity, family and social relationships, social presentation, emotional and behavioural development and self care skills), age-related schedules ask how far children's needs are being met by those people who have caring responsibilities for them: parents, other relatives, foster carers, residential workers, social workers, teachers, health visitors and older children themselves (see Chapter 13).

Moreover work undertaken by the *Looking After Children* research team, in the development of the Assessment and Action Records, demonstrated that the issues covered are regarded as important by almost all parents. A study of the parenting values and practices of 400 families where children were living at home in the community showed that most parents shared common aspirations for their children, and regarded it as important to provide them with the opportunities recommended by the Records. Not all parents, however, were able to do so (Moyers and Mason 1995).

Nevertheless the Assessment and Action Records were developed specifically for children looked after away from home. They have since informed the construction of the Core Assessment Records (Department of Health and Cleaver 2000) to be used by social services departments in gathering information about the relationship between parenting capacity, family and environmental factors and children's developmental needs under the new *Framework for the Assessment of Children in Need and their Families* (Department of Health, Department for Education and Employment, Home Office 2000a; see Chapter 8). However while both groups of assessment records detail the components of satisfactory parenting, they do not identify commonly acceptable standards, nor do they set thresholds for increasing involvement with families by public services and voluntary agencies.

Nevertheless the conceptual framework that underpins the assessment records provided a basis upon which to develop the work. The seven developmental dimensions and the link between environment, quality of care and children's progress were both of key importance to this issue. Messages from the literature search (Peel and Ward 1997), together with the items used in the *Looking After Children* Assessment and Action Records (Department of Health 1995a) were therefore used as a basis for identifying indicators of concern. These could be used to alert professionals to families where children's experiences and progress fall below certain thresholds, and where additional services are required in order to ensure that their developmental needs are met.

The indicators covered eight dimensions: the seven areas of development identified in the *Looking After Children* materials, plus the child's physical environment. Additional indicators, that could be used to assess the quality of the child's emotional ambience, or the parents' capacity to promote wellbeing, were included in the dimensions already noted. In each of the seven developmental dimensions, two types of concern were identified: concern about the parenting experiences being offered, and concern about the child's rate of progress. Although often the latter will be related to the former, a causal relationship is not always either evident or demonstrable.

Within each dimension, indicators were classified by the researchers as demonstrating areas of mild, moderate or serious concern. These thresholds correspond to Hardiker's levels one, two and three, and also to the definitions of need specified in Sections 17(a) and 17(b) of the Children Act 1989 (see Chapter 1). Indicators of mild concern identify those families that may need to make better use of support universally available from health or education services, but will normally not require additional assistance from social services. Indicators of moderate concern show that 'a child is unlikely to achieve or maintain, or to have the opportunity of achieving or maintaining, a reasonable standard of health or development without the provision of services' (Peel and Ward 2000). Support is likely to be required from a range of agencies, possibly including social services, but not as a matter of urgency. Serious concerns indicate that 'a child's health or development is likely to be significantly impaired, or further impaired, without the provision of services'. Immediate action is required to provide support from a range of agencies, led and co-ordinated by social services (Peel and Ward 2000).

For instance, in the education dimension, the following indicators might raise concerns about the parenting experiences of children under five years old.

Mild concerns:

- a pre-school child has no experience of nursery/playschool before formally starting school
- the child is not being prepared for school (e.g. learning to count, recognise letters, and identify colours).

Moderate concerns:

- the parent does not encourage the baby/pre-school child to play with a range of objects and materials or to explore his/her environment
- the parent does not read or show picture books to him/her.

Serious concerns:

- the parent/carer rarely talks to or plays with the baby/child and/or leaves him/her alone for most of the day
- a child with a major learning disability has no individual education plan
- the child is not sent to school (if of school age).

Similar types of indicator identify different thresholds of concern about other dimensions of the child's developmental progress, the emotional ambience in the home and the child's environment.

Establishing a consensus

Up to this point the research team had been engaged in a purely theoretical piece of work. However the purpose was to lay the foundations for the development of practical tools for needs assessment that could be used by any front line professional and that would be, as far as possible, acceptable to service users. As the research programme moved from the theoretical to the developmental stage, so the inter-agency commitment moved from the identification of a common purpose towards the establishment of a consensus about relevant indicators and agreed thresholds of concern.

Professionals from all agencies likely to come into contact with families in need were invited to attend workshops in which they were shown a randomised list of the indicators in each of the dimensions. They were asked first whether there were any that they wished to add or delete, and second if they could allocate the indicators to categories representing mild, moderate and serious concerns. Similar exercises were carried out with parents and with groups of children aged ten and eleven.

It would not have been possible to gather together a representative sample of potential participants in the time available before the pilot began. Moreover although the exercise was intended to discover how far the views of potential participants differed over the severity of various indicators of need, it also had other purposes. These were to publicise the work of the research team and to ensure that a wide range of those people with direct concerns in this area had an opportunity of contributing to the finished product. The exercise was therefore undertaken with a number of focus groups, whose function was to advise the researchers. Initially there were difficulties in gaining access to sufficient numbers of all participants in the commissioning authority, and so groups of parents, professionals and children from a similar district in another authority were also brought into the original consultation. However as interest spread within the locality, the views of the 'outsiders' became a less important part of the overall discussion.

In general terms there was a high degree of agreement between the groups concerning the ranking of indicators; with very few exceptions, they also agreed with the allocations made privately by researchers. Where differences were identified, parents tended to rank indicators more seriously than did professionals, possibly because of difficulties previously experienced in accessing services. There was also evidence that parents tended to accept that professionals had both the duty and the power to police quite basic aspects of family lifestyles.

Children's views were elicited through discussions held in response to selected video clips shown during school Personal Social and Health Education (PSHE) lessons. They considered the emotional environment within the home as of much greater consequence than the physical environment, emphasising that it was important for parents to 'be there' and to 'do right' by their children. Children thought that child welfare agencies should provide help when parents were unwilling or unable to offer a positive emotional environment; in the most serious circumstances they thought young children should be cared for away from home.

The work with the focus groups was designed to ensure that the assessment materials were based on commonly agreed parenting standards. Responses from these groups were therefore used to make adjustments both to the list of indicators and to their allocation to different threshold classifications in the pilot version of the materials. The materials were initially piloted intensively in two areas of the local authority. Prior to their introduction, virtually all social workers, health visitors, police officers, representatives of voluntary child welfare agencies, education welfare officers, and teachers with pastoral responsibilities in those areas were trained in their use. The focus groups continued to operate throughout the nine month pilot period. Feedback both from professionals using the materials and from the focus groups, which included parents, was used to develop the final version which is in the process of being implemented throughout the authority.

Although there was some difficulty in accessing sufficient numbers of parents and professionals within the locality prior to the pilot, the indicators included in the final version are, as far as possible, representative of the views of the community as a whole. In total, 250 professionals, 46 parents and 79 children were consulted in this authority and their views taken into account in developing the materials.

It should, however, be noted that even if common agreement was reached at this stage, standards will not remain constant. Although children's developmental needs do not change, threshold decisions concerning the level of deprivation at which agencies have a right or responsibility to intervene will alter over time, partly in response to changes in our knowledge and understanding of the consequences of deprivation and partly in response to the availability of resources. Assessment tools such as those under discussion will constantly need updating. Moreover, as has already been noted, the materials are now being developed and piloted in a number of other authorities. Within each of these additional authorities, the indicators and ratings are being discussed, explored and adjusted before the pilot version of the materials is produced. Although we expect some indicators of serious concern to remain constant (such as evidence of incest or physical assault necessitating medical attention), where issues are less clear-cut, and the consequences of unmet need less universally apparent, the indicators and thresholds are likely to vary from one locality to another.

The Children and Families Assessment Form

The current version of the Children and Families Assessment Form takes professionals through a structured assessment of indicators of concern raised by the material circumstances in which the family lives, the parent's capacity to respond to a child's needs and the child's progress in seven developmental dimensions. Separate assessments for each individual child in a family are completed in the home, as far as possible in partnership with parents. In making the assessment, respondents are asked to provide specific, factual information and to state whether concerns are mild, moderate or serious. Where indicators are noted but there are thought to be no grounds for concern, they are asked to provide evidence of mitigating circumstances. Throughout, the assessment is designed to identify the family's strengths as well as any weaknesses or difficulties. Thus respondents are asked first to determine whether support is available from within the child's family or the immediate community to meet identified areas of concern, before considering what should be addressed by statutory or voluntary agencies.

Once all areas of concern have been identified, respondents are asked to decide whether further action is necessary, and if so, whether this should be undertaken by their own agency, or whether the case should be referred elsewhere, most probably to social services. If further action is to be undertaken by their own agency, they are asked to draw up specific plans with identified objectives and a recognised timescale and to decide who will take responsibility for putting them into practice. They are also asked to identify those indicators that will need to be monitored in order to assess the effectiveness of whatever services are provided and to specify arrangements for reviewing progress.

Reciprocity and trust

So far, the various agencies within the authority have reached agreement on a number of points. They have identified a common objective, and set up a management structure to oversee its achievement; they have established the existence of a substantial area of common ground in the identification of need and agreed to subscribe to a consensus view both on relevant indicators and on thresholds at which action might be taken; they have also undertaken a common training programme and agreed to use common materials. The remaining part of the research programme demonstrates how far the other components identified by Hudson as integral to a successful inter-agency relationship – reciprocity and trust – have influenced and been influenced by the introduction of these materials.

The construction of a methodology to which all agencies agree to subscribe, provides a procedure for effective inter-agency working, but data from a formal evaluation of the pilot project was also necessary to identify how far the new procedures were likely to affect practice in the agencies concerned. To this purpose the research team gathered data on all cases referred by external agencies to social services in the 12 months prior to the introduction of the materials (1998–1999), and compared these with data on all cases referred by agencies in the 12 months after the pilot began (1999–2000). During the period of the pilot a number of factors, most particularly the introduction of the new *Framework for Assessment of Need in Children and Families* (Department of Health *et al.* 2000a), required managers in all child welfare agencies to devote considerable attention to the assessment of need. It was important to ensure that the findings from the Assessment Project did not simply reflect changes happening in all authorities over this period. The research team therefore also matched the data from the commissioning authority with comparative information on all referrals made to a similar district in another local authority social services department over the same period (Peel and Ward 2000).

The data were gathered in order to identify whether the introduction of the pilot materials affected the answers to the following questions:

- does introduction of an inter-agency method of assessment improve joint working between health, education and social services?
- does it reduce duplication of effort?
- does it affect partnerships between professionals and parents?
- does it result in increased rates of referral?
- does a common, structured methodology improve the quality of information offered at referral?

The findings suggest first that the introduction of the materials in the pilot authority led to a dramatic increase in the extent and quality of information offered by referring agencies. Whereas in the pre-pilot stage, referrals often recorded concerns of professionals in general terms, after the introduction of the new methodology there was substantially more specific evidence of need and its relationship to the child's wellbeing (Peel and Ward 2000, pp.18–20). Work currently being undertaken in another authority may, however, demonstrate that the introduction of *any* structured methodology for assessment may produce similar findings (Ward, Garnett and Everett forthcoming).

Second, there was evidence that both professionals and families benefited from a reduction in duplicated assessments and an increase in inter-agency trust, as social services accepted assessments completed by workers from other agencies without requiring the investigation to be repeated. An education worker commented:

> They (social services) have never been interested in my assessment skills before, and even though they were very nice about it, it was as if they felt I wasn't up to it. It's difficult with families as well, you tell them you are referring them to social services for help with X, but they assess the family and say 'no it's Y that's the problem'. It makes you look stupid in front of your families. (Peel and Ward 2000, p.17)

Third, while child concern referrals dropped in both the pilot and the comparison site over the pilot period, the decrease was substantially greater in the former (64%) than in the latter (11%). Just over half of the decrease in the pilot site could be attributed to investigating agencies deciding to meet the needs of families themselves or to take no further action after they had completed an inter-agency assessment. Fears that a drop in child concern referrals would be matched by a rise in child protection referrals proved to be unfounded (Peel and Ward 2000, pp.24–25).

Such findings suggest that the introduction of the Assessment Project in the pilot authority was largely beneficial. Referral rates were reduced as child welfare practitioners from other agencies operated agreed thresholds in deciding whether social services should be alerted to a child's circumstances; better quality referrals made it easier for social services to prioritise cases; a common standard for basic assessments reduced duplication of effort and also made it easier for professionals from different disciplines to work together and in partnership with parents.

However these findings raise a number of important questions. The advantages to a social services department of introducing a formalised assessment procedure that is used by all referring agencies are relatively straightforward: 'unnecessary' referrals are reduced, and those which are made come with clearer, more specific information concerning the nature and extent of need within a family, reducing some of the work of the duty team. The advantages to referring agencies are not so obvious. As a matter of policy, cases referred by other professionals are not currently accepted by social services in this local authority unless accompanied by a completed Children and Families Assessment Form. The formal assessment takes about

45 minutes to complete, and may be regarded as time-consuming by professionals who have previously simply asked social services to investigate a case. The introduction of the new procedures also required a considerable change in the working practices of some agencies, and led to important debates concerning the role and responsibility of certain professionals, such as schoolteachers, in identifying need.

On the other hand, there are suggestions that the adoption of a common system will give greater credibility to referrals made to social services, and provide greater transparency concerning the reasons why some are taken up and not others. Initial fears – that the introduction of the new methodology would be regarded as an attempt by social services to offload their work onto other agencies – did not appear to be realised during the pilot stage. However we do not yet know how far the new system will, in the long term, increase the work of both assessment and service provision in agencies outside social services; nor do we know whether the perceived advantages will be seen as sufficient compensation.

At the basis of the Assessment Project lies the question of trust. The various agencies concerned may agree to adopt common thresholds of need and a common methodology for identifying children who fall below these thresholds. They may decide that there are sufficient reciprocal advantages to continue with a methodology that, at least on the surface, might appear to benefit some agencies more than others. However unless they can be certain of both the motives and the competency of the staff in the other agencies involved, the initiative is unlikely to succeed. The programme would not have advanced as far as it has without the establishment of considerable trust between the representatives of the various agencies involved, but this will need to be reinforced if the initiative is to be sustained. If agencies outside social services are likely to be more involved in the work of initial screening, and if this leads to their providing services to more children and families at the first and second levels of intervention, then there will need to be some reallocation of resources. If social services are unwilling to contemplate this, then their motive in supporting an initiative which appears to reduce the burden on their staff will be called into question, as will the trust that has been so carefully established. One way forward might be to establish a common pool of resources to which staff from other agencies could apply when identifying needs that can best be met without further referral. Such resources might be held, and their use monitored, by the ACPC.

Finally, if as appears, referrals to social services from other professionals are substantially reduced, there should be a reciprocal arrangement whereby those that are received will be given added weight. If all professionals involved have agreed a common threshold of need, and have been trained to implement a common methodology, then the adoption of a common standard should be acknowledged. This will not, however, be easy to achieve if all participants have not the same degree of skill or level of training. Moreover there may be occasions when one department may consider that its statutory responsibilities require it to override the views of representatives from another agency with a lesser degree of accountability. Nevertheless the rationale behind such decisions will need to be clearly expressed and openly debated if the requisite level of trust between the agencies concerned is to be maintained.

Conclusion

The Children and Families Assessment Project is designed to introduce a systematic and holistic approach to needs assessment to all agencies within an authority, in order to set the question of abuse within the much broader framework of the identification of unmet developmental needs. However its construction and piloting has been fundamentally an exercise in the development of robust inter-agency working practices. At its conception, the initiative contained all the necessary elements for successful collaboration: a common, identified purpose; consensus; reciprocity; choice and trust. However these will need to be continually reinforced if the programme is to be sustained. The initiative can perhaps best be seen as a step-by-step approach to the construction of more successful inter-agency working practices. There are still likely to be numerous setbacks on the way, but if the programme can continue to be sustained, it should bring identifiable benefits to the children and families with whom it engages.

CHAPTER ELEVEN

Addressing Family Needs when a Parent is Mentally Ill

Adrian Falkov

This chapter addresses key themes and concepts which are relevant to the assessment of needs when mentally ill parents/carers and their children are living together. An epidemiological perspective is provided to assist in identification of need, together with examples from daily practice. A systemic conceptual framework which incorporates developmental, family, social and mental health domains is presented together with a framework for consideration of the range of parent–child–professional interactions and opportunities for intervention are highlighted.

Introduction

> It took me six months to come to terms with my diagnosis and during that time I lost most of my self confidence, which does not make a good parent. I felt they (the children) knew better than I did what was right for them. Slowly I returned to normal feeling older and wiser but let down by the system.

There has been interest in the needs of children whose parents are mentally ill for much of this century (Rutter 1966). Compelling evidence now exists from a growing number of systematic studies indicating that such children are at increased risk of adverse psychosocial adaptation (Downey and Coyne 1990; Laucht, Esser and Schmidt 1994; Watt *et al.* 1984). Increasingly studies of emotional and behavioural problems in children have begun to address interactions between multiple child, family and socio-demographic variables in an attempt to quantify mechanisms of risk transmission and the operation of protective factors (Anthony and Cohler 1987; Rolf *et al.* 1990). The impact of children's problems and disorders on their parent's mental health has also been noted, as has the persistence of mental health problems into adulthood and across generations (Andrews, Brown and Creasey 1990; Quinton, Rutter and Gulliver 1990).

Yet despite this evidence and increasing prominence given to the interface between parental mental health and child maltreatment, to date there are no generic services within health or local authorities that are specifically configured to address the needs of *both* mentally ill parents and their children (Nicholson *et al.* 1993; Gopfert, Webster and Seeman 1996; Cleaver, Unell and Aldgate 1999; Weir and Douglas 1999).

Within the context of a needs assessment framework this chapter will discuss some possible explanations for barriers to service development and, more importantly, what can be done to improve awareness, knowledge and skills amongst practitioners working with family members, across all services. A necessarily selective overview on key themes will be provided which serves to justify both interest and action. This will include identifying and defining needs of children and their mentally ill parents/carers, including needs for safety. Examples from practice will be used to illustrate the opportunities and rewards that can be gained from talking directly with children and their mentally ill parents.

Key themes

Reasons for interest

CARE IN THE COMMUNITY

Since the mid-1950s, the introduction of medication – anti-psychotics and antidepressants – together with ongoing social changes have led to a dramatic reduction of institution-based psychiatric care. Most prominent amongst these changes has been the large-scale exodus of long-stay patients from asylums to the community. In the UK, 350 psychiatric beds per 100,000 population were occupied in 1954 compared with 133 per 100,000 population in 1989 (O'Driscoll *et al.* 1993). An American survey from the early 1980s estimated that each year 65 per cent of patients discharged from psychiatric hospitals return to their families (Goldman 1982).

One of the unplanned benefits of this policy has been to make children more visible to those with responsibility for supporting mentally ill adults in the community. This policy has also enabled mentally ill parents and their dependent children to spend more time together which has, in turn, created a dual burden of increased childcare responsibilities for parents and greater exposure of children to problematic symptoms and behaviours when they arise. Professionals across all services are therefore facing dilemmas resulting from the diverse and at times competing needs of parents and their children.

Furthermore, recurrent hospitalisation of parents has the potential to seriously disrupt the continuity of care provided for children and the formation of stable, harmonious family relationships. For example, psychiatric admission rates for England (1991–1992) indicated that women in the 20–44 age band accounted for nearly 20 per cent of all in-patient episodes (Department of Health 1995e).

MEDIA EXPOSURE

There is intense, media-driven, high profile, but selective attention given to fatalities committed by mentally ill adults and their victims as evidence of the failure of community care. A recent analysis of homicides by people with mental illness based on Home Office generated criminal statistics for England and Wales between 1957–1995 showed that there was little fluctuation in numbers of people with a mental illness committing criminal homicide over the period studied. The authors concluded that there are many reasons for improving the resources and quality of care for people with a mental disorder, but there is no evidence that it is anything but stigmatising to claim that their living in the community is a dangerous experiment that should be reversed (Taylor and Gunn 1999).

Lack of understanding about mental illness, ongoing discrimination against those who are mentally ill and our society's intolerance allow for myths to be perpetuated about dangerousness and mental illness. When the victims are children and their parents are the perpetrators who are mentally ill, the issues are greatly magnified. Here the negative associations go a step further in linking poor parenting with mental illness. Examples are the extreme view that any parent with mental illness could not be a good parent or the opposite but similarly extreme view that a parent with mental illness must be allowed to look after her/his children (whatever the cost to the child's welfare). The end point of this debate is the question as to whether those with mental illness have rights to becoming parents (Sayce 1999).

The pervasive fear of children being removed from their families continues to affect the quality of child, parent and practitioner relationships. There is evidence that some parents who are severely mentally ill are at greater risk of losing their children (Grunbaum and Gammeltoft 1993; Isaac, Minty and Morrison 1986; Oliver 1985; Sheppard 1993) but child maltreatment is *not* an inevitable accompaniment to parental mental illness. The consideration of the welfare needs and safety of all children when a parent experiences mental ill health is an essential part of good practice across all services.

SERVICE USER PERSPECTIVES

> I can well see that in the present climate it is important to offer confidentiality, but why all the secrecy? The public has, if any, a very poor perception of mental health. These days many people on mental drugs live normal lives but they feel ashamed of being labelled 'mental' and hide their illness. I asked my GP whether I ought to tell my older daughter's school about my problem in case they thought her 'moods' odd. His advice was no, which I didn't think unreasonable but I can't help feeling that unless we get across the message that it isn't the end of the world being mentally ill, that things won't improve.

Taken individually issues such as gender, race, mental illness and parental status each carry the risk of discrimination. When they occur together in the same family the (adverse) effects can be cumulative – women who are mentally ill, who belong to minority ethnic groups and who are parents repeatedly appear as a very vulnerable group – socially alienated, materially deprived, with least access to support (Darton, Gorman and Sayce 1994).

Feedback from users – parents and young people – is unanimous. They want appropriate understanding and support based on the (different) needs of individual family members, sustained over time but varying according to prevailing circumstances, and for children to have access to support without necessarily needing to acquire a mental illness label to be eligible (Falkov 1998).

The changing but enduring nature of mental illness – a lifespan perspective

Loss and its consequences

The consequences for families of changing patterns of care are a central feature of the impact on family life when an adult is mentally ill. Besides parental hospitalisation, suicide, accommodation of children and adoption are some of the circumstances that generate uncertainty, confusion and despair. Even when physical separations between parents and children have not occurred, there is a complex interplay between mental illness and loss. Descriptions of the experiences of young people, parents and adults who grew up with a mentally ill parent have vividly illustrated the impact on daily life for all family members (Crosby 1989; Dunn 1993).

A lifespan approach recognises the impact on children in the present as well as longer term influences into adulthood, parenthood and perpetuation of difficulties into the next generation – cycles of adversity (Oliver 1988). Adversities may be both genetic and psychosocial and there is increasing recognition of the interplay between biogenetic features, social circumstances and life events. However adaptation also brings with it the possibility of successful coping despite adversity (Anthony and Cohler 1987). The long-term nature of mental illness thus provides opportunities for earlier intervention to reduce difficulties in the short term and to enhance adaptation over time (Silverman 1989).

Looking back – 'Many frames make the movie'

This approach recognises the relevance of links between past (childhood) experiences and current and future functioning of individuals (Landerman, George and Blazer 1991; Bifulco and Moran 1998). Retrospective analysis has demonstrated associations between experience of early adversity and psychological trauma in generating susceptibility to later difficulties – the transition to parenthood and/or occurrence of psychiatric disorder. For example:

- childhood sexual abuse and the onset of depression in adulthood (Bifulco, Brown and Adler 1991)
- links between disturbed early attachments and later difficulties in forming stable relationships, the most extreme being personality

disorder (Bowlby 1969; Fonagy, Steele and Steele 1991; Paris and Frank 1989).

However retrospective research does have limitations. Associations have tended to be based on individuals with more severe difficulties in adulthood, attending specialist services. Not all individuals who experience childhood adversity will necessarily experience difficulties in adulthood. Clearly there is much scope for further work which addresses the mechanisms whereby some individuals experience difficulties whereas others adapt more successfully (resilience and protective factors).

Mental illness within a social and family context

A letter from a 43-year-old married mother of two children, with a ten year history of manic depression:

> ...I am the first to admit that I am one of the lucky ones. I've had support from my parents as well as my husband. But it has put a great strain on the family and I have many complaints about the lack of help we have had. As a parent I had to understand that while I was ill in hospital I couldn't ask much of my husband. He had to put the children first and try to perform normally at work. How could he understand what I was going through without any 'counselling'? When I was sent home with my diagnosis we were given no guidance or even an appointment to see anyone. At that time I hadn't started taking lithium and my depression reached suicide level before a desperate letter from my husband got things moving.

A partner wrote three months after an assessment:

> It is now 1pm I have decided to do this rather than get out of bed. Rosemary has been in hospital for over ten weeks with mental illness. For the first few weeks Linda (friend) and relatives have helped look after the children but this has waned to more moral support rather than practical. (The exception being my father who runs me to hospital every day.) For the last three weeks I have been signed off on the sick. I worry a lot about our futures and am taking prescribed sleeping tablets. I am looking after my children but don't know how long I can continue. I feel depressed and have periods of gross paranoia. I hope your research goes well and this will be of some help.

These quotes illustrate the relevance for individuals of the quality of their relationships and experiences as essential core components in addressing their needs. These needs can be significantly exacerbated when mental illness and social adversity co-exist. It is when mental illness occurs together with, for example, parental hostility, discord and violence or the combination of mental illness and substance misuse, together with adverse social circumstances, that children are much more likely to develop emotional and behavioural problems and parents to struggle to meet their needs.

Links between social class, adversity and mental ill health have been demonstrated in the work of Brown and Harris (1978) and Harris, Brown and Bifulco (1987). Their findings revealed that working class women with children were more than four times as likely as middle class women to become depressed in the presence of an adverse life event. The presence of three or more children in the home, the absence of a close confiding relationship and absence of paid employment increased the risk of depression, as did the *vulnerability factor* of having lost a mother before age eleven.

A family perspective

An integrated, ecological model of influences and interactions between mental illness, parenting, family relationships, child development and environmental risk factors and protectors was developed in the Department of Health sponsored training materials on the impact of parental mental illness on children entitled *Crossing Bridges* (Falkov 1998). This model emphasises the relevance of a systems approach to assessment and intervention. Each component affects and is affected by every other component. Such an approach requires consideration of:

- the tasks and responsibilities of parenthood and an individual's coping resources; this includes family of origin and childhood experiences as well as susceptibility to difficulties in the transition to parenthood
- unique aspects of the relationship between a parent and child
- the nature of the mental illness experienced by the adult

- the child's own needs according to their developmental stage and ability, as well as temperament, physical and mental/emotional health
- the family, social and environmental context in which these interactions take place, and the impact of this context on those interactions.

How these core components interact and influence each other determines the quality of an individual's adjustment within his or her family, as well as the adequacy of the whole family's adaptation to living with a mentally ill member.

A continuum in the quality of parent, child (and professional) interactions

There is a wide diversity of capability amongst parents experiencing mental ill health. Some display impressive parenting, including warmth, sensitivity and understanding of children's developmental needs, despite the presence of significant mental health problems (Cox *et al.* 1987). At the opposite extreme are those whose children have died (Falkov 1996). Children of parents with a mental illness should therefore be seen as part of a broad continuum within which several sub-groups can be identified. The sub-groups, defined according to currently perceived levels of need and/or contact with existing services include children and young people who are:

- *not known* to services (e.g. well children and those with hidden needs)
- resilient *but* in need of support (e.g. young carers)
- vulnerable *and* in need of services (e.g. children in need)
- vulnerable *and* in need of services *and* protection
- severely maltreated or killed (child fatalities).

Needs, risks and resources change dynamically over time. Different individuals within the same family have different needs. For example, the needs of a young carer will be different from those of an infant or toddler. Similarly the needs of an ill, isolated lone parent will be different from those of a mentally ill parent who has a stable relationship with a supportive partner. Furthermore, needs will change during and between crises and it is likely that shifts between groups will occur as a consequence. This schema is an attempt to provide a conceptual framework within which to consider the range of needs relevant to children of parents experiencing mental illness and clearly requires further validation and refinement. This framework is discussed in *Crossing Bridges* (Falkov 1998).

The challenge for all professionals is to match needs and resources utilising good quality local data and appropriately skilled practitioners. For example, the combination of practical supports (help within the home, childcare facilities to provide respite for a parent) is more likely to lead to attendance for therapeutic work and greater capacity to use specialist resources than either one provided alone, particularly when multiple difficulties exist.

Children and young people not known to services

This group includes children who are well and not in need of services at a particular point in time. They display good coping strategies, experience warm and harmonious family relationships, and there is good quality social support. Nevertheless circumstances may change gradually or suddenly. Those who are managing well will be unlikely to need specialist services, but a lifespan approach would recognise the potential for needs to change in the future, given the presence of a mentally ill adult in the family. Furthermore, professionals could learn from such individuals and families about how they have managed to cope successfully.

Michael, aged fourteen, on being questioned about his father's chronic schizophrenia, said that the person who had helped him the most was his (non-ill) mother who would always talk with him if he were worried. This illustrates the important protective influence for a child or young person of having a confiding relationship with a well parent who is able to talk openly and answer questions. Regarding his understanding of his father's illness he said:

> It's to do with chemicals in the brain. Part of the brain has a fault or a disease and it doesn't work properly. It might start giving the wrong amounts of chemicals to other parts of the brain. Like too much or too little, or the wrong part.

Regarding hereditary factors he said:

> At the hospital they talked about that – they were asking if there were any family illnesses and I asked is there a chance I'll get it? And I think they were talking about 10 per cent or 1 per cent. I think 1 per cent is too low it's probably 10 per cent because my dad's got it.

This group also includes children in need of support and/or protection but not known to services (hidden morbidity). There is evidence of under-representation of family needs amongst minority ethnic communities (for example, Asian families). This raises concerns about stigma associated with access to services which are insufficiently attuned to the range of cultural beliefs and practices of minority ethnic groups.

However it is not just lack of access to services but a lack of appropriate provision for those who are in contact. Here the concern is the divide between children's and adult services across agencies that can prevent a co-ordinated family-oriented response when mental health, social care needs and parenting issues occur together.

> I have heard it said that manic depression can be hereditary but I don't think that it is proven. I did go through a period of worry about my elder daughter because she is like me in temperament and did start trying to get advice. I drew a blank. No one had any advice or experience.

Children and young people who are resilient *but* in need of support

This group includes children who are not suffering from or at imminent risk of physical abuse or neglect, and whose levels of vulnerability do not reach obvious thresholds for statutory intervention. A fifteen-year-old wrote:

> My mother is a Manic Depressive (MD) and therefore myself and my sisters and brother have grown up with MD... I myself think that there is not enough help available for families and friends of sufferers and that it would be helpful if the illness was explained properly and also if help was given to the children who have to cope without a parent to look after them.

Young carers, for example, are recognised as a *hidden* group but when they become known to services, their resilient capabilities are frequently allowed to predominate in the assessment of *their* needs. As a consequence their underlying emotional needs frequently remain neglected as the absence of readily observable emotional or behavioural problems reduces the perception of need. The longer term costs – emotional, social and financial – of their apparently successful adaptation must be incorporated into any assessment of need.

At the same time, it is vital to recognise the importance for a young person to be able to undertake responsibilities as a carer. The challenge for practitioners is to achieve a reasonable balance between competence-enhancing tasks and responsibilities which overwhelm the young person. These difficulties highlight the lifelong implications of mental illness in families and provide further evidence for the importance of support for young carers as a long-term preventive strategy.

Children and young people who are vulnerable *and* in need of services

Children whose vulnerability by virtue of living with a mentally ill parent has led to observable difficulties (for example: educational under-achievement; peer/family relationship difficulties; discrimination; isolation; bullying; emotional or behavioural problems) constitute a substantial proportion of the caseloads of those working within primary care or specialist children's services.

Children of parents known to Adult Mental Health (AMH) services constitute a population of predominantly non-referred children amongst whom there will be a continuum of need, both recognised and hidden. Important opportunities exist for detecting hidden need, reducing difficulties in the short term and for prevention of future difficulties. This is an issue of particular relevance given the enduring nature of mental illness and because of the strong continuities that have been demonstrated between the experience of early adversity and later difficulties in adulthood (Quinton, Rutter and Gulliver 1990).

Amongst children's social services, children and young people will, by definition, all have been referred and their needs will be wide ranging and substantial. Many of their parents will have mental health problems which have been direct or indirect reasons for referral as a result of their inability to meet children's needs and/or to ensure their safety. Many will be children in need. They therefore present an opportunity to engage in earlier intervention with the potential to prevent escalation of difficulties and further crises. Defining more clearly how the presence of mental ill-health affects a parent's capacity to meet children's needs is essential in order to recognise those families who would benefit most from earlier support and collaboration.

Children and young people who are vulnerable *and* in need of services *and* protection

A letter to Jo, aged ten, from his mother:

> Dear Jo,
>
> If anything happens to me you must go to the police. If I disappear and you don't know what's happened to me, I'll probably be dead. It's Louise and Mary that are doing it – they've been trying to get rid of me for years. I know they say I'm mad but I'm not – ask at my Doctor and at Smith Street Practice – they know all about it
>
> Just Know that I love you and I never want to leave you
>
> Love Mum

Studies conducted over the past fifteen years document the strongest associations between parental illness and maltreatment in court and clinic-referred samples where families are known to child protection services. These studies rightly emphasise the non-causal nature of the relationship and the interplay between multiple indices of social disadvantage. Whilst parental psychotic disorders feature prominently in child fatalities, the main parental psychiatric disorders implicated in substantiated non-fatal child maltreatment are depression, alcohol and drug dependence and personality disorders. The triad of episodic parental depression and underlying personality disorder complicated by substance misuse appears to carry a particularly poor prognosis for children (Falkov 1997).

The role of mental illness in impairing a primary carer's capacity to ensure a child's safety where a partner is displaying hostile, critical or physically abusive behaviour is another key dimension to the comprehensive assessment of need. Amongst those referred to child abuse treatment programmes, severe parental personality problems, persistent substance misuse and parental psychosis with delusions involving a child have all been implicated as poor prognostic factors (Jones 1991). There are a number of sub-categories in this group. For example:

- *Children entering the care system as a direct or indirect result of acute parental illness.* This will include those who require brief fostering because of the ill parent's social isolation and absence of adequate family or friends to assist with childcare during the crisis of parental hospitalisation. A needs-led approach might include attempts to provide the type of support that minimises separation trauma (for *both* parent and child) and promotes appropriate communication (for example, hospital visits, letters and phone calls). Discharge planning must include consideration of the effects on the family and parent of returning home. Support following discharge and ways of minimising relapse and ensuring prompt, early treatment of symptoms is essential, as are ways of promoting harmonious relationships, including mutual understanding of parental illness and its consequences for all family members.
- *Children subject to childcare court proceedings* as a result of longer term inability to meet a child's needs and ensure their safety. This includes factors such as poor response to treatment, poor compliance and poor engagement, associated with other adversities (personal, family and environmental) and where support has failed to facilitate positive change. The appropriateness of contact between parent and child must be considered both during crises as well as long-term plans to ensure the child's welfare and safety (e.g. care proceedings, long-term fostering and adoption).

Therapeutic issues include the impact of losses for both child and parent. Losses include parental loss of the ability to be the child's parent and the child's loss of that parent as primary carer. Issues of importance include consideration of the appropriateness of future contact between parent and child, helping the child understand reasons for the separation and support for foster and adoptive parents.

Child protection and parental mental health – the issue of unintended emotional neglect

Although the majority of mentally ill parents do not abuse their children (and the majority of those who abuse children are not mentally ill), it is important that the needs of children and parental capacity to meet those needs, including ensuring their safety, are routinely considered.

The issue of child maltreatment is therefore a key factor in joint working between adult and children's services, which may facilitate or block collaboration. It does raise anxieties and highlights competing needs and agendas, especially if maltreatment is not intentional. The need for advocacy by adult professionals becomes more understandable. The parent did not intend to harm and is doing her/his best for the children whilst also struggling with a devastating illness. From an adult perspective that person appears to be being victimised further through no fault of her/his own. No surprise then that the advocacy may easily become overzealous, polarising professionals and blocking joint working.

Emotional abuse and neglect thus remains the least studied and potentially most problematic type of maltreatment. It does not present in the readily observable way that physical abuse and neglect manifests but, if actively sought, is certainly evident in families whose children are known to Child Protection Services (CPS). A study by Glaser and Prior (1997) of children registered for emotional abuse found that 61 per cent of families/children had been referred to child mental health services, and 43 per cent were either known to or later referred to adult mental health services.

Evaluating the long-term outcomes of court decisions is also vital. Decisions taken with children's best interests uppermost may be correct, but outcomes for those children may be hampered or even fail because of poor quality (or insufficient) support for family members beyond the period of court involvement. Anecdotally, a recurring theme is the inadequate support for foster carers and for work with children at an appropriate stage beyond proceedings to help them understand the circumstances and reasons for the decisions that were taken about them and their parent(s).

Children and young people who have died

Studies of selected samples of children and mentally ill adults where fatal child abuse and homicide have occurred highlight links between parental mental illness and severe maltreatment (Wilczynski 1997; Special issue in Child Abuse Review 1995; Spotlight on Practice in Child Abuse and Neglect 1995). Children who are killed constitute an important but very small proportion of all maltreated children. The low base rates of fatalities –

rare events – make prediction in individual cases extremely difficult. Nevertheless there is no place for complacency. Much can be learned from tragedy whilst being mindful of the limitations of hindsight and retrospective analysis of individual cases and small samples.

The recommendations from both adult homicide inquiries and child death reviews are remarkably similar: improving communication, co-ordination and collaboration within and between all services and agencies to better support parents who are struggling to meet the needs of their children, including their safety (Boyd 1996; Falkov 1996; Woodley Team Report 1995).

Identifying need – an epidemiological perspective

By their nature, specialist services will always deal with fewer families than the primary care sector, illustrating the pyramid of need whereby fewer families with disproportionately greater needs are known to specialist services. Chapter 8 (Figure 8.1) has demonstrated how the total child population of England includes 32,000 on the child protection register, 53,000 looked after, 3–400,000 children in need and four million who are regarded as vulnerable. As Chapter 10 has indicated, *Messages from Research* (Department of Health 1995b, p.28) provides annual prevalence estimates for children entering and exiting the child protection system. The numbers range from 160,000 referrals to child protection services, 40,000 child protection conferences and 6000 children accommodated (including voluntary). The Department of Health receives, on average, about 50 Part 8, Child Fatality Reviews annually. In each of these samples the core question is: *how many parents have a mental illness?*

However specialisation in training and service development has meant that the core focus for adult mental health services is on the affected adult whilst in children's services the emphasis is on children and parents but not adult mental health. It is therefore not surprising that the overlap between adult mental illness, parental status and child development has not been addressed and that very little systematic data is currently available on the number of mentally ill adults who are parents and on the number of referred children whose parents are mentally ill (Falkov 1998).

Although the actual numbers of families where parents are struggling to meet children's needs and ensure their safety may be small in comparison to the overall population of children whose parents are mentally ill, their needs will be substantial, diverse and disproportionate to their numbers. Amongst these families lie the greatest challenges for inter-agency collaboration to ensure children's safety and provide support that is relevant to the needs of individual family members.

Quantifying need

Attempts to estimate the number of families who would be eligible for services constitute a heterogeneous group of large and small studies of variable methodological rigour in which direct or extrapolated conclusions about the numbers of children and parents can be drawn. These surveys have occurred in a range of settings across various tiers of service provision and are summarised in the Reader accompanying *Crossing Bridges* (Falkov 1998).

In west Lambeth, south London, a three month census of professionals working in mental health and social care settings was undertaken. The aim was to ascertain, via questionnaire, how many families in contact with services had *both* a mentally ill parent and dependent children. Besides raising awareness, this was an attempt to gauge the number of families who might be eligible for the service being developed (Falkov, Murphy and Antweiler forthcoming). From a total of nearly 1600 individuals known to the participating teams on each of the eight survey sites (six adult mental health settings, an adult social services resource centre and a children's social services area office), there was a return rate of 63 per cent. There were 185 positive returns (18%) that met the inclusion criteria. This indicated that nearly one-fifth of individuals known to a mental health or social care agency in a defined area of a deprived inner London borough had significant mental health problems *and* dependent children.

Across all sites, the quality of information provided about children was poor. Such basic information as numbers of children, their age and gender was missing in at least one-third of returns. In over a third (65 families), no information was provided about who looks after the children.

These findings compare with a selection of other studies, summarised in *Crossing Bridges*. Key points are as follows:

- Various data suggest that a substantial proportion (at least 20%, probably a third and in some cases up to 50%) of adults known to mental health services have children but that much less is known about the extent and nature of children's needs, including their needs for safety and protection.

- Current estimates suggest that amongst children whose parents are known to adult mental health services between one- and two-thirds will experience difficulties, dysfunction or disorder, depending on the nature of the sample and the criteria used for determining morbidity.
- Epidemiological studies highlight the widespread prevalence and complex interplay between mental health problems, childcare burden and social adversity.
- Given the number of mentally ill adults of child-bearing and rearing age and the adverse impact on children's psychosocial adaptation, there are substantial public health implications for better detection, intervention and prevention of parental mental illness.

Taken together, these surveys highlight the importance of considering childcare and protection issues amongst mental health services and the development of a mental health perspective amongst child protection agencies.

Meeting need – liaison between child and adult mental health services

The FaMHLiS: Families and Mental Health Liaison Services

Those who are mentally ill and who have experienced lifelong adversity will have multiple needs which impinge on many services. Clarifying roles, establishing coherent professional networks and assessing capacities for change amongst family members is a complex inter-agency challenge.

Close links have been developed between the specialist child and adult mental health services in west Lambeth (previously Lambeth Healthcare NHS Trust and now the South London and Maudsley NHS Trust). The service is small and has evolved gradually over the past three years. It began with funding for a community psychiatric nurse (CPN) and social worker from a joint finance bid. There have been various contributions from different sources and professionals at different stages, and the exit strategy for the project was based upon the successful links established between the child and adult mental health services. There are ongoing efforts to establish similar links with children's social services. Need continues to exceed provision and roles and responsibilities for different professional groups have now been developed as part of a service specification for a formalised liaison service.

Principles underpinning the service include:

- working within the context of the Children Act 1989 and Mental Health Act 1983
- a *child welfare perspective* in which children's needs (including their safety) and parental capacity to meet those needs are routinely considered
- a *family perspective* in which the health and social care needs of all members are considered
- a *parenting perspective* which brings with it recognition of the needs of patients/clients as parents and that all adults experiencing mental ill health have a right to expect that the needs of their children will be routinely addressed
- a *preventive approach* whereby explicitly addressing parental fears (e.g. expressing concerns about children or their capacity to cope leading to children being removed) can facilitate collaborative relationships and support which promotes strengths and coping skills
- drawing on the *combined skills and experience* of adult and child mental health practitioners, whilst ensuring clarity in roles, tasks and responsibilities
- recognition that the *needs of children and their parents are different*; they may at times be in direct competition but *both are valid*
- the adverse impact of mental illness on parenting and on children's adaptation is well documented *but not all children will be adversely affected* and many parents cope exceptionally well despite the presence of a mental illness
- *most mentally ill parents do not maltreat their children* but some are unable to meet their children's needs and ensure their safety; *unintended emotional neglect* is an important issue.

The FaMHLi service

A child psychiatrist provided the equivalent of one to two sessions a week, a specialist registrar in child psychiatry provided two sessions and an adult CPN devoted one session a week. Negotiations are under way for a specialist liaison mental health worker, to be based within the Child and Adolescent Mental Health (CAMH) service and to work across the interface, spending time on wards, at the community mental health centres (CMHCs), developing links with local agencies (social services, voluntary sector, primary care) and undertaking teaching, implementation of protocols and audit. An audit of clinical activity has been undertaken and is available from the author.

Referrals

Initially many referrals from adult services had been of complex and multiply disadvantaged families in which there were concerns about a child's safety which were not straightforward. Poor parental compliance and variable engagement with professionals were especially notable. As a consequence there were difficult dilemmas in trying to support keyworkers and build relationships with parents, whilst ensuring that children remained safe.

The objective, through closer working, was to become more proactive and encourage *earlier discussion and referral* so that the needs of the less visible majority of parents and children could be considered. A balance was thus required between the complex cases where poor prognostic features predominated and less extreme situations where there were opportunities for treating parental psychiatric disorder, improving parent–child relationships and preventing abuse.

Joint working

Adult mental health practitioners' perceptions

Feedback from team members indicates that, in the early stages, discussions and teaching (undertaken by Adrian Falkov) felt artificial and too theoretical, detached from the reality of day-to-day work. It was initially 'padded out' with model constructs and statistical cautions, with lists of 'do's and don'ts'. This has now been complemented with the authenticity of 'live' joint work involving cases well known to the team and serving to validate the clinical contribution of all team members. Over time clearer roles and remits have been established; for example, on how to ensure that children and parents' needs are recognised and appropriately prioritised throughout the assessment and intervention process. Over time, joint working and regular supervision has enabled AMH team members to elicit information from patients/clients at an earlier stage about the effects of:

a) Parental mental illness on children including:

- parental awareness of the effects of their illness or distress on the child
- parental capacities within the parent–child relationship (for example, parental warmth, hostility or criticism)
- the quality of inter-parental relationship (for example, discord or domestic violence versus mutual support)
- the child's ability to make sense of parental symptoms and behaviour.

b) Children's behaviours and needs on their parents including:

- parental burden with childcare responsibilities
- exacerbation of parental symptoms/stress
- difficulties with parenting (for example, the ability to set limits, to provide for the child's psychological/emotional and material needs) as well as strengths.

Child mental health practitioners' perceptions

CAMH service collaborators have been able to develop greater tolerance for working with very unwell parents in the community, with clearer awareness of AMH management plans; they have also gained additional insights into how psychiatric symptoms and the task of parenting influence each other. This has helped to achieve a balanced approach in recognising the needs of both children and parents and in particular the impact of children's problems on parents' mental health.

The current situation

Staff in adult services now regularly telephone for advice to plan joint work and CAMH professionals attend team meetings and provide regular supervision. Where a child protection issue is clear, AMH practitioners refer directly to the relevant social services team. A keyworker in AMH may ring to check out actions already taken. Sometimes this may be to plan a joint home visit or clinic-based assessment. Joint work may involve initial assessments (home visits, at CMHCs or on wards) or ongoing therapeutic intervention.

Adult workers focus on mental state assessments, monitoring of symptoms and medication and support for the parent. In particular the relevance of childhood experiences as key aspects in the susceptibility both to mental health problems and difficulties in the transition to parenthood is emphasised. Child mental health workers focus on parenting strategies, parent–child relationships and children's emotional wellbeing, including facilitating children's understanding of parental illness.

Sarah, an eleven-year-old girl, provided a description of past problems when her mother was acutely psychotic:

> She was sick – when I was younger, mum had a problem. She had difficulty with us four kids – sorting us out for school – she wasn't getting a lot of help and she was shouting a lot. Her words were all jumbled up – didn't come out properly. She was having too many cups of tea ... always asking me for cups of tea so I was late for school. I told the teachers an excuse that mum overslept and I had to make breakfast for the younger ones – mum didn't want them to know she was sick because she thought they were watching her and coming round.

She went on to state that she thought it very unlikely anyone was watching because: 'if there were watchers I'd have seen them – but I didn't tell mum this because she would have said – how do you know?'

Tom, an eight-year-old, thought that the cause of his mother's illness was confusing:

> It's not like a tummy ache or a cold – but she's not feeling well. She thinks she's the king, then I know something's wrong...in the neck – where she speaks, (or maybe) the heart – it's a very important part of the body – makes you do things, or maybe the mind – not the brain because the brain is just to make you think and the illness is the things she says...

Through talking with parents about their children we have found that, rather than jeopardising therapeutic relationships, more open discussion has served to provide them with an opportunity to ask for help, to express fears and obtain advice. These conversations have revealed a wide spectrum: from impressive coping despite significant adversity through to vulnerability, risk and serious child protection concerns. A lone mother, socially isolated and depressed, who was wanting to run away said: 'I only enjoy the company of my children when I feel happy myself – I can't remember when I last felt happy'.

Seeing mentally ill parents together with their children

A defining feature of the service has been the opportunity for adult and child practitioners to talk together with parents and their children in the same room. This joint approach has highlighted the differences in parents' and children's needs. These differences can be a useful focus for discussion. One conversation with a parent who had a severe, long standing mental illness and who had not been able to talk with her children revealed some insights into the approaches taken by different professionals. The discussion had centred on the basis for a mother's inability to talk with her children about her illness:

> Child psychiatrist: 'Do you worry you might upset your children if you talk to them about your difficulties?'
>
> Adult psychiatrist: 'Do you worry you might upset yourself?'

Different perspectives, common challenges – the task of working across multiple interfaces

Common preoccupations include:

- a fixed, blinkered focus on the core *client* (child *versus* adult) rather than child *and* parent (family)
- anxiety about what is *child protection* and what is *mental illness*
- concern about lack of appropriate skills and knowledge or the converse: overconfidence (*we do it anyway*)
- confidentiality

- under-resourced and overstretched services
- assessment of risk, provision of support and prevention.

Both over and under-reaction by social workers to referrals from AMH workers have been reported. These have included expressions of concern because of the apparent delay or lateness of the referral as well as lack of action and decisiveness by social workers, for example, delayed or absent feedback or refusal to allocate a social worker or convene an initial child protection case conference. Lack of action or substantial delays in response to referrals of a child in need have also been a source of frustration for AMH workers. Feedback following a social work assessment has at times been difficult to obtain, compounded by having to deal with an overstretched duty system.

Children and families social workers have, in turn, been frustrated at times by AMH workers' decisions about the absence of a mental illness or treatable illness or the view that mental health problems exist but are outweighed by social problems. As a consequence, social workers have on occasions become preoccupied with the need for a diagnosis at the expense of good observations about the quality of parent–child interactions as part of their assessment. Social workers' anxieties in the face of uncertainty about a parent's mental state have probably been under-estimated by those familiar with mental health issues.

Clearly there is much scope for common-sense approaches to improving opportunities for practitioners across all agencies to meet. This would facilitate developing greater awareness about each other's tasks, responsibilities and pressures. Such an approach requires active support across all management tiers in both agencies as well as a corporate strategy which encompasses the needs of families with mentally ill members and dependent children. Joint debate and clarification about child protection, child in need and mental illness thresholds and eligibility criteria is essential (see Chapter 10). Facilitation of joint case discussions by an experienced child mental health professional may assist the process of workers in different agencies acquiring better shared understanding about family needs and the resources (skills) available to meet them.

The lack of clear boundaries between mental ill-health and social care needs of mentally ill parents and their children is a reflection of the realities of family life. The blurring will continue to challenge practitioners, but this should not become a barrier to good practice in which active debate and clarification of roles, tasks and responsibilities occurs. A supportive organisational framework will assist practitioners to discuss jointly how their combination of skills can improve the daily life of all family members. For example, it should help them consider jointly how mental ill-health impairs or prevents a parent from meeting a child's needs.

A practical approach which enables practitioners in children's services to describe accurately how parental preoccupation with symptoms is associated with neglect, how distorted thought processes impede practical care tasks, or how tearfulness and despair impair a parent's relationship with her/his child will facilitate assessment of needs.

The *Framework for Assessment of Need in Children and Families* (Department of Health, Department for Education and Employment, Home Office 2000a) (see Chapter 8) will be a helpful tool in assisting practitioners to undertake systematic assessments of the needs of *all* family members. It will therefore help to identify gaps in provision and provide opportunities for establishing better links with mental health service practitioners. The *National Service Framework for Mental Health* (Department of Health 1999i) will, in turn, provide mental health practitioners with support for mental health promotion and earlier intervention/prevention (Standard One). It will also assist provision of support for carers (Standard Six) which should be interpreted as applicable to all carers – those who care for individuals experiencing mental ill-health, young carers who look after a mentally ill parent/carer and those who are themselves experiencing mental ill-health and who also have responsibilities for dependent children.

Combined efforts which effectively harness mental health and childcare assessment skills will ensure much richer, comprehensive views about need than either approach in isolation.

Conclusions

There is abundant evidence that parents with severe mental illness are known to both adult *and* child welfare agencies. Lack of awareness about even basic information concerning children and parents amongst *all* services helps to justify the increasing emphasis being placed on improving joint working.

Adult mental health services are strategically placed for initiating assessments of children and their parents. However the traditional agency, speciality and geographic divides between and within services for children and adults makes co-ordinated provision of comprehensive family-oriented services a major inter-agency challenge. There are short and long-term benefits if earlier intervention programmes and strategies can be achieved. Parents of children who are known to children's services, especially child protection services, are at particular risk for a range of mental health problems, especially depression and substance misuse. However mental illness must be seen as but one of a number of factors and processes which operate in a complex web of influences to adversely affect the quality of life for many families.

A broader approach to assessment and a conceptualisation of services which incorporates the health and social care needs of children and parents is required. To support these changes a systematic and accessible mechanism for recording which adults known to services have dependent children and which parents have mental health problems is required. Initiating earlier communication between different agencies could reduce the need for traumatic separations and enhance quality of life for all family members.

Training to improve practitioners' recognition of and responses to the needs of children and parents is necessary. For AMH teams this requires consideration of the interpersonal context of their patients, in particular their role as parents, their childcare responsibilities and the nature of their children's experiences within the parent–child relationship. For practitioners in children's services, achieving a mental health perspective is essential, including developing greater awareness of the impact of parental psychiatric disorder on child development and on childcare practice decision making. The Department of Health has taken a lead in supporting the development of training materials for practitioners across all agencies. One of the aims is to achieve better integration of research findings into practice.

Loss is a pervasive theme for children and parents. Failed hopes, aspirations and expectations involving both parents and children have life-changing implications within and between generations, highlighting the need to address the consequences of loss in a variety of practical and therapeutic ways.

Whilst not all children should be referred for treatment, parents have a right to expect that, despite being mentally ill, their childcare burden will be recognised and to know that their children will be given the best possible chance for optimal development and fulfilment of their hopes and dreams. The growing interest in this area is welcome but it remains to be seen whether interest and awareness will be translated into meaningful benefits for families.

CHAPTER TWELVE

Assessing Children's Needs and Parents' Responses

Hedy Cleaver

This chapter discusses the evidence from a research review concerning the extent to which mental ill-health, problem drinking, drug misuse and domestic violence affect parents' capacity to meet their children's needs. The ways in which parents' problems can affect their children's development are discussed and evidence about which children are most likely to experience adverse consequences is explored. The research findings were used as a basis for developing the Assessment Recording Forms, designed to help practitioners operationalise the Framework for the Assessment of Children in Need and their Families.

To raise a family is possibly the most challenging task adults have to face in their lifetime. To be confronted with a crying baby, a demanding toddler or a truculent teenager can reduce most adults to despair, regardless of how successful they are in their chosen job or profession. But despite the pressures of child-rearing, practically all parents wish to look after their children and provide them with the best possible start in life. Indeed, the Children Act 1989 is founded on the assumption that it is generally best for children to grow up within their own family and that most parents want to carry out their parental responsibilities autonomously. The Act also recognises that it is normal for families to have problems from time to time and to turn to the state for help.

> Parents are individuals with needs of their own. Even though services may be offered primarily on behalf of their children, parents are entitled

> to help and consideration in their own right. Their parenting capacity may be limited temporarily or permanently by poverty, racism, poor housing or unemployment or by personal or marital problems, sensory or physical disability, mental illness or past life experiences. (Department of Health 1990, p.8)

Although many families cope adequately with their problems, others, particularly those experiencing multiple and complex stressors, would benefit from the assistance of professional agencies. These parents need help to ensure that the hardships they are experiencing do not adversely affect the health and development of their children. As other chapters have already indicated, the criteria under which Section 17.10 of Children Act 1989 identifies children as being in need are specified in *developmental* terms (see Chapter 1).

The importance of identifying the stressors experienced by parents and mobilising the relevant services is highlighted by the findings from the recent body of research on child protection (Department of Health 1995b). This showed that, although only a small proportion (some 15%) of families drawn into the child protection system resulted in the child being registered, many would have benefited from social work services. Indeed, in more than half the cases parents had problems of their own which had negative consequences for their children (Cleaver, Unell and Aldgate 1999). Most of these families laboured under a number of difficulties including mental illness, learning disability, problem drinking or drug misuse, domestic violence, homelessness and extreme poverty, without the help of support services (Department of Health 1995b). Parents frequently had to manage alone because:

- the allocated social worker had not identified the family problems; problems only came to light during the course of the research
- family problems had been recognised but information had not been systematically recorded
- family problems had been identified but their impact on children and other family members had not been fully understood.

This evidence led the Department of Health to commission two pieces of work: first, a review of relevant research from both the adult and children's arena in order to identify how parental mental illness, problem drinking and drug misuse, and domestic violence impacts on children's health and development; second, the development of assessment schedules based on the findings from the research review. The schedules were to be aimed primarily at helping social workers assess children's needs and parents' capacity to respond appropriately. This chapter focuses initially on the key findings from the research review (Cleaver *et al.* 1999) before giving a brief description of the assessment schedules (Department of Health and Cleaver 2000).

Findings from the review of relevant research: the prevalence of parental mental illness, problem drinking and drug misuse, and domestic violence

General population studies

Many adults have times when they suffer from anxiety or depression, have unstable relationships with partners or drink alcohol to excess and increasing numbers have used drugs, both licit and illicit, but this does not mean they are poor parents. It is the extremity or combination of these stressors, particularly the association with violence, which may place children at risk of significant harm.

To estimate the size of the problem depends on knowing the prevalence of mental illness, problem alcohol/drug use and domestic violence within the parenting population. Unfortunately the ability to gauge accurately the extent of these issues is hampered because prevalence depends upon the population group being studied. For example, community-based samples will be more representative than research which focuses on specific groups, such as hospital patients, outpatients, women in refuges, or those who attend clinics or courts. However the severity of the condition under study is likely to be much greater in specific sample groups, as is the coexistence of problems. But regardless of the type of sample group under consideration, any generalisations to populations beyond that being studied should be made with considerable caution.

An additional problem, demonstrated by Falkov in Chapter 11, is that research which gives information on the extent of mental illness, problem alcohol or drug use, or domestic violence in the adult population, rarely tells us much about the parental status of sufferers. The Government Household Survey, however, does throw some light on this because it breaks down the data by the type of family unit (Office of Population and Censuses and Surveys 1996). This analysis (Table 12.1) shows that both psychiatric morbidity and problem drinking and drug misuse are associated with family characteristics.

Table 12.1. Prevalence of mental illness, problem drinking and drug use amongst parents in the general population

Parental problem	Couple & child %	Lone parent & child %
Neurotic disorders	15.5	28
Functional psychoses	0.4	1.1
Alcohol dependence	2.7	3.8
Drug dependence	0.9	2.4

The survey reveals that the prevalence of parental problems is higher amongst lone parents than for parenting couples. This has repercussions for children's welfare, because when no other parent is available to take on the caring role the impact of parental problems on children is likely to be greater.

The household survey does not give similar information on the prevalence of domestic violence amongst parents in the general population. What is known is that in the majority of recorded instances of domestic violence (90–95% of cases) women are the victims of male violence (Dobash and Dobash 1992). Understandably, therefore, most research has focused on this pattern of family violence and indicates that approximately one in four women have experienced domestic violence (Mooney 1994).

Although we have increasing information about the prevalence of male-perpetrated domestic violence, the degree of violence is less well documented. Nevertheless, it is very disturbing to discover that 18 per cent of all injuries seen in hospital emergency rooms are the result of domestic violence and on average two women per week are killed in England and Wales by partners or former partners (Home Office 1994).

Studies of mutual violence or violence perpetrated by women on men are more unusual. However, recent work suggests that partner violence is not role specific. In many violent households mutual combat may be the norm, although female violence is only reported in extreme cases (Moffitt and Caspi 1998). But regardless of which parent is being aggressive, witnessing adults being violent to one another gives children the notion that such behaviour is an acceptable way of dealing with frustration or conflict.

Indeed, the children exposed to family violence are among the most vulnerable to long-term emotional and behavioural problems (Jones and Ramchandani 1999).

Child protection studies

An additional source of information on the prevalence of parental mental illness, problem drinking and drug misuse, and domestic violence is data from child protection research. As already indicated, a considerable proportion of children who come into the child protection system are from families where parents are experiencing one or more of these problems (Department of Health 1995b). Moreover children in families exposed to a multitude of stressors, both acute and chronic, are three times more likely to be re-abused than children from families experiencing fewer problems (Cleaver and Freeman 1995). Children are particularly at risk of significant harm when parental mental illness, problem drinking or drug misuse occurs in conjunction with domestic violence (Rutter and Quinton 1984; Velleman 1993).

Although particular types of parental problems are associated with certain types of child abuse, for example maternal problem drinking with child neglect, mental illness with emotional and sexual abuse, and domestic violence with physical abuse, when research focused on all types of child abuse the prevalence of identified parental problems increased with the level of enquiry (Cleaver *et al.* 1999).

Table 12.2. Prevalence of parental problems identified at different stages in the child protection process

Level of intervention	Mental illness %	Problem drink/drug %	Domestic violence %
Referral	13	20	37
Initial SW visit	20	25	40
Case conference	25	25–60	35–52
Case proceedings	42	70	51
Fatal child abuse	33–90	Not known	

Caution is needed in interpreting this data because we do not know whether the increase reflects a true picture or simply that, at the early stages of the assessment process, social workers either do not know about the stresses parents are experiencing or fail to record their observations. Indeed, the findings from the child protection research suggest that incidents of parental mental illness, problem alcohol or drug misuse and domestic violence are under-recorded during the early stages of an enquiry (Department of Health 1995b). Under-recording may be caused by two factors. First, parents may conceal problems because they fear that revealing their own difficulties will result in their losing their children. Second, social workers may not always investigate their suspicions as thoroughly as they might otherwise do when families have a history of violent or bizarre behaviour.

What services are needed

In order to match children's needs with relevant services, a comprehensive assessment of the family's circumstances is required. Such an assessment must be based on an understanding of how parental mental illness, problem alcohol and drug use, and domestic violence impact on the children and affect the parent's ability to respond to their children's needs.

To suggest that in all instances parental mental illness, problem drinking or drug use, or domestic violence place children at risk of significant harm would be misleading. Indeed, research indicates that many children who live with families where a parent is experiencing such problems suffer few long-term adverse consequences. For example, Rutter and Quinton (1984) found that two-thirds of children in families where there was parental mental illness have no long-term behaviour or emotional difficulties. Most children in families where a parent had an alcohol or drug problem grow up to be balanced and productive adults (Orford and Velleman 1990; Tweed 1991). Similarly, Jenkins and Smith (1990) found that few children living with marital disharmony exhibit long-term psychiatric problems.

While caution is needed in making assumptions about the impact on children of parental mental illness, problem alcohol or drug use, or domestic violence, when these issues coexist the risk of significant harm to children increases considerably; of particular significance is the association with domestic violence (Cleaver *et al.* 1999).

Although not all families require professional intervention when a parent is experiencing such problems, nonetheless many children's health and development will be impaired if they do not receive social work services. To identify which children are 'in need' depends on understanding how parental mental illness, problem alcohol and drug use, and domestic violence impact on parents' capacity to look after their children. Such parental problems may influence parenting in three ways:

- emotional and behavioural responses change
- the family's social circumstances deteriorate
- the capacity to respond to their children's needs is impaired.

Parental problems affect emotional and behavioural responses

Mental illness – depression

Although functional psychoses could be considered to have a more dramatic impact on sufferers, because depression is the most prevalent form of mental illness its effects on parenting are explored here. For a description of how other forms of mental illness impact on parenting see Cleaver *et al.* (1999).

Depression affects all aspects of life: sleep is disturbed, appetite lost, thoughts are heavy, slow and gloomy, concentration becomes difficult and decisions impossible, actions slow down, and many sufferers are overwhelmed with feelings of worthlessness. Life for the depressed appears hopeless, torpor defeats them and even the most mundane aspects of living, such as getting out of bed, appear momentous. For children one of the most disturbing symptoms of depression is the apparent inability of the depressed parent to show affection.

Problem alcohol or drug use

Problem drinking or drug use can also have psychological and behavioural outcomes. Users may experience a range of adverse effects including impaired memory, reduced psychomotor co-ordination and slurred speech. Drink or drugs may also affect the users' inhibitions, resulting in diminished self-control and outbursts of violence that may be directed at the child.

To anticipate the impact of drink or drugs is difficult because drugs, including alcohol, affect different people in different ways. The situation is further complicated because drugs may have different behavioural consequences even within the same individual, depending on:

- current mental state
- experience and/or tolerance of the drug
- expectations
- personality
- the quantity taken
- the combination of drugs taken.

Domestic violence

Research has shown that many women who experience domestic violence also suffer psychologically: 'I just didn't care. He was so cruel that I didn't take any pride in myself...I lost the baby...I was only seven stone' (NCH Action for Children 1994, p.47).

Abused women experience a loss of confidence, depression, problems with sleep and increased isolation, and use medication and alcohol more frequently. Many women in these circumstances feel degraded and see themselves merely as objects: 'was a nervous wreck. I was just like a gibbering idiot. I had no confidence, no self esteem. I thought I was the most useless thing...because when you are being told all the time that you are crap, you sort of eventually begin to believe it' (NCH Action for Children 1994, p.45).

Parental problems affect the family's social circumstances

Although mental illness, problem drink/drug use, and domestic violence affect the sufferer in different ways, it could be argued that all have similar social consequences for families: living standards are reduced, contact with friends and family is curtailed, and marital/partner disharmony is increased.

Living standards are reduced

Living standards may be reduced because parents who are suffering from extreme problems are unable to sustain their jobs. For example, excessive alcohol or drug use, mental illness or domestic violence may all result in parents being absent from work, or late arriving, or functioning inadequately when at work. As a result jobs may be lost and family income reduced.

Parental problems may also adversely affect living standards because parents are using money for drink or drugs rather than to buy food and clothing. Alternatively the psychological effects of mental illness, drugs or domestic violence may mean that parents forget or disregard essential household bills.

Fights and rows are common features of domestic violence, problem drinking and the lifestyle associated with drug misuse. In the process of such violent outbursts adults may deliberately damage or destroy property making the home an unsafe environment and leaving children traumatised.

In addition to children being exposed to physical dangers, parents' preoccupation with their own problems may result in children being neglected. Homes need to offer warmth, sanitation and shelter. Unfortunately the effect of mental illness, problem alcohol or drug use, or domestic violence may mean the home is neglected and children are dirty and unfed: 'She described their home as cold and dirty. They did not have hot water or any food at home' (the experience of a 10-year-old in Swadi 1994, p.239).

Contact with friends and family is curtailed

Parental problems may result in families losing contact with relatives and friends. For example, mental illness and problem alcohol/drug misuse can lead to a withdrawal from reality or violent and unexpected mood swings. Such behaviour generates unease and fear even in close friends and relatives. As a result, visiting and telephone contact may be avoided and families can become isolated, a factor which increases the vulnerability of children.

Contact with family and friends may also be curtailed because parents are ashamed of their circumstances and wish to hide their experiences. For example, problem drinking or drug use is often a secret, shameful and solitary affair. To ensure friends and family do not find out, social events are shunned: 'Once upon a time you drank with your friends, to be sociable. Slowly you start to avoid them. Terrified of being seen to be drunk you dread invitations' (Innes 1998).

Similarly, in cases of domestic violence the victim is often ashamed of what is happening to them. Indeed, research suggests few men and only a third of abused women tell anyone of their experience (Dominy and Radford 1996; Cook 1997). Secrecy and separation from family and friends may also be imposed on the children: 'He says that if we ever tell anyone he will kill us...I'm scared...it's getting worse' (12-year-old whose father drank and was violent, quoted in ChildLine 1997, p.23). Finally, when parents are involved in a lifestyle which is based around excessive drinking or illicit drug use, it influences their choice of friends and social activities.

Marital/partner disharmony

Mental illness, problem alcohol/drug use and domestic violence can severely strain relationships between spouses and intimate partners. For example, coping on a day-to-day basis with the self-absorption and disinterest of the depressed or the constant lies and deceit of many problem drinkers can be very exhausting and dispiriting: 'Within the home you withdraw from your family, urging your partner to take the children out for the day, pushing them hastily through the front door so you can drink in peace' (Innes 1998).

Moreover problem drinking and drug misuse have been shown to be associated with domestic violence. Indeed, research suggests that 80 per cent of all violent incidents are alcohol-related (Velleman 1993). One explanation is that because alcohol and drugs lower inhibitions, violence is resorted to more readily when users are angry or frustrated. The link between mental illness, problem drinking/drug misuse and violence, however, is complex. An alternative explanation for the link is that many victims of domestic violence develop mental health problems or find solace in alcohol or drugs. Finally, the association between mental illness, problem alcohol/drug and domestic violence may owe more to a common antecedent such as childhood adversity.

But regardless of how or why they are associated, when parental problems coexist with domestic violence children are at increased risk of significant harm. Mental illness or problem drinking/drug use that exist in isolation have fewer adverse consequences for children (for mental illness, see Quinton and Rutter 1985; for problem drinking, see Velleman 1993).

Parents' problems affect their capacity to respond to their children's needs

The research findings suggest mental illness, problem alcohol/drug use and domestic violence adversely affect parenting for the following reasons:

- parents have difficulty organising their lives
- parents neglect their own and their children's physical needs
- parents have difficulty controlling their emotions
- parents are insensitive, unresponsive, angry and critical of their children
- children have to be cared for by someone else.

Parents have difficulty organising their lives

The behavioural and emotional consequences of mental illness, problem alcohol/drug use, and domestic violence mean that parents have difficulty organising their lives. Young children are particularly vulnerable if parental disorganisation leaves them unsupervised or in the care of inappropriate adults. Additional problems may arise when appointments for health checks are missed or when school attendance is not a priority. To assume older children escape unscathed from a disorganised lifestyle would be unwise. When families include a troubled parent many older children assume the role of carer, which may interfere with school attendance, homework and time with friends: 'Anthony said that he is left to look after his baby brother. He hasn't been to school all week' (child whose parent had an alcohol problem, quoted in ChildLine 1997, p.24).

Parents neglect their own and their children's physical needs

When a parent suffers mental illness, or when alcohol or drugs become the prime focus of their attention, children's physical needs may be neglected. But neglect is not restricted to young children. When parental problems divert monies that would ordinarily be used for household essentials and clothes, children may find it difficult to keep up an acceptable appearance and friendships may be jeopardised: 'They spend all the money on drink. There's no soap in the house and all my clothes are too small. I lost my girlfriend because she said I smell. Others call me names and make fun of me. It hurts' (Paul, 14, quoted in ChildLine 1997 p.37).

Most mothers who are victims of domestic violence continue to meet the physical needs of their children, although some reported periods of despair when they did not care what happened either to themselves or their children: 'I didn't bother to do the housework, and I didn't bother to wash myself...I didn't give a shit about who said what about how the children looked...' (NCH Action for Children 1994, p.47).

Parents have difficulty controlling their emotions

When parents display violent mood swings and ineffective and inconsistent behaviour, children may become very frightened. For example, drugs such as cocaine, crack or alcohol, and certain types of mental illness can result in unpredictable behaviour. Parents may quickly change from being caring, loving and entertaining to being violent, argumentative and withdrawn. In these circumstances children often believe that the rapid mood swings of their parents are the result of their own behaviour.

Parents are insensitive, unresponsive, angry and critical of their children

The attachment process between children and their parents depends on parental sensitivity, responsiveness and support. Insecure attachments have implications for the child's intellectual, emotional, social and psychological functioning.

When a parent is suffering from mental illness, has a problem with alcohol or drugs or is the victim of domestic violence, the effects may render them physically unable to respond to the needs of their children. Alternatively, the effects of their own problems may leave parents emotionally flat with little or no desire to interact with their children. For example, acute depression is associated with the mothers being cold and unresponsive to their children. Personality disorders have been found to be related to a 'callous unconcern for others, a low threshold for frustration, a discharge of aggression and an inability to feel remorse' (Stroud 1997, p.158). In addition, problem alcohol/drug use can result in a parent being emotionally unavailable to the child.

The difficulties of attachment may be confounded when excessive drinking or drug use during pregnancy has resulted in babies being born with damage to the central nervous system, or with behaviours such as poor feeding, tremors, irritability and occasional seizures. High levels of criticism and rejection are also associated with insecure attachments in children.

Research suggests that opiate-using mothers rely on harsh verbal responses when communicating with their children, thus increasing risk of significant harm (Hogan 1998).

Children may have to be cared for by someone else

Parents may be unable to look after their children when the resolution of their own problems depends on residential treatment. For example, domestic violence can result in a mother seeking safety in a refuge, an acute episode of mental illness in a parent's hospitalisation, or problem alcohol/drug abuse in a parent being treated away from home. When this happens the care of children may fall to others. If the other parent or close relative can provide a stable environment the negative effects of separation are much reduced. However some children will need to be looked after by the local authority, with all the well-known concomitant difficulties surrounding placement.

Which children are most vulnerable?

Most studies of resilience conclude that children can be protected from the adverse effects of parental mental illness, problem alcohol or drug misuse, but there is little evidence for this in the case of domestic violence. Indeed, as already noted, it is the association of parental mental illness, problem alcohol/drug use with parental violence that is most frequently cited as presenting the greatest risk of significant harm.

Research by Quinton and Rutter (1985) suggests that the degree to which children are affected by their parents' problems is related to the level of their involvement. For example, the following factors have been shown to aggravate the impact on children of parental mental illness, problem alcohol/drug use, and domestic violence:

- parental violence, neglect or rejection directed at the child
- the coexistence of parental problems such as mental illness, illicit drug use, problem alcohol use, domestic violence criminality, and poverty
- witnessing the parent's sexual and physical abuse
- being drawn into participating in the abuse of a parent
- colluding in the secrecy and concealment of parental problems
- the home being used by other heavy drinkers or drug users.

No one age group of childhood appears to be particularly protected from, or vulnerable to, the impact of parental mental illness, problem alcohol/drug use, and domestic violence. How children respond is related to the severity, characteristics, and social context of their parents' problems.

Research suggests children are less likely to be adversely affected when:

- parents' problems are mild and of short duration
- one parent has no such problems
- other responsible adults are involved in childcare
- the adult with the problem is in treatment
- there is a stable home and adequate financial resources
- there is no association with family violence, conflict and disorganisation
- parents' problems do not result in the family breaking up.

(see Cleaver *et al.* 1999)

It is important that professionals do not pathologise all children who live in families where a parent suffers mental illness, is a problem drinker or drug user or where there is domestic violence. As already noted, many children who grow up in these circumstances are not at risk of significant harm. The challenge facing social workers is to identify:

- which children and families need help – and the level of concern
- in which areas of their development children are suffering
- what type of services would be most effective.

The assessment records

Evidence from research and from social services inspectorate inspections has shown the poor quality of written assessments and the absence of plans for children in need. As a result, the Department of Health established a working partnership with researchers and practitioners to develop records for assessing children in need and their families. These records are not intended to replace social workers' professional judgement. They provide a systematic means of recording and analysing information gathered during the process of assessment, which leads to plans which are then subject to review.

The development of the materials

The work on developing the assessment records was closely co-ordinated with a number of the government's other key policy initiatives:

- the *Framework for the Assessment of Children in Need and their Families* (Department of Health, Department for Education and Employment, Home Office 2000a)
- *Working Together to Safeguard Children* (Department of Health, Home Office, Department for Education and Employment 1999)
- *The Government's Objectives for Children's Social Services* (Department of Health 1999a).

As a result, the assessment records for children in need are evidence-based, operationalise the assessment framework and reflect the principles that underpin these three government initiatives. They have been based on the findings from the review of research outlined above and have become part of the *Framework for the Assessment of Children in Need and their Families* (see Chapter 8).

There are three assessment records with accompanying guidance:

The Referral and Initial Information Record:

- to be completed in one working day
- records initial information about the child and family
- records the action to be taken.

The Initial Assessment Record:

- to be completed within a maximum of seven working days of referral
- records whether this child is a child in need
- records what services are required and the timescales
- records whether a core assessment should be carried out.

The Core Assessment Record:

- to be completed within a maximum of 35 working days
- assessment records are age-related

- records details of child's development needs
- records details of parenting capacity: strengths and difficulties
- records family and environmental factors: adverse and protective features
- objectives are clearly stated and a plan of action identified
- plans are subject to regular review (at least every six months).

The records are based on an interactive approach to the family. This acknowledges the circular way in which the emotions and behaviours of the parents are affected by their background and present circumstances, which in turn affect the emotions and behaviour of the child. The consequent feedback results in a further modification in family relationships. The records focus on the inter-relationship between children's behaviour, parenting capacity and environmental circumstances. To help social workers identify where services may be needed, the records explore the strengths and difficulties families may be experiencing, and the health and development of the children. Core Assessment Records have been designed to be used with the following age groups: 0–2; 3–4; 5–9; 10–14 and 15 and over. The records focus on the seven child-related dimensions featured in the *Looking After Children* materials.

The findings from the research in *Children's Needs – Parental Capacity* (Cleaver *et al.* 1999) and from the implementation of the assessment records have fed into the development of the government policy of creating an integrated children's system, described in Chapter 14. They are establishing a framework to monitor and evaluate government strategies, and to identify areas which require further investigation. For example, development work on the assessment records led in 1999 to a study commissioned under the Department of Health's Costing and Outcomes research initiative.

The significance of the records goes beyond the social work profession. They are helping to reframe the perceptions of other relevant professionals, particularly those of psychiatrists, paediatricians, heath visitors, teachers and police. They are enabling social workers and their professional colleagues to develop a more holistic approach to children's needs and families' capacity to respond appropriately.

CHAPTER THIRTEEN

Assessing Emotional and Behavioural Development in Children Looked After Away from Home

David Quinton and Clare Murray

Although emotional and behavioural problems are known to have a major influence on placement outcomes and the long-term wellbeing of looked after children and young people, there is a paucity of information about them. The Looking After Children *Assessment and Action Records represent the first attempt to provide consistent data on this issue. Data from 100 Assessment and Action Record emotional and behavioural development scales completed by 10–18-year-olds in seven local authorities were tested for reliability, and in 50 cases were compared with data from the Strengths and Difficulties Questionnaire and psychiatric interviews in order to test for validity. The results showed a high level of emotional and behavioural problems, with young people more likely to complete the scales and to report difficulties when rating alongside carers.*

Introduction

Children who have been separated from their parents and are looked after by statutory or voluntary agencies are amongst the most vulnerable in Western societies; the services they receive are also extremely expensive to provide. It is therefore unsurprising that one of the earlier attempts to introduce a systematic assessment of the relationship between need and outcome amongst users of children's services in England focused specifically on the experiences of the small group of 50–60,000 children who are looked after away from home.

Throughout the 1980s and 1990s a series of research reports, Social Services Inspectorate inspections and government inquiries produced increasing evidence of the failure of services to meet the often extensive developmental needs of children placed in care or accommodation by local authorities (see Chapter 1). Poor outcomes for these children led to a recognition that it was necessary to introduce a more structured approach that would help agencies to identify need, monitor progress and take action by providing appropriate services as and where necessary. In particular local authorities would need to demonstrate that they were acting as responsible parents to children who were placed in their care.

The *Looking After Children* system was developed as a response to these concerns. Introduced in 1995 by the Department of Health after a lengthy pilot period, it has now been implemented in virtually all local authorities in England and Wales as well as in a number of other countries (Parker *et al.* 1991; Ward 1995).

Central to the system are a series of six age-related Assessment and Action Records (AARs), designed to help practitioners assess children's progress in each of seven developmental dimensions: health, education, identity, family and social relationships, social presentation, emotional and behavioural development and self care skills. By asking not only how far children are progressing, but also whether they are receiving those parenting experiences that are thought to be necessary to successful development, the AARs are intended to 'bring to the attention of those responsible for children's welfare the probable consequences of certain actions – in other words to introduce ideas about outcome into everyday social work practice' (Ward 1995).

The AARs have been set within a comprehensive system for gathering information, making plans and reviewing children's progress. In theory they can provide systematic, longitudinal data concerning the relationship between needs, services and outcome for all children in each of the seven developmental dimensions. They are specifically designed to highlight deficits in the care that children receive, particularly when parenting responsibilities are shared between several parties. They were intended to be used at both an individual level, to set the agenda between young people, carers, birth parents, social workers, and other child welfare workers, and at an aggregate level, to provide data that might be used in planning services. As such, they are designed to act both as tools that guide practice and as instruments that have the potential to assess outcomes of social work interventions.

The original AARs were an innovative procedure that required substantial changes to both the culture and the practice of social services departments. They represented the first attempt to introduce systematic measurement of the effectiveness of social interventions over time. How well they are taken up and how well they perform is thus an important part of the development of more systematic care for vulnerable children and young people. However successive audits have shown that implementation has proved problematic in England and Wales, and that it is rare for the AARs to be used on a routine basis (Moyers 1996; Peel 1997; Nicholson and Ward 1999; Scott 1999), although there is some evidence to suggest that they are more successfully used in Canada (Flynn and Biro 1998). In England and Wales, there are also concerns about the accuracy of the data recorded on these, as well as on other *Looking After Children* materials (Ward and Skuse 1999).

For these and other reasons, it has long been clear that the *Looking After Children* materials, and the AARs in particular, would eventually need to be extensively revised if they were to be used more effectively in England and Wales. New arrangements for monitoring the health and educational development of looked after children have already been announced (Department of Health 1999j; Department of Health and Department for Education and Employment 2000) and will require substantial changes to the content of the relevant dimensions of the AARs. At the time of writing, the nature and extent of such changes are being explored within the broader context of the development of the Integrated Children's System (see Chapter 14).

A further dimension that is likely to require extensive revision is the assessment of children's emotional and behavioural development. One of the first steps in preparing for this has been to undertake a detailed examination of the reliability and validity of the data gathered from this section of the AARs, completed in three local authorities with young people aged ten and over. This age group was chosen because emotional and behavioural problems are believed to be especially marked for them and because some specific assessment issues arise in their case through the use of the AARs as a practice tool and as a measure of outcomes. The results from this study are discussed in this chapter, which considers how the system could be better developed to address these issues.

Emotional and behavioural problems in looked after children

Before presenting some data on how the emotional and behavioural development section of the AARs works, it may be helpful briefly to review what we know about such problems in looked after children and to provide some background on their classification.

Until recently, concern over the mental health problems of this group has focused predominantly on the difficulties they raise for service providers rather than on their effects on the lives of the children and young people. For example, they tend to be discussed as 'risk factors' for breakdowns in foster care (reviewed in Berridge 1997) rather than as problems for the children themselves. Despite such recognition, there are remarkably few – it does not go too far to say scandalously few – data on the prevalence of such disorders or systematic programmes to alleviate them. There are virtually no studies that are epidemiologically based, use standard instruments or criteria, and collect data from children, carers and schools. Despite attempts to introduce some measurement through the *Looking After Children* system, we know little about the prevalence of such difficulties and collect no routine information on them. In the absence of such data we do not know whether interventions supposed to help children and young people do any good, nor do we know how to design services. If we do not know what the problems are we cannot begin to assess 'what works'.

However the few investigations that have been based on systematic measures do, indeed, show that emotional and behavioural problems are very common. Earlier questionnaire studies suggested that as many as 30–40 per cent of children 'in care' showed such difficulties (Lambert, Essen and Head 1977; Wolkind and Rutter 1977) . Similar rates were found for children in residential homes, with over 40 per cent showing problems (Quinton and Rutter 1988; Wolkind and Renton 1979). These rates are strikingly higher than those in the general population, even in deprived inner-city areas.

The difficulties the children have are mostly problems of conduct; that is, oppositional and antisocial behaviour, but disturbances in the emotions involving high levels of anxiety and misery are also much higher. Strikingly, gender differences are much less evident than in the general population, with boys and girls often showing similar levels of difficulties. Recent improvements in measurement have also highlighted high levels of restless and distractable (hyperactive) behaviour. For example, over 20 per cent of children late-placed in permanent substitute families show clinically significant problems of this kind both at home and at school (Quinton *et al.* 1998).

One recent study in Canada compared children placed in foster care with clinic and with community samples (Stein *et al.* 1996). Not surprisingly, the clinic children had the highest mean scores on the Child Behaviour Checklist (CBCL) – a widely used questionnaire measure – but the fostered children had problem profiles much more like the clinic than the general population.

The only comparable recent epidemiologically-based data on looked after children in the UK is the study by McCann and her colleagues of 13–17-year-old young people in foster and residential care in Oxfordshire (McCann *et al.* 1996). They also used the CBCL (Achenbach 1991a, 1991b, 1991c) as a screening instrument and then interviewed young people who scored high on the questionnaire. These were compared with a school-based control group. This study produced astonishingly high prevalence rates for disorder in the looked after group according to standard diagnostic criteria (DSM IV) when weighted calculations were made: 96 per cent for young people in residential care and 57 per cent for those in foster care. The most common problems were conduct disorder, over-anxiety and major depression. These figures are clearly very high. They may overestimate prevalence rates because of interview factors or missing cases, although missing information was taken into account statistically. However the 15 per cent prevalence rate in the controls is not out of line with the recent general population survey of children's mental health which showed disorders in 15 per cent of boys and 10 per cent of girls aged 10–15 (Department of Health 1999k).

Outcomes

Just as we have very little systematic data on the mental health of looked after children and young people, so we have little information on the influence of these problems on outcomes for them more generally, either in the short term or later in life. However we know that emotional and behavioural problems play a major role in continuities from poor childhood experiences to a range of difficulties in psychosocial functioning in adulthood. Continuities from conduct disorders to problems in personal relationships, parenting, friendships, criminality and work are very strong. This is true for the general population as well as for looked after groups (Quinton *et al.* 1993). Analyses of data from the national cohort studies have shown that emotional problems in childhood also have strong links to anxiety, depression and personal problems in adulthood (Cheung and Buchanan 1997).

We now have some understanding of the indirect nature of the continuities from childhood to adulthood in such psychosocial problems. The persistence of difficulties is far from inevitable but it is clear that emotional and behavioural problems are a key link between adverse childhoods and poor functioning and unhappy lives in adulthood (Rutter 1989; Quinton *et al.* 1993).

Three things are clear from this brief summary:

1. Rates of emotional and behavioural problems are very high amongst looked after children and young people and at a level of difficulty nearer to that of children attending clinics than to the general population.
2. To date we have collected *no* systematic data on these problems and their development over time.
3. Such problems are of central importance in explaining psychosocial problems later in life and, therefore, a critical link in the intergenerational transmission of parenting and other problems.

If we do not collect systematic data we shall not be able to design or evaluate services or interventions. It is clear that some measurement is essential, whatever kind of measure finally proves the most satisfactory and manageable.

Classification in child and adolescent psychiatry

Before examining the performance of the AAR scales it may be useful to have some overview of issues in the classification of emotional and behavioural problems in children and young people and the relationship of measurement scales to these classifications.

The systematic classification of child and adolescent psychopathology is of fairly recent origin (Cantwell 1996). There are two regularly used schemes: that devised under the auspices of the American Psychiatric Association, the series of Diagnostic and Statistical Manuals (DSM 1 to IV) produced between 1952 and 1994 and the World Health Organisation's International Classification of Diseases (ICD), now up to ICD 10 (World Health Organisation 1992). Before this the main attempt at a systematic classification was that by Anna Freud (1965), which was based on psychoanalytic *theory*. The DSM and ICD classifications followed a different principle. This was that classification should be based on what was reported and observed rather than on theories of their cause. The reason for this is that it is not possible to study causes if the classification is based on ideas of what they are.

In these modern schemes, in order to be classified as having a 'disorder', individuals have to show a particular patterning of symptoms that interfere with their lives in one way or another. The description of the disorder is based on clinical observation and also tested through research that confirms that the clinically identified groups of symptoms do usually go together. Thus definitions of 'disorder' attempt to provide characterisations of problems that are both coherent in research terms and agree with clinical observations.

These categorical schemes are extremely useful, indeed essential, in order to compare groups and populations and as a basis for refining and testing concepts and definitions of disorders. However it is important to recognise that the use of the term 'disorder' does not necessarily define a clearly established and distinguishable entity like measles or meningitis.

The classification of common emotional and behavioural problems

The primary classification of common emotional and behavioural problems is implied by that phrase itself. That is, the term 'emotional disorders' refers to problems whose main feature is abnormal mood or emotion and 'behavioural disorders' to aggressive, unco-operative and antisocial behaviour, especially when it is unacceptable to adults and peers. This basic division is essentially the same as the commonly used distinction between 'internalising' and 'externalising' disorders, a terminology made popular through the use of the CBCL. The emotional/internalising disorders include withdrawal, inhibition, anxiety, panic and depression and the behavioural/ externalising disorders involve disinhibition, aggression, oppositional/defiant behaviour, antisocial acts and other kinds of under-socialised behaviour.

These two broad groups of problems account for most of the disorders found amongst young people. To these should be added those problems that come under the heading of 'hyperactivity' (ADHD). ADHD is not just another manifestation of externalising problems. It is different from these in terms of the structure and cluster of symptoms (Fergusson, Horwood and Lynskey 1994), developmental antecedents, course and response to medication (Sanuga-Barke 1998).

There are, of course, other much rarer disorders that also occasionally occur in looked after children such as schizophrenia, obsessive-compulsive disorder or autism. The social disabilities usually associated with these make it much more likely that they will come to professional attention.

Assessment and measurement

The clinical assessment of both common and rare mental health difficulties requires a careful examination of information from a variety of sources: parents/carers, children and young people and teachers, as well as a range of medical and psychological tests and examinations.

Modern screening questionnaires, like the one found in the AARs, are not intended to provide clinical diagnoses. Rather, they are designed to pick up the more usual emotional and behavioural problems and hyperactivity. Assessments of peer relationships are commonly also included. Peer relationships do not form a 'mental health' dimension in the same sense as the other three, but are strongly related to such problems and have a serious impact on children's current lives and their future development. A second purpose of these instruments is to serve as a broad measure of continuity and change over time.

The most commonly used questionnaires in Britain are the Rutter parents and teachers' scales (Elander and Rutter 1996) , and newer instruments developed from these, especially Goodman's 'Strengths and Difficulties' questionnaire (Goodman 1997; Goodman, Meltzer and Bailey 1998). These scales contain a series of descriptive statements about the child's behaviour – for example, 'frequently fights with other children' –

and the rater is asked to check whether this 'does not apply', 'applies somewhat' or 'definitely applies' to the child.

Measuring emotional and behavioural development in *Looking After Children*

The Goodman scales have certain advantages over the Rutter scales from which they are derived: first, the sub-scales contain the same number of items, which makes interpretation easier; and second, some problem items are positively worded, which makes the scales more popular with parents and teachers.

The original intention was to use these scales in the emotional and behavioural development section of the AARs and to add four items to cover problems that are rare in the general population but more common in looked after children: indiscriminate friendliness, self-harm, over-suspiciousness and bed-wetting. A final set of new items, which were intended to assess the children's relationship with their carers (i.e. 'attachment' in the broadest sense) were also added. Thus, there was an intention to provide an overall problem score and 'sub-scales' measuring:

- emotional problems (fears, unhappiness, depression etc.)
- conduct problems (fighting, destructiveness, stealing etc.)
- over-activity (restlessness, failure to settle to tasks, poor concentration etc.)
- peer relationships
- pro-social disposition (positive behaviour towards others).

These scales were to be scored like the Goodman scales and rated in the orthodox (confidential) manner. However in order to meet social workers' concerns, the scales in the AARs were changed to their current format (see Figure 13.1 the questionnaire about Emotional and Behavioural Development, below).

EMOTIONAL AND BEHAVIOURAL DEVELOPMENT

The questions in this section are designed to draw attention to how you have been feeling and how this has affected the way you behave. They also find out whether you are getting help if you need it.

Here are some descriptions of the way many young people behave and feel.

- Read each description and decide how like you it is and then tick the box that applies best.
- Think about how you have felt and behaved over the last three months, not just today.
- Then ask your carer(s) to fill in their opinion.

Key:
1. Definitely like me
2. Quite like me
3. A bit like me
4. Not at all like me
5. Definitely like you
6. Quite like you
7. A bit like you
8. Not at all like you

B1 Relationships with others

	Your opinion				Your carer(s) opinion			
Some young people:	1	2	3	4	5	6	7	8
feel able to trust and confide in adults	☐	☐	☐	☐	☐	☐	☐	☐
go to their carer(s) when they need reassurance	☐	☐	☐	☐	☐	☐	☐	☐
like their carer(s) to show them physical affection	☐	☐	☐	☐	☐	☐	☐	☐
get demanding and impatient with their carer(s)	☐	☐	☐	☐	☐	☐	☐	☐
can be over-friendly with people they don't know well	☐	☐	☐	☐	☐	☐	☐	☐
are extremely suspicious of other people's motives	☐	☐	☐	☐	☐	☐	☐	☐
are considerate of other people's feelings	☐	☐	☐	☐	☐	☐	☐	☐
comfort other people who are upset	☐	☐	☐	☐	☐	☐	☐	☐
are popular with other young people	☐	☐	☐	☐	☐	☐	☐	☐

find it hard to mix with other young people or are very shy	☐	☐	☐	☐	☐	☐	☐	☐
are often in trouble for being defiant, disobedient or disruptive in school or at home	☐	☐	☐	☐	☐	☐	☐	☐
comfort other people who are upset	☐	☐	☐	☐	☐	☐	☐	☐
are popular with other young people	☐	☐	☐	☐	☐	☐	☐	☐
find it hard to mix with other young people or are very shy	☐	☐	☐	☐	☐	☐	☐	☐
like to share things with others	☐	☐	☐	☐	☐	☐	☐	☐
often show they are angry and lose their temper	☐	☐	☐	☐	☐	☐	☐	☐
find it easy to make and keep close friendships	☐	☐	☐	☐	☐	☐	☐	☐
like to let others join in things they are doing	☐	☐	☐	☐	☐	☐	☐	☐
get into fights or pick on other young people	☐	☐	☐	☐	☐	☐	☐	☐

Concentration and behaviour

Some young people:

find it easy to concentrate when they want to	☐	☐	☐	☐	☐	☐	☐	☐
rush into things without thinking	☐	☐	☐	☐	☐	☐	☐	☐
find it difficult to stick to things for more than a few moments	☐	☐	☐	☐	☐	☐	☐	☐
deliberately break or steal things	☐	☐	☐	☐	☐	☐	☐	☐
are very restless and fidgety	☐	☐	☐	☐	☐	☐	☐	☐
are responsible and can be trusted	☐	☐	☐	☐	☐	☐	☐	☐

Anxieties and worries

Some young people:

have poor appetite or are very concerned about dieting	☐	☐	☐	☐	☐	☐	☐	☐
worry a lot	☐	☐	☐	☐	☐	☐	☐	☐
often get aches and pains (including headaches and stomach aches)	☐	☐	☐	☐	☐	☐	☐	☐
have difficulty in sleeping because of worry or anxiety	☐	☐	☐	☐	☐	☐	☐	☐
sometimes wet the bed	☐	☐	☐	☐	☐	☐	☐	☐
have strong feelings of misery or sadness	☐	☐	☐	☐	☐	☐	☐	☐
are frightened of particular things or situations (e.g. open spaces, going to school or being alone)	☐	☐	☐	☐	☐	☐	☐	☐
deliberately injure themselves (e.g. by scratching, cutting or taking an overdose)	☐	☐	☐	☐	☐	☐	☐	☐

Are any of the above a cause for concern to you or your carer(s)? If so, please describe

Are there any other concerns which have not been mentioned above? If so please describe:

Figure 3.1 *Assessment and Action Record Questionnaire*

Modifications to the scheme and the 'administration' issue

The compromise between the practice and outcome purposes of *Looking After Children*, alluded to earlier, created potential difficulties in using the AARs to screen for emotional and behavioural problems. Their use as a practice tool was intended to take young people's own perspectives into account and to promote constructive discussion between the children, their carers and their social workers. However their use as outcome instruments required that raters did not bias each other's accounts. This would be the normal reason for carers and young people to fill in the forms *separately and confidentially*. This is the essential tension in the 'practice' *versus* 'outcome' measure dilemma.

In order to meet practitioners' concerns that the carers' ratings should not be secret and that filling in the scales should involve a discussion between carers and young people, the confidentiality principle was abandoned. This led to the parallel presentation of the carers' and young people's scales in the 10–18 age group. As part of this change the carer and young person scales were set out side by side on the same page and the rating format was revised.

In order to meet the concern that young people should not have to rate negative things about themselves directly, they were asked, instead, to compare themselves with a description of what 'some young people' were like and to rate how much they were like that young person. That is, a comparative and not a 'direct' self-rating approach was used.

These changes raised certain fundamental issues for the interpretation of the ratings. First, the side-by-side presentation would mean that one rater would be able to see the other's views when rating. Second, if the AAR was completed in the way intended, the ratings would reflect a discussion between carer and young person: that is, they would reflect some negotiated consensus. The biases in this would be unknown. In some cases one rater might get their way, in others extreme ratings might be toned down out of kindness or sensitivity or out of anxiety about self-revelation, and in others items might be omitted completely because of the extent of disagreement.

Assessing the performance of the scales

In assessing how well the emotional and behavioural measures work we are concerned with such questions as: do carers and young people agree on what the problems are? Do the items in the scales form patterns that are meaningful in terms of current classifications of emotional and behavioural problems? Does the AAR scale agree with other measures that attempt to identify the same problems? How well do the scales agree with more detailed interview-based assessments of difficulties? How well does the scale identify those for whom a more detailed assessment is needed? In short, we were concerned with the reliability and validity of the scales.

The common sense understanding of *reliability* is whether the administration of an instrument produces sufficiently similar results when it is repeated within some interval by the same rater (*test-retest reliability*) or when it is completed by different raters (*inter-rater reliability*). Test-retest reliability was not possible in this study because of the difficulty in getting the scales completed once, let alone twice. Because of this, reliability was examined with respect to *internal structure and consistence* of the scales. That is, factor and reliability analyses were used to see how well the scale items hung together and to what extent they formed meaningful, i.e. believable, patterns.

The common sense meaning of *validity* is that the scale measures what it is intended to measure, that is, that it is a satisfactory reflection of the concept of which it is taken to be an indicator. Two principal tests were applied: first, whether the scale agreed with another well-tested scale designed to measure the same things (*concurrent validity*); in this case the Strengths and Difficulties Questionnaire (SDQ), and second, how well it predicted disorder as revealed through a standard psychiatric interview: the DAWBA (*criterion validity*).

Data

The data come from 100 AARs completed by 10–18-year-old young people in seven local authorities. The comparisons between the AAR and the SDQ, and the AAR and the psychiatric interview come from 50 young people and their carers, the great majority of whom were recruited through two local authorities in south London. Contact was first made with their social workers and then with the young people and their carers, either through the social workers or directly to the young people and carers themselves. The carers and young people were then interviewed in their own homes or residential facilities using the DAWBA. At the same time each of them completed the SDQ *independently and confidentially.*

In addition to the 50 AARs available from the interview/SDQ study, we attempted to collect as many additional emotional and behavioural sections as possible from our most co-operative authorities for the factor and reliability analyses. CM visited local area offices and collected these data on an additional 32 young people. In a last attempt to increase the numbers further, two social services departments in the west of England sent us information on a further 18 young people. We thus had AAR data on 100 young people for the factor analyses and internal reliability assessments. These were adequate for the second of these tasks but fell short of what is ideal for the former (Child 1990). Nevertheless both kinds of analysis are outlined.

Summary of data available

Table 13.1 gives a summary of the available data on which these analyses are based. These data show a reassuringly good distribution by age and gender. The same is true for the SDQ, which had a maximum of 50 questionnaires completed by young people or carers with an overlap of 42 cases. The interview was successfully completed with 40 young people and carers. Once again the age and gender distributions were satisfactory. Some AARs did not have data on type of placement or age.

Table 13.1 Number of cases with different kinds of data

	Boys	Girls	Foster	Residential	10–11	12–13	14–15	16–18
SDQ	27	23	26	22	10	14	16	10
Interview	20	20	26	13	10	11	11	8
AAR	46	54	52	31	13	22	28	21

Results

It is important first to emphasise that in all the analyses that follow the scoring of items does not match the numbering conventions in the AARs. Rather both the carer's and the young person's scale items are scored from 0 to 3, with a higher score always meaning more problems, except for the pro-social items where a high score indicates a more pro-social disposition.

Scale completion and missing items

First we looked for patterns in the completion of items and examined whether these showed differences between the carers and young people. We looked at three issues: first, whether certain items were more frequently left out than others; second, whether young people or carers were more likely to leave out items the further they went through the scale; and finally, whether young people were more likely to miss out items if their carers did, or vice versa. The number of missing items is summarised in Table 13.2.

Table 13.2. Missing items on the AAR

Number of items missing	Young person n=100%	Carer n=100%
0	76	66
1 or 2	16	10
more than 2	8	9
all	0	15

Chi sq=17.15, 3.d.f p=0.0007

The first point to notice is that the young people were significantly more likely to complete the forms than their carers. Thirty-four per cent of carers did not fully complete the forms, 19 per cent partially completed and 15 per cent not at all. Young people failed to complete the forms only when carers also failed to do so. Thus 46 per cent of young people failed to complete when carers also failed. In contrast *all* the young people made their ratings when their carers did so as well. These data suggest that the carer's involvement is essential to the success of the *Looking After Children* enterprise.

Lack of carer involvement had a marked effect on the young people's involvement in the task. This was most clearly seen when the *pattern* of missing items was examined. Table 13.3 gives the total of missing *items* for each group of five as they appear successively in the scale. (Note that this is not a count of the number of young people with missing items. Many young people will appear in more than one group.) This is a test to see whether the young people get bored as they go through the scale or whether missing data were more related to their unwillingness to fill in certain items.

Table 13.3. Number of young person's missing items according to carer engagement and item position in scale.

	Items 1–5	Items 6–10	Items 11–15	Items 16–20	Items 20–25	Items 26–30
Carer engaged	2	2	2	0	1	0
Carer not engaged	8	12	15	17	23	28

Chi sq for trends p<0.000

It is clear from this analysis that missing items occurred increasingly frequently as the young people went through the scale when they were left to complete the AARs on their own. Missing items on the carer ratings showed no trend of this kind. That is, when carers completed the scale they did so without any tendency increasingly to omit items as they progressed through the scale.

There was no evidence that some items were left out more often than others nor that carers and young people omitted the same items – perhaps because they were in marked disagreement about them or agreed not to fill them in for some other reason.

Frequency of individual problems

Table 13.4 shows the data on the frequency with which carers and young people rated individual problems (a rating of 'quite like' or 'definitely like' the young person) and the agreement between carers and young people on these. Items with positive wordings (e.g. 'trusts adults') are reversed in the analysis so that the percentages reflect problems: in this case the young people's rating of 33 per cent means that 33 per cent did *not* trust adults. The only items for which this reversal is *not* the case are the 'pro-social items' indicated by *. Thus 73 per cent of children rate themselves as considerate.

Table 13.4. Frequency of individual problems and agreement between young persons' and carers' ratings

Item	% rating 2–3: child	% rating 2–3: carer	Agreement (weighted Kappa)
trust adults	33	28	0.61
goes for reassurance	34	24	0.74
likes affection	45	32+	0.63
demanding with carer	34	46+	0.69
over-friendly	17	25	0.43
suspicious	35	26	0.78
considerate*	73	62+	0.36
defiant	23	31	0.54
comforts others*	74	71	0.63
popular	30	35	0.54
finds it hard to mix	28	24	0.66
likes to share*	74	75	0.47
anger, temper	38	36	0.58
makes friends easily	28	38+	0.40
lets other join in*	71	66	0.43
gets into fights	15	14	0.50
poor concentration	25	29	0.48
rushes into things	49	49	0.73
can't stick at things	29	30	0.67
breaks things, steals	9	14	0.68
restless, fidgety	38	34	0.84

trustworthy	24	32+	0.55
poor appetite	8	15	0.59
worries a lot	23	30+	0.46
aches and pains	21	22	0.65
sleep problems	14	18	0.65
wets the bed	4*	9*+	0.34
misery or sadness	21	27	0.56
fears	11	16	0.52
self harm	11*	14*	0.27

*Percentages calculated where any problem reported rating 1, 2 or 3
+Differences significant at the 5% level or better
All Kappas are significant at the 0.000 level or better

In general these analyses show good agreement between the carers and young people but with some significant differences. Carers were significantly more likely to rate the young people as: demanding with them, having problems making friends, untrustworthy, worrying, and as wetting the bed. Young people were more likely to indicate that they had problems or reservations in their relationships with carers, although this was only significantly different with respect to physical affection.

Summary and conclusions on the analysis of individual items

The main problems in the completion of the scales were associated with the extent of carer involvement:

- Thirty-four per cent of carers did not complete the scales fully, including 15 per cent who did not fill them in at all.
- Young people always completed the scales when their carers did so, but 71 per cent failed to complete them when carers did not.
- When carers were not 'engaged' in the task the items were progressively less likely to be filled in by the young people the

further down the scale they were. No such effect was apparent when carers also completed the scales.

- An examination of missing data in those cases where most items were completed showed no clear pattern. That is, no items appeared 'unpopular'.
- In general, carers rated the young people as having more individual problems than the young people did themselves. However young people were more likely to rate their relationships with their carers as problematic.
- The frequency of individual problems appeared quite high, with 30 per cent or more of young people showing problems that were 'quite like' or 'definitely like' them.

Structure and internal reliability of the Assessment and Action Record scales

In this part of the discussion we present the data concerned with checking the consistency and reliability of the sub-scales using exploratory factor analyses and reliability analyses.

Factor analyses

Factor analyses using principal components extraction and varimax rotation were performed on the young people's and carers' ratings, omitting the items that were not relevant for the sub-scales. It should be emphasised that the number of AARs available was not sufficient for these analyses to be considered reliable. The factor analyses were used instead as a rough guide in choosing the sub-scale items. The analysis of the young people's scales produced eight factors with an eigenvalue of over one and accounted for 66.1 per cent of the unique variance. The carers' scales similarly produced seven factors with 67.2 per cent of the variance accounted for.

In general the analyses of both the young people's and the carers' responses reflected the *a priori* structure in the scale's items. The factors that appear most 'cleanly' were emotional problems, conduct problems and relationships with carers. The over-activity/restlessness items were clearly associated with each other in both carers' and young people's accounts but in both cases went together with other difficulties as well. These patterns were more clear-cut on the carers' scales where the emotional, carer relationship, conduct and pro-social factors emerged reasonably cleanly. Distinct factors were less clear in the young people's accounts, although the emotional, over-activity and conduct problem dimensions were apparent, as were relationships with carers. It was striking that a pro-social factor did not emerge from the young people's self-ratings. Instead higher pro-social behaviours went along with the young people's views of themselves as having *poor* peer relationships.

Reliability analyses

The second approach to the exploration of the overall scale and the construction of the sub-scales was to apply a standard reliability analysis using Cronbach's alpha. The more interpretable factor structure of the carers' accounts was reflected in the reliability analyses. The alpha statistic was always higher for the carers' scales – indicating that the scales have more internal consistency or coherence. The alphas (Table 13.5) are generally adequate but never more than modest. It should be said that the same was true for the data from the SDQ.

It was clear from these analyses that the 'emotional' sub-scale was marginally improved on both accounts by removing the 'appetite' item. Likewise, the relationship with carers' sub-scale was better if the 'demanding and impatient' item were dropped. Both of these conclusions were consistent with the factor analyses. However problems on the latter item were rated very frequently by carers (46%) and by young people (34%). This compared with only 15 per cent and 8 per cent for the 'appetite' item. It therefore seemed appropriate to drop the 'appetite' item from the emotional scale but to keep the 'demanding and impatient' item in the total scale (but not to include it in any of the sub-scales).

Table 13.5. Summary of sub-scale reliability analysis

Scale	Young person n=79 Alpha	Carer n=70 Alpha
emotional	0.74	0.84
conduct	0.65	0.69
overactivity	0.65	0.72
prosocial	0.60	0.70
peers	0.53	0.70
carers	0.45	0.54

Final selection of sub-scale items

Following the factor and reliability analyses the final selection of items was as follows:

Emotional problems: worries; has aches or pains; poor sleep; misery, sadness; fears.

Conduct problems: defiant; disobedient; anger or temper; fighting; breaks or steals things.

Overactivity: poor concentration; rushes into things; can't stick to things; restless; fidgety.

Pro-social: considerate; comforts others; likes to share; lets others join in.

Peers: popular; finds it hard to mix; makes friends easily.

Carers: trusts and confides; goes for reassurance; likes affection.

Total score

The total score is made up of the above items, except for the pro-social items, plus the item 'demanding and impatient with carers': a total of 20 in all. The total score is thus a problems score. All the items in the total scale are coded or re-coded so that the higher the score the greater the number of problems.

Table 13.6. Total and sub-scale scores for carers and young people from the full AAR sample

Scale	Young person				Carer			
	n	range	mean	s.d.	n	range	mean	s.d.
Emotional	90	0–14	3.76	3.38	98	0–15	4.18	3.92
Conduct	91	0–12	3.42	2.65	77	0–12	3.48	2.73
Overactive	94	0–12	4.71	2.93	76	0–11	4.68	3.06
Peers	94	0–8	2.89	2.02	78	0–9	3.30	2.23
Relationship with carers	98	0–9	3.40	2.37	81	0–8	3.03	2.22
Pro-social	94	2–12	8.41	2.44	78	2–12	8.01	2.69
Total score	82	2–47	19.23	1.03	70	2–43	19.84	1.17

Table 13.6 compares the young persons' and carers' scores on these scales. The mean scores are generally similar. A comparison of differences between the two scores when both sets of ratings were available showed two interesting findings. First the carers' and young people's sub and total scores were very highly correlated and, as a consequence, few of the scores were significantly different. Second, there were differences on problems in peer relationships and relationships with carers. In both cases the young people rated more problems than their carers did.

The 'administration' issue

A comparison of carers' and young people's scores on the sub-scales showed few differences except that young people were somewhat more likely to rate difficulties with peers and with carers. In general however, the two sets of scores were clearly very highly correlated.

This very high level of agreement made it necessary to address the 'administration issue', that is, the effect of the parallel and non-confidential presentation of the scales. There were three different questions here: first, whether the administration procedure created a consensus rating, second, whether the ratings leant towards one or other account, and finally, whether the jointly made ratings showed a lower or higher level of problems than were revealed when the ratings were made confidentially. We used the data from the SDQ to explore these issues because these scales were completed independently and confidentially.

Table 13.7. Correlations of carers' and young people's total and sub-scale scores for the SDQs and AARs

	Between SDQs n=42–47	Between AARs n=68–82
Total score	0.40**	0.76***
Emotional	0.36**	0.70***
Conduct	0.40**	0.72***
Hyperactivity	0.51**	0.78***
Peers	0.27 n.s.	0.64***
Pro-social	0.23 n.s.	0.79***
Carers	No scale	0.75***

Table 13.7 addresses the question of whether the AAR administration approach created a consensus rating. If this were the case we would expect the correlations between the carers and the young people to be much higher on the AAR than on the SDQ. This was the case to a striking extent: the AAR system of administration produces a composite rating.

Table 13.8 deals with the second question: whether the composite account leans more towards the carers' or the young people's views. In this case we would expect the correlations between the AAR and the SDQ to be stronger for the dominant account, since there would be less reason for the dominant parties to alter their ratings when they had a chance to act on their own.

Table 13.8. Total and sub-scale correlations between AAR & SDQ

	Carers n=37–48	Young people n=45–48
Total score	0.5**	0.29
Emotional	0.14	0.19
Conduct	0.37**	0.34*
Hyperactivity	0.53***	0.58***
Peers	0.51***	0.11
Pro-social	0.60***	0.46**

The correlations were strong and statistically significant for the carers apart from the 'emotional' sub-scales, which are not significantly correlated. The correlations were lower for the young people with the 'total', 'peer relationships' and the 'emotional' sub-scales not significantly correlated across the two scales. These findings suggest that the carers' AAR scores reflect the carers' view of the young people's problems more than they reflect the young people's own opinion – or at least what they rate when they are allowed to do so on their own.

Validity

Of course, these analyses deal only with the patterns and levels of agreement within and across the scales. At this stage they do not show if one or other set of ratings is more predictive of problems. For example, do the AARs reflect an unfairly negative view of the young people by the carers or do the young people's SDQ ratings reflect an over-normalised account of themselves? In this final section we look at the two approaches to assessing the validity of the emotional and behavioural development section of the AARs. The first involved the comparisons between the AAR Emotional and Behavioural Development Scales and the Goodman SDQ; that is, the test of *concurrent* validity. The second involved the relationship between the AAR scales and the assessments of psychiatric disorder obtained from the 40 interviews with carers and young people using the structured interview (the DAWBA); that is, the test of *criterion* validity.

Concurrent validity

The young people/carer agreement in our study can be compared with Goodman's pilot evaluation of his young people's scale, which compared ratings within a general population and a clinic sample (Goodman *et al.* 1998). The age ranges for the three samples are similar (*Looking After Children* 10–18; Goodman 11–16). Table 13. 9 supports the notion that the administration approach used in the AARs leads to an artificially high level of agreement between the ratings of carers and young people.

Table 13.9. Comparison of young people/carer agreement on the AAR and SDQ with agreement between self and parent ratings on the SDQ

	AAR n=68–82	SDQ n=42–47	Goodman Clinic n=116	Goodman Community n=83
Total score	0.76***	0.40**	0.46***	0.43***
Emotional	0.70***	0.36**	0.52***	0.52***
Conduct	0.72***	0.40**	0.68***	0.36**
Hyperactivity	0.78***	0.51**	0.58***	0.29*
Peers	0.64***	0.27n.s.	0.57***	0.29*
Pro-social	0.79***	0.23 n.s.	0.65***	0.31*
Carers	0.75***	–	–	–

The correlations between the young people's and carers' ratings on the SDQ in the *Looking After Children* study show very similar patterns to those in the other two samples, although some correlations are nearer to those of the clinic sample (conduct, hyperactivity) and others to the general population (peers, pro-social). The 'emotional' sub-scale shows a lower correlation than is the case for either the clinic or community samples. This may be related to the reluctance of the looked after young people to rate negative feelings or to a more general instability in this sub-scale. Unfortunately we do not have the correlations between carers and young people rating the AAR confidentially. This would be a key comparison in testing the performance of the AAR in comparison with the SDQ.

Discriminant validity

Finally we looked to see whether the confidential ratings by the carers and young people were accurate reflections of the likely level of disturbance. This is a proxy version of discriminant validity, which examines whether a measure reflects the different levels of disorder that might be expected in different populations. This is a common way of testing scales. For example, children attending mental health clinics may be compared with children attending clinics for other conditions that are unlikely to have a mental health component, such as dental clinics. In this case we looked to see whether the carers' or the young people's SDQ reflected the expected level of disturbance in this high-risk group.

Table 13.10. Proportions in LAC and community controls in the SDQ abnormal band

	Parents/carers		**Teachers**		**Young people**	
SDQ Scale	LAC N=49 %	Controls N=160 %	LAC 20 %	Controls 103 %	LAC %	Controls %
Total	37	10***	40	7***	14	5
Emotional	31	16*	10	8	8	10
Conduct	51	15***	50	7***	20	6*
Hyperactivity	20	14	25	8*	12	16
Peers	47	16***	20	8	6	5
Pro-social	22	4***	35	11*	8	2

(We are indebted to Robert Goodman for these data and analyses)

Table 13.10 compares the SDQs for our sample of looked after children with Goodman's community controls. The data are very striking. The carers in the LAC study rate the young people as having substantially more problems than the community controls and at a level consistent with other data on looked after children. The data from the small sample of teachers who completed ratings for the LAC study provide a similar picture. The young people's own ratings are remarkably different. Only the self-ratings of conduct problems show more difficulties than in the general population. There seems no doubt that the young people were under-reporting or 'normalising' their own feelings and behaviour.

The implication of this is that the AAR ratings in their present form may be adequate for assessing emotional and behavioural problems only to the extent that the carers' views dominate. Although this seems to be the case, the main issue remaining – and unresolvable at this stage – is whether the administration bias pulls the carers' ratings towards an agreed middle account and therefore weakens the discrimination.

Criterion validity

The assessment of criterion validity involved the ability of the emotional and behavioural development section of the AARs to identify young people with different levels of mental health difficulties as indicated by the interviews with them and their carers. It was clear from the analysis of the interviews that the looked after young people had high rates of disorder. Even allowing for the lack of complete data from teachers, 30 per cent of the young people had disorders, the majority being conduct problems but with a substantial level of anxiety and depression also.

Predicting disorder from the AAR scale

The association between SDQ and AAR total scores and the presence or absence of disorder are given in Table 13.11. The SDQ categories are based on the recognised cut-offs (14 and above for carers and 16 and above for young people). No similar cut-off is available for the AAR because no looked after/general population comparison exists. In its place the dichotomous categories are based on a median split (20 and above for young people, 21 and above for carers).

Table 13.11. Association between low and high scores on the SDQ and AAR and ratings of disorder

	Categorical Questionnaire Rating		
	Low	**High**	**Exact significance**
	% with disorder	% with disorder	
SDQ child	25	42	0.45
SDQ carer	14	64	0.003
AAR child	18	41	0.258
AAR carer	22	40	0.44

The children with disorders were twice as likely or more to be rated highly on the questionnaires, but this only reached statistical significance for the carers' SDQ. The lack of more significant discrimination by the AAR may reflect a lowering of ratings due to the administration effect. However the relationship between the AARs and disorder ratings is clearer in Table 13.12, which considers the relationship when the questionnaire scores are based on a statistical division of the categories into thirds.

Table 13.12. Association between low and high scores on the AAR and ratings of disorder based on a tripartite division

	Categorical Questionnaire Rating			
	Low	**Medium**	**High**	**Exact * significance**
	% with disorder	% with disorder		
AAR child	9	42	40	0.16
AAR carer	16	20	54	0.027

* *Cochrane-Armitage trend test*

In this comparison the probability of a rating of disorder increases significantly as the carers' ratings increase, with scores in the top third being strongly predictive of disorder. This is not true for the young people. For them, ratings of disorder are as likely when they rate themselves as having only a medium level of difficulties as they are when the ratings are high. The conclusion would be that looked after young people's self-ratings – whether they are based on the independently rated SDQ or on the jointly rated AAR – are, on their own, a poor indicator of emotional and behavioural disorders, possibly because the young people feel a need to protect rather than express themselves.

Discussion and conclusions

This chapter has sought to highlight the lack of information on looked after young people's emotional and behavioural problems, even though these are acknowledged to be a major influence on placement outcomes in the short term, on psychosocial development more generally, and on longer term social functioning. It is in this context that initiatives such as *Looking After Children* need to be set, especially in the attempt to provide consistent and interpretable information that will allow the tracking of the development of young people. If we have no way of collecting consistent information we have no way of doing this and no way of knowing 'what works'.

The emotional and behavioural development section of the AARs has been a first attempt to introduce consistent data collection on this topic within social services. Its effectiveness depends, of course, on the extent to which the forms are completed and the quality of the data collected. For this reason, the success of the emotional and behavioural development section is dependent on how well the AARs are used more generally. However some additional checks on the effectiveness of the content of the section are possible because they are organised in a form that is amenable to assessments of reliability and validity. It was with these that the chapter has been principally concerned.

The data that were presented (although the sample should not be taken as representative) confirmed the sparse data from elsewhere on the extent of emotional and behavioural problems, with the level of difficulties much in excess of the general population and nearer to that of clinically treated samples. Carers and teachers were clear about the excess of problems, especially those concerned with conduct, overactivity and peer relationships. The 'administration issue', that is, the parallel and open ratings of the AAR section, led to a much greater concordance between carer and young person accounts than in comparisons that involved separate and confidential ratings. The evidence suggested that this form of administration favoured the views of the carers.

The accounts from the young people themselves were harder to interpret. It seems clear that the low levels of problems identified by them when they could rate confidentially are not a good reflection of their level of difficulties. If they were, then care experiences would seem to imply no harm at all, which is against all the evidence. Rather, it seems possible that they felt it necessary to 'normalise' their distress or to protect themselves from the dangers of open expression of their feelings.

This makes the administration issue quite a conundrum because, under the *Looking After Children* procedure, the looked after young people do rate themselves as showing higher levels of difficulties than they do when rating on their own. Is this just a reflection of contextual coercion or is the section, when done properly, serving its intended purpose of bringing emotional and behavioural problems to the fore? It is clear that the section highlights problems. What we do not know at the moment is whether it raises the level of awareness of carers and therefore *increases* the rating of problems or tends somewhat to *lower* the level of difficulties recorded through some kind of bargaining process.

In the course of this sometimes technical discussion, however, a more general issue around the AAR data became apparent: that the key *practice* aspect of the administration of the forms – that is, that they should be completed as a collaborative effort between the carers and the young people – is essential to the effectiveness of the AARs as *outcome* measures. The young people in this study *always* completed the forms when their carers did but showed an increasing lack of commitment when they were left to their own devices.

It can be concluded that the AAR approach to highlighting emotional and behavioural problems is sound, raises issues for young people and carers that ought to be addressed, and provides a useful mapping of the type and severity of problems in relation to formal diagnostic schemes. This is a considerable advance. The analysis of the administration issue, seen initially as a problem, highlights the need to complete the AARs properly for both the practice benefits and the outcome data. Things initially seen as forced into an unnatural union prove to be natural bedfellows. Refinements to the

AARs need to take these lessons into account since they tell us something about the circumstances under which we shall get any consistent data for either practice developments or the understanding of outcomes.

CHAPTER FOURTEEN

Two Steps Forward, One Step Back

Issues for Policy and Practice

Wendy Rose

This chapter explores some of the key themes which have emerged in this book and relates them to policy and practice issues. An explicit developmental/ecological perspective underpins the systems and processes for assessing children's needs. The search for more rationality, rigour and an evidence basis to both individual casework and service planning is examined, which the development of the Integrated Children's System is intended to support. However factors such as the current state of new technology, the professional workforce and the complexity involved in new systems may inhibit the pace and scale of implementation in practice.

Introduction

The relationship between need, service and outcome has been the pervading theme of this book. The critical role which assessment of need plays in the route through to provision of services and to improving the life chances of vulnerable children has been reflected in many of the chapters. The effectiveness of intervention is acknowledged as being dependent on the quality of assessment. Gough's (1992) formulation of the relationship between assessment and outcome (cited by Pinnock and Garnett in Chapter 4) is reinforced in similar terms by Saunders, Berliner and Hanson (2001), that 'the likelihood of a successful outcome is enhanced substantially when effective interventions are matched correctly to specific problems discerned through appropriate assessment' (p.14). We cannot, therefore, expect to see an improvement in the outcomes for our most vulnerable children unless we first address how we identify their needs and understand what is happening to them.

The preceding chapters have told a tale of two parallel but not unrelated developments in the assessment of need in children and families over the last decade, one concerned with a community level of service planning and delivery, and the other with improving direct work with children and families. These developments encompass a rich and diverse range of approaches and initiatives, and record the progress that has been made in evolving conceptual frameworks, systems and processes. However whether these are aimed at planning services to meet the needs of a population of children living in a geographical area or at developing a better understanding of what is happening to an individual child in order to plan an effective intervention, there is a surprising and important degree of consonance in the emerging themes. In this concluding chapter, we gather together some of the key points which have arisen and relate them to current policy and practice issues.

A developmental perspective

It is clear that there is widespread acceptance at both a policy and practice level of a developmental perspective for understanding the needs of children. Such a perspective emphasises that children develop along several dimensions, often simultaneously, and that a series of developmental tasks must be completed successfully if optimal outcomes are to be achieved (Rose and Aldgate 2000). As the child attains a degree of competence at each stage, so this lays the foundation for further increasingly complex and integrated development (Jones 1997). Adopting a developmental approach has a number of consequences for those with responsibility for identifying need and providing services to vulnerable children. These include recognising the importance of timing in a child's life in achieving certain developmental tasks, and understanding the impact of interruption or impairment at particular stages of development. The approach also incorporates a multi-dimensional view of children, involving the interplay between different aspects of development. When concerns are raised, a range of agencies with responsibility for those different aspects of children's lives, such as health and education, are inevitably drawn in, as well as family and carers, in order to understand the whole child.

This is not new. A developmental perspective was enshrined in the groundbreaking Children Act 1948, as outlined by Ward in Chapter 1, and has continued at the foundation of child welfare services throughout the second half of the twentieth century. In her description of the responsibilities of the new children's committees established by the 1948 Act, Pugh makes this point:

> The Act explicitly states the duty of the committee towards the child in their care: 'to exercise their powers with respect to him so as to further his best interests, and to afford him opportunity for the proper development of his character and abilities'. Children in care were seen not as paupers or criminals, but as individuals with needs and potentialities which the new committees must help to fulfil. (1968, pp.6–7)

Nevertheless whilst the rhetoric of childcare since then has supported the principle of a developmental approach to children's welfare, this has not been embedded in the systems underpinning service delivery. Indeed, the loss of focus on children as individuals in their own right and on their needs, at the expense of a more diffuse concern about parental and wider family problems, was best summed up in the admonition in the Cleveland Report of 1988 (Butler-Sloss 1988): 'the child is a person and not the object of our concern'. The work of the Department of Health Working Party on Assessing Outcomes in Child Care, reported by Parker and colleagues (1991), was a major breakthrough in developing a more systematic approach. Their aim was to provide a method of assessment for children looked after in public care 'that covered all those milestones in growing up which are informally monitored and promoted by 'reasonable' parents' (Ward 1995, p.10). Their identification of seven developmental dimensions made feasible the measurement of progress of children by child welfare agencies, both on an individual basis and at an aggregated level to inform service planning. It became possible for social services departments to answer the critical question of 'how well are our children doing?'

The developmental perspective now underpins the assessment of all children in need. Thus, as Gray reports in Chapter 8, one of the principles in the government guidance on assessing children in need and their families is that the work must be rooted in child development. However the concepts of children's development are not uncontested. Some argue that a much broader view should be taken of children's development which acknowledges the heterogeneity of childhood experiences and that 'different societies have their own ideas about children's capacities and vulnerabilities, the ways in which they learn and develop and what is good for them and what is bad' (Boyden, Ling and Myers 1998, p.32). Others express concern that optimal outcomes for children are defined by adult preferences, implying that the focus is on preparing children 'for their transition into adulthood' (Ben-Arieh 2001, p.30) and that their progress is measured in those terms. Ben-Arieh makes a strong argument for a newly defined and appropriate concept of children's wellbeing that takes into account their activities and experiences while they are children, valuing childhood as a stage in itself. Such debates suggest that while an explicit developmental approach now underpins the assessment of vulnerable children, further work may be required on agreeing a consensus around the building blocks of development.

An ecological model

As is indicated throughout the chapters, a broad view is being taken of the influences on children's development, which Jones (1997) summarises as 'ranging from genetic and constitutional influences, via physical and psychological factors, to influences emanating from the family, neighborhood, and cultural spheres of life' (p.521). Not only are the influences of immediate family recognised but also the significance of friends, adults special to a child, school and other social networks, which all form an important part of the child's world. Furthermore, the impact of growing up in circumstances of poverty, disadvantage, harassment, discrimination and social isolation is acknowledged. Such conditions can have a direct effect on the child, on the parents or carers and their capacity to respond to the child's needs, and on the quality and accessibility of community resources. This ecological model of a child's wellbeing has a considerable history and has been widely developed and explored (for example, in the writings of Bronfenbrenner 1979; Belsky and Vondra 1989; Prilleltensky and Nelson 2000). Jack (1997, 2001) and Stevenson (1998) have strongly encouraged its application to work by social care agencies with children and families. However, it is only beginning to be built into policy and practice more systematically and the full implications of its adoption understood.

If it is accepted that 'a child's wellbeing is determined by the level of parental, familial, communal, and social wellness' (Prilleltensky and Nelson 2000, p.87), then a number of critical issues follow. Life for the practitioner or the service planner is inevitably more complex. It requires an understanding of the interactions, transactions and compensations between different parts of the system. It requires a continuum of information to be gathered from work with individual children and their families through to the community as a whole. Judgement is called for about the different weighting of factors, and where the stresses and strains lie in the system. Multiple levels of analysis need to be applied. Consideration has to be given to the point and timing of intervention, and to the consequential impact of change in one part of the system on another. Co-ordinated strategies will be needed which 'will necessarily involve inter-professional and inter-agency co-operation at quite a sophisticated level' (Stevenson 1998, p.18).

In Chapter 2, Page identifies the importance of the overall policy context. If there is recognition at a government level of the interconnections of policies on the wellbeing of its citizens, then this can create more propitious conditions for action at a community and individual level. Whilst there is a better understanding of the interactions at an individual level, for example the part that success at school may play in terms of a child's sense of identity and self esteem when coping with difficult circumstances at home, problems arise in translating this into a framework for interventions to promote child and family wellness at a community and strategic level. Many of the chapters demonstrate the progress that is being made in responding to these challenges both conceptually and in practice, although they also identify the distance there is still to go.

Measuring outcomes

Even when a framework for assessing need has a sound theoretical underpinning, systems are required which translate it into practice and ensure that specified outcomes are achieved. It is clear that it is only by placing an emphasis on improving outcomes and trying to find ways of measuring them that the aspirations for safeguarding and promoting the wellbeing of children will be achieved. Children defined as in need under the Children Act 1989 will inevitably require considerable attention and investment of resources if they are to achieve life chances that are equal to those of their more fortunate contemporaries. It is this imbalance that government initiatives such as Quality Protects and Children First have tried to address. A better evidence base is therefore required to inform key stakeholders – the public, government, professionals, and children and families themselves – whether improvements are occurring in the lives of children in need.

Finding out who are the children in need is perhaps the first step, although establishing satisfactory systems for doing so has proved difficult. The government Working Party on Observation and Assessment, set up in 1978, recorded its concern that 'we were unable to find out how many children are assessed by social services departments and what is the cost' (Department of Health and Social Security 1981, p.3). This has continued to be the picture, although the Department of Health's *Child in Need Census*, started in 2000, has been an important move in the right direction (Department of Health 2000b), see Chapters 1 and 4. As Gray has pointed out in Chapter 8, many of the government objectives for children's social services are now framed in developmental and outcome terms, such as 'to ensure that children in need gain maximum life chance benefits from educational opportunities, health care and social care' (Department of Health 1999a, p.12). Measuring progress in achieving those outcomes has required the development of a range of performance indicators, which has raised questions about the nature of evidence being used and how adequately it reflects what is happening to children in different circumstances (Ward and Skuse 2001). There have been particular concerns about how far the measures are sensitive to children with disabilities. Concern has also been expressed that outputs become confused with outcomes, and measures of agency performance become muddled with measuring children's progress. This is an issue which has been well debated in other parts of the public sector (Carter, Klein and Day 1992; P. Smith 1996, for example) but until recently less attention has been given to children's services.

An evidence-informed approach

Many of the chapters indicate the search by service providers for more rationality, rigour and coherence in the systems they are developing. They need to generate better and more reliable information on which to base decisions and also to ensure greater transparency in order to justify and be accountable for what is happening. Although grounding practice in evidence is one of the principles underpinning the *Framework for the Assessment of Children in Need and their Families* (Department of Health *et al.* 2000a), this remains a contested area. There is little or no consensus about what constitutes evidence, let alone how it should be measured or judged (see Cheetham *et al.* 1992; Everitt and Hardiker 1996; Hill 1999; Davies, Nutley and Smith 2000; Webb 2001). It is easy to be seduced by the idea that there can be a clear body of evidence contributing to practice to the point that this becomes the holy grail. Lewis (2001) urges caution about looking for certainties and suggests that evidence-informed work may be a more appropriate goal. 'Evidence can only ever be a small part of what constitutes practice' she argues, because other factors will be important, such as the availability of resources, staff skills, organisational stability or upheaval or performance indicators that have to be met (Lewis 2001, p.1). There is also a danger that there will be a tendency to concentrate on readily quantifiable information at more strategic levels of planning (P. Smith 1996).

We are beginning to become more sophisticated in recognising that there are different types of evidence which can be used for different purposes. There is a place for randomised control trials alongside qualitative studies which can provide insights that could be missed by the use of quantitative data alone. Rigour will always be necessary in any evidence-informed approach but the nature of that rigour will vary according to the type of evidence being weighed. The way in which different professions have been taught to identify and describe evidence becomes an important consideration if a holistic view of children is being taken. There has to be a common language by which children's needs and the aspirations for those children can be described, which transcends professional boundaries and interdisciplinary differences. Only by agreement about the language to be used will it be possible to draw the evidence-informed and developmental/ecological approaches together effectively.

Developing an Integrated Children's System

Work by Ward and her colleagues (Ward forthcoming; Ward and Skuse 2001) has shown that systems currently in use for collecting key information about children's progress are poorly implemented. As a result, information is often collected from sources other than interactions between practitioners and children and families, such as databases held within education departments. Not only is this a fragmentary and unreliable basis for monitoring a child's progress, the information becomes divorced from the individual it concerns. As discussed in Chapter 1, the Integrated Children's System is designed to address this and other issues that have proved problematic in the introduction of outcome measures into children's services. It aims to provide a coherent model for assessment, planning, intervention and reviewing for use with all children in need. It will set out the information to be collected by practitioners in the course of their work with children in need, 'including those looked after away from home, those for whom the plan is adoption and care leavers. It is envisaged that practitioners will be able to enter this information directly into a computerised system with software and visual displays designed to assist them in the organisation of the material' (Department of Health 2000e, p.1). The aim is to produce a seamless methodology that squares the circle between identification and assessment of need on the one hand, and the provision of services and the monitoring of outcomes on the other. Its primary purpose is to support and improve direct work with children and families but its secondary and equally important purpose is to gather information about children on an aggregate basis to assist local and national service planning and delivery.

Obstacles or challenges?

The themes emerging from the chapters suggest a high degree of agreement and support for more structured and systematic approaches to assessment of need, which take a developmental/ecological perspective, and attempt to relate more closely the identification of need with service provision and monitoring outcomes. There are, however, a number of potential obstacles which may impede progress. First, there is the issue of ownership and participation by all those involved; second, the capacity of new technology to deliver more integrated systems; and third, the increasing complexity of the tasks, particularly in an inter-agency context and during a period of public sector reform.

The importance of key stakeholders having a sense of ownership of the systems should not be underestimated. Practitioners, not only in social services, need to be convinced that new systems will help them with their tasks. Nocon and Qureshi (1996) stress the importance of working closely with practitioners to establish the value of information systems 'rather than instituting complex additional procedures which practitioners may see as unnecessary bureaucratic impositions' (p.143). It is important to retain the principles of professional intervention as well as to develop systems to measure performance and outcomes. The systems should be seen to serve the interests of improving the quality of life of children in need and their families. This is graphically illustrated by Ballard (2001) who describes his recent return to practice from a period of living abroad and having been a lecturer in social work in the 1970s and 1980s:

> I found that the social work scene had changed utterly. Children and families were brought together with professionals in large child protection case conferences where private details of their lives were being aired in what was almost a public setting.
>
> Our professional job title had, in some places, been eliminated and replaced by such terms as 'care manager', where the administration of cases seemed more important than the relationship between worker and client…
>
> I recently spent six training days funded by the Quality Protects Programme learning how to fill in an enormously complicated and lengthy form. Its aim is to help us carry out better assessments of children at risk of significant harm. However, the questions did not match the vital issues confronting the children we struggle to help. (p.15)

This is a salutary warning about maintaining the balance between administrative systems and human relationships, and professional autonomy and bureaucracy. We must help practitioners to grasp that, in their interactions with individual children, they need to gather accurate, structured information that allows them to assess how far services are affecting developmental progress and interventions are having the impact intended.

Although discussion of these tensions has focused on practitioners, there are other important stakeholders, namely children themselves and their families, who in the past have often experienced exclusion from the decisions and processes affecting them. Their involvement in a more active and participative way also merits close attention. Creating child-centred services requires commitment and imagination by child welfare agencies. The overview of 24 studies on the implementation of the Children Act 1989 identified some clear messages about the need for agencies to adopt approaches that are sensitive to children's priorities and perspectives (Department of Health 2001c):

> Children are honest and often have very sensible views on what they see as helpful, both to themselves and to their families. If children were allowed to design the nature of meetings, communication with them might improve considerably. If children had a hand in designing the forms that record their lives as looked after children, we might see some changes in how best to safeguard them and promote their welfare. (p.95)

The second major concern must be about the capacity of new technology to support the systems being developed. Technology has advanced rapidly and, as a result, it has been possible for information about children's needs to be collected and data analysed in a way unthinkable less than twenty years ago. Following a programme of inspections of social services departments, the Social Services Inspectorate drew the conclusion that the single most important factor in improving service quality in social care was the use of effective information and communication systems (Social Services Inspectorate 2001a). The Integrated Children's System is designed on the basis of single data entry, in order to eliminate the repetition inherent in the widely used paper-based recording forms, and it will enable data collected about individual children and families to be used for planning at individual and strategic levels. Without the technology underpinning it, the system will not work. Social services departments are worried as to whether there will be sufficient government support to ensure they have access to both appropriate hardware and software. Although the introduction of such a system is designed to help agencies improve the wellbeing of children in need, the technology will be a major determinant of its success.

Finally, but not least, the third key issue is about the impact of increasing complexity and its management. Conceptually, a developmental/ecological perspective in assessment of children's needs extends the scope and interactions of a child's world beyond the immediate family into the wider environment of the community, and beyond a local level into national policies across government. It requires that all agencies with responsibility for children's welfare plan and work together through co-ordinated strategies. In order to make sense of the interactions and transactions in different parts of the child's world, it requires large amounts of data to be collected and subject to multiple levels of analysis. At the same time, the concern for children in need, and the planning expectations which accompany that concern, have now been extended to all vulnerable children. The government recognises that, ideally, planning services should encompass all children and families in a community, undertaken through one co-ordinated exercise (Department of Health 2001k). Although it will not happen immediately, policy makers are making it clear that the move is in that direction. In the meantime, local councils working in partnership with the community and with local service providers are required to produce a plethora of plans at different levels, for different purposes, and under different government guidance (see *The Children's and Young People's Planning 'Bookcase': a Practical Chart from Strategy to Implementation* in Department of Health 2001k, p.8). Against a background of public service reform and organisational turbulence, there must be concern about the capacity of community level agencies to meet the aspirations for service planning and delivery, to improve the outcomes for vulnerable children.

The more complex systems become, the more sophisticated interventions become, the more important it is that children remain central, not only in terms of their participation in key processes, but also in shaping the services intended to promote their wellbeing. Even so, there will still be the need to marry society's obligations towards its most vulnerable children with appropriate services, which in turn requires some evidence of progress. Hence the importance of establishing consistent and, as far as possible, objective measures of outcome. The authors have demonstrated the number of ways in which authorities are seeking to meet these objectives at the population and the individual level.

References

Achenbach, T. (1991a) *Manual for the Child Behaviour Checklist/4–18 and 1991 profile.* Burlington: University of Vermont, Department of Psychiatry.

Achenbach, T. (1991b) *Manual for the Teacher's Report Form and 1991 profile.* Burlington: University of Vermont, Department of Psychiatry.

Achenbach, T. (1991c) *Manual for the Youth Self-Report.* Burlington: University of Vermont, Department of Psychiatry.

Acheson, D. (1998) *Independent Inquiry into Inequalities in Health.* London: The Stationery Office.

Adcock, M. and White, R. (eds.) (1998) *Significant Harm: Its Management and Outcome.* Croydon: Significant Publications.

Alcock, P. and Craig, G. (1998) 'Mapping Local Poverty.' *Monitoring and Evaluation of Anti-Poverty Strategies, Discussion Paper No. 3.* Local Government Anti-Poverty Unit, LGMB.

Aldgate, J. and Bradley, M. (1999) *Supporting Families Through Short-Term Fostering.* London: The Stationery Office.

Aldgate, J. and Tunstill, J. (1995) *Making Sense of Section 17: Implementing Services for Children in Need within the 1989 Children Act.* London: The Stationery Office.

Alexander, Z. (1999) *Study of Black, Asian and Ethnic Minority Issues.* London: Department of Health.

Allen-Meares, P. and Lane, B.A. (1987) 'Grounding Social Work Practice in Theory: Ecosystems.' *Social Casework*, November, 515–521.

American Psychiatric Association (1994) *Diagnostic and Statistical Manual of Mental Disorders.* Fourth edition. Washington, DC: APA.

Andrews, B., Brown, G. and Creasey, L. (1990) 'Intergenerational Links between Psychiatric Disorder in Mothers and Daughters: The Role of Parenting Experiences.' *Journal of Child Psychology and Psychiatry 31*, 7, 1115–1129.

Anthony, E.J. and Cohler, B.J. (eds.) (1987) *The Invulnerable Child.* New York: Guilford Press.

Archer, J. and Lloyd, B. (1995) *Sex and Gender.* Cambridge: Cambridge University Press.

Armstrong, H. (1997) *Refocusing Children's Services Conference, 26 September 1996.* London: Department of Health.

Association of Directors of Social Services (1997) *Refocusing Children's Services.* East Midlands Working Group Report.

Atkinson, A.B. and Hills, J. (eds.) (1998) *Exclusion, Employment and Opportunity, Case Paper No.4.* Centre for Analysis of Social Exclusion, London: LSE.

Audit Commission (1994) *Seen But Not Heard: Co-ordinating Community Child Health and Social Services for Children in Need.* London: The Stationery Office.

Axford, N., Little, M. and Morpeth, L. (2000) *Patterns and Thresholds of Need in an Ordinary Community.* Dartington: Dartington Social Research Unit.

Baldwin, N. and Spencer, N. (1993) 'Deprivation and Child Abuse: Implications for Strategic Planning.' *Children and Society 7*, 4, 357–375.

Baldwin, S. (1996) 'Two Different Worlds? Planning and Delivering Services for Adults and Children.' *Research, Policy and Planning 14*, 1, 62.

Ballard, R. (2001) 'Fewer Meetings and Pointless Rules, Please.' *Community Care*, 9 –15 August, 15.

Bamford, F. and Wolkind, S. (1998) *The Physical and Mental Health of Children in Care: Research Needs.* London: ESRC.

Bebbington, A. and Miles, J. (1989) 'The Background of Children who Enter Local Authority Care.' *British Journal of Social Work 19*, 5, 349–368.

Bee, H. (1995) *The Developing Person.* Sixth edition. London: Harper Row.

Bell, R., Nguyen, T., Warheit, G. and Buhl, M. (1978) 'Service Utilisation, Social Indicator and Citizen Survey Approaches to Human Service Need Assessment.' In C. Atkinson, W. Hargreaves, M. Horowitz and J. Sorenson (eds.) *Evaluation of Human Service Programs.* New York: Academic Press.

Belsky, J. (1993) 'Etiology of Child Maltreatment: A Developmental-ecological Analysis.' *Psychological Bulletin 114*, 3, 413–434.

Belsky, J. and Vondra, J. (1989) 'Lessons from Child Abuse: The Determinants of Parenting'. In D. Cicchetti and V. Carlson (eds.) *Child Maltreatment.* Cambridge: Cambridge University Press.

Ben-Arieh, A. (2001) *Evaluating the Outcomes of Programs vs. Monitoring Wellbeing: A Child Centred Perspective.* Paper presented to the International Research Seminar on 'Outcome-Based Evaluation: A Cross-national Comparison'. Fondazione E Zancan and Boston College, Volterra, 26–30 March.

Bennett, P. and Smith, C. (1992) 'Parents' Attitudes towards Immunisation in Wales According to Socioeconomic Group: A Preliminary Investigation.' *Health Education Journal 51*, 3, 127–131.

Benzeval, M., Judge, K. and Whitehead, M. (eds.) (1995) *Tackling Inequalities in Health.* London: Kings Fund.

Benzeval, M. and Webb, S. (1995) 'Family Poverty and Ill Health.' In M. Benzeval, K. Judge and M. Whitehead (eds.) *Tackling Inequalities in Health.* London: Kings Fund.

Beresford, B. (1996) *Research with Disabled Children: Issues and Methods.* University of York: SPRU.

Berridge, D. (1977) *Foster Care: A Review of Research.* London: The Stationery Office.

Best, R. (1995) 'The Housing Dimension.' In M. Benzeval, K. Judge and M. Whitehead (eds.) *Tackling Inequalities in Health.* London: Kings Fund.

Biehal, N., Clayden J., Stein, M. and Wade, J. (1995) *Moving On: Young People and Leaving Care Schemes.* London: The Stationery Office.

Bifulco, A., Brown, G and Adler, Z. (1991) 'Early Sexual Abuse and Clinical Depression in Adult Life.' *British Journal of Psychiatry 159*, 115–122.

Bifulco, A. and Moran, P. (1998) *Wednesday's Child: Research into Women's Experience of Neglect and Abuse in Childhood and Adult Depression.* London: Routledge.

Black, D. (1990) 'What do Children need from Parents?' *Adoption and Fostering 14*, 1, 43–50.

Blackburn, C. (1991) *Poverty and Health.* Buckingham: Open University.

Blair, T. (1998) *The Third Way: New Politics for a New Century.* London: Fabian Society.

Blair, T. (1999) 'Beveridge Revisited: A Welfare State for the 21st Century.' In R. Walker (ed.) *Ending Child Poverty.* Bristol: Policy.

Blaxter, M. (1981) *The Health of the Children.* London: Heinemann.

Botting, B. and Crawley, R. (1995) 'Trends and Patterns in Childhood Mortality and Morbidity.' In B. Botting (ed.) *The Health of Our Children.* Decennial Supplement Series DS, No.11., London: OPCS.

Bowlby, J. (1969) *Attachment and Loss: Attachment.* New York: Basic Books.

Bowlby, J. (1988) *A Secure Base: Clinical Applications of Attachment Theory.* London: Routledge.

Boyd, W. (1996) *Report of the Confidential Inquiry into Homicides and Suicides by Mentally Ill People.* London: Royal College of Psychiatrists.

Boyden, J., Ling, B. and Myers, W. (1998) *What Works for Working Children.* Sweden: UNICEF/Save the Children Sweden.

Bradshaw, J. (1972) 'The Concept of Need.' *New Society 30 3,* 640–643.

Bradshaw, J. (1990) *Child Poverty and Deprivation in the UK.* London: National Children's Bureau.

Bradshaw, J. (ed.) (2001a) *Poverty: The Outcomes for Children.* London: Family Policy Studies Centre.

Bradshaw, J. (2001b) 'Child Poverty under Labour.' In G. Fimster *Tackling Child Poverty in the UK: An End in Sight?* London: Child Poverty Action Group.

Brandon, M., Thoburn, J., Lewis, A. and Wade, J. (1999) *Safeguarding Children with the Children Act 1989.* London: The Stationery Office.

Brighouse, H. (200) *A Level Playing Field: The reform of private schools.* Policy Report No.52. London: Fabian Society.

Broad, B. and Saunders, L. (1998) 'Involving Young People Leaving Care as Peer Researchers in a Health Research Project: A Learning Experience.' *Research, Policy and Planning 16,* No.1.

Bronfenbrenner, U. (1979) *The Ecology of Human Development.* Cambridge, MA: Harvard University Press.

Brown, G. (1999) 'Equality – Then and Now.' In D. Leonard (ed.) *Crosland and New Labour.* London: Macmillan/Fabian Society.

Brown, G.W. and Harris, T. (1978) *Social Origins of Depression: A Study of Psychiatric Disorders in Women.* London: Tavistock.

Bullock, R., Little, M. and Mount, K. (1995) *Matching Needs and Services.* Dartington: Dartington Social Research Unit.

Butler, I. and Payne, H. (1997) 'The Health of Children Looked After by the Local Authority.' *Adoption and Fostering, 21,* 28–35.

Butler-Sloss, Lord Justice (1998) *Report of the Inquiry into Child Abuse in Cleveland 1997.* London: The Stationery Office.

Cameron, H. (1997) *Early Infant Settlement, Research Implications.* Paper to the Family Proceedings Conference, 12 December. Birmingham.

Campion, M.J. (1995) *Who's Fit to be a Parent?* London: Routledge.

Cantwell, D. (1996) 'Classification of Child and Adolescent Psychopathology.' *Journal of Child Psychology and Psychiatry 37,* 3–12.

Cantwell, D. and Rutter, M. (1994) 'Classification: Conceptual Issues and Substantive Findings.' In M. Rutter, E. Taylor and L. Hersov (eds.) *Child and Adolescent Psychiatry: Modern Approaches.* Oxford: Blackwell.

Carr-Hill, R. (1990) 'The Measurement of Inequalities in Health: Lessons from the British Experience.' *Social Science and Medicine 31,* 3, 393–404.

Carr-Hill, R., Dixon, P., Mannion, R., Rice, N., Rudat, K., Sinclair, R. and Smith, P. (1997) *A Model of the Determinants of Expenditure on Children's Personal Social Services.* York: University of York.

Carr-Hill, R. A., Rice, N. and Smith, P.C. (1999) 'The Determinants of Expenditure on Children's Personal Social Services.' *British Journal of Social Work 29,* 679–706.

Carter, N., Klein, R. and Day, P. (1992) *How Organisations Measure Success.* London: Routledge.

Catlow, R. and Cole, J. (1992) *Fifty Rochdale Records.* Derby: Breedon.

Challis, L., Fuller, R., Henwood, M, Klein, M., Plowden, W., Webb, A., Whittingham, P. and Wistow, G. (1988) *Joint Approaches to Social Policy.* Cambridge: Cambridge University Press.

Cheetham, J., Fuller, R., McIvor, G. and Petch, A. (1992) *Evaluating Social Work Effectiveness.* Buckingham: Open University Press.

Cheung, S.Y. and Buchanan, A. (1997) 'Malaise Scores in Adulthood of Children and Young People who have been in Care.' *Journal of Child Psychology and Psychiatry 38,* 575–580.

Child, D. (1990) *The Essentials of Factor Analysis.* (2nd. ed.) London: Cassell Educational.

ChildLine (1997) *Beyond the Limit: Children who Live with Parental Alcohol Misuse.* London: ChildLine.

Children in Need Assessment Project (1998) *Joint Approaches to Evidence-Based Planning.* Conference Proceedings.

Children's Rights Development Unit (1996) *Checklist for Children: Local Authorities and the United Nations Convention on the Rights of the Child.* London: AMA.

Cicchetti, D., Rogosch, F.A., Lynch, M. and Holt, K.D. (1993) 'Resilience in Maltreated Children.' *Development and Psychopathology 5,* 629–647.

Cleaver, H. (2000) *Fostering Family Contact: A Study of Children, Parents and Foster Carers.* London: The Stationery Office.

Cleaver, H. and Freeman, P. (1995) *Parental Perspectives in Cases of Suspected Child Abuse.* London: The Stationery Office.

Cleaver, H., Meadows, P. and Walker, S. (forthcoming) *A Structured Approach to Assessing Family Capacities and Children's Needs: Report to the Department of Health.* London: Royal Holloway College.

Cleaver, H., Unell, I. and Aldgate, J. (1999) *Children's Needs – Parental Capacity: The Impact of Parental Mental Illness, Problem Alcohol and Drug Use, and Domestic Violence on Children's Development.* London: The Stationery Office.

Collins, P. (2001) 'A Story of Justice.' *Prospect,* May 28–33.

Colton, M., Drury, C. and Williams, N. (1995) *Children in Need: Family Support under the Children Act 1989.* Aldershot: Gower.

Commission on Social Justice (1994) *Social Justice.* London: Vintage.

Committee on Children and Young Persons (1960) *Ingleby Report.* Cmd. 1191. London: The Stationery Office.

Compton, B.R. and Galaway, B. (1989) *Social Work Processes.* California: Wadsworth.

Convery, P. (1997) 'The New Deal Gets Real.' *Working Brief 88,* October, 7–14.

Cook, P.W. (1997) *Abused Men: The Hidden Side of Domestic Violence.* Westport: Praeger.

Cox, A., Puckering, C., Pound, A. and Mills, M. (1987) 'The Impact of Maternal Depression in Young Children.' *Journal of Child Psychiatry 28,* 917–928.

Crosby, D. (1989) 'First Person Account: Growing Up with a Schizophrenic Mother.' *Schizophrenia Bulletin 15,* 3, 507–509.

Cubey, D.C. (1999) 'Deprivation Indexes: Do They Measure Up?' *Research, Policy and Planning 17,* 2, 23–32.

Dale, P., Davies, M., Morrison, T. and Waters, J. (1986) *Dangerous Families: Assessment and Treatment of Child Abuse.* London: Tavistock.

Daniel, P. and Ivatts, J. (1998) *Children and Social Policy.* London: Macmillan.

Dartington Social Research Unit (1995) *Matching Needs and Services: The Audit and Planning of Provision for Children Looked After by Local Authorities.* Dartington: Dartington Social Research Unit.

Dartington Social Research Unit (1996) *Matching Needs and Services.* Dartington: Dartington Social Research Unit.

Dartington Social Research Unit (1998) *Towards a Common Language for Children in Need.* Discussion paper. Dartington: Dartington Social Research Unit.

Dartington Social Research Unit (1999a) *Matching Needs and Services.* Second edition. Dartington: Dartington Social Research Unit and www.dartington-i.org

Dartington Social Research Unit (1999b) *Structure, Culture and Outcome: How to Improve Residential Services for Children.* Dartington: Dartington Social Research Unit.

Dartington Social Research Unit (2001) *Matching Needs and Services – A Dartington-I Practice Tool.* Third edition. Dartington: Dartington Academic Press.

Dartington-I (2001) *Paperwork.* http://www.dartington-i.org/paperwork1.html

Darton, K., Gorman, J. and Sayce, L. (1994) *Eve Fights Back – The Successes of MIND's Stress on Women Campaign.* London: MIND Publications.

Davies, B. (1978) *Universality, Selectivity and Effectiveness in Social Policy.* London: Heinemann Educational.

Davies, C., Morgan, J., Packman, J., Smith, G. and Smith, J. (1994) *A Wider Strategy for Research and Development Relating to Personal Social Services.* London: The Stationery Office.

Davies, H.T.O., Nutley, S.M. and Smith, P.C. (eds.) (2000) *What Works? Evidence-based Policy and Practice in Public Services.* Bristol: The Policy Press.

de Geus, A. (1988) 'Planning as Learning.' *Harvard Business Review*, March/April, 70–74.

Denzin, N. (1978) *Sociological Methods: A Sourcebook.* New York: McGraw Hill.

Department for Education and Skills (2001) *Special Educational Needs: Code of Practice.* Nottingham: DfES Publications.

Department of Health (1988) *Protecting Children. A Guide for Social Workers undertaking a Comprehensive Assessment.* London: The Stationery Office.

Department of Health (1990) *The Care of Children: Principles and Practice in Regulations and Guidance.* London: The Stationery Office.

Department of Health (1991a) *The Children Act 1989 Guidance and Regulations, Volume 2, Family Support, Day Care and Educational Provision for Young Children.* London: The Stationery Office.

Department of Health (1991b) *Child Abuse. A Study of Inquiry Reports 1980 – 1989.* London: The Stationery Office.

Department of Health (1991c) *Patterns and Outcomes in Child Placement.* London: The Stationery Office.

Department of Health (1991d) *The Children Act 1989 Guidance and Regulations, Volume 3, Family Placements.* London: The Stationery Office.

Department of Health (1992) LAC (92) 18, *Children's Services Plans.* London: Department of Health.

Department of Health (1994a) *Children in Need: Report of Issues Arising from Regional Social Services Inspectorate Workshops January – March 1994.* London: Department of Health.

Department of Health (1994b) *Report on the National Survey of Children's Services Plans.* London: Department of Health.

Department of Health (1995a) *Looking After Children: Assessment and Action Records for children aged under 1; 1–2; 3–4; 5–9; 10–14; 15; plus Essential Information Records, Care Plans, Placement Plans and Review Forms.* London: The Stationery Office.

Department of Health (1995b) *Child Protection: Messages from Research.* London: The Stationery Office.

Department of Health (1995c) *Children's Services Plans: An Analysis of Children's Services Plans 1993/94.* London: Department of Health.

Department of Health (1995d) *The Genetics of Common Diseases.* London: Department of Health.

Department of Health (1995e) *Mental Health in England: 1982–1992.* London: Government Statistical Services.

Department of Health (1996a) *Refocusing Children's Services, Conference Proceedings, 26 September 1996.* London: Department of Health.

Department of Health (1996b) *Focus on Teenagers: Research into Practice.* London: The Stationery Office.

Department of Health (1998) *In the Public Interest – Developing a Strategy for Public Participation in the NHS.* London: Department of Health.

Department of Health (1998a) *Modernising Social Services: Promoting Independence, Improving Protection, Raising Standards.* Cm. 4169. London: The Stationery Office.

Department of Health (1998b) *Modernising Health and Social Services: National Priorities Guidance 1999/00 – 2001/02.* London: Department of Health.

Department of Health (1998c) *Partnership in Action: New Opportunities for Joint Working between Health and Social Services: A Discussion Paper.* London: Department of Health.

Department of Health (1998d) *Children and Young People on Child Protection Registers, Year Ending 31 March 1998.* London: Government Statistical Services.

Department of Health (1998e) *Caring for Children Away from Home: Messages From Research.* Chichester: Wiley.

Department of Health (1998f) *Children Looked After by Local Authorities, Year Ending 31 March 1998.* London: Government Statistical Services.

Department of Health (1999a) *The Government's Objectives for Children's Social Services.* London: Department of Health.

Department of Health (1999b) *Performance Assessment Framework for Social Services.* London: Department of Health.

Department of Health (1999c) *Mapping Quality in Children's Services: An Evaluation of Local Responses to the Quality Protects Programme.* London: Department of Health.

Department of Health (1999d) *Planning to Deliver: Inspection of Children's Services Planning.* London: Department of Health.

Department of Health (1999e) *Modern Social Services – A Commitment to Improve: The 8th Annual Report of the Chief Inspector of Social Services.* London: Department of Health.

Department of Health (1999f) *Children Looked After by Local Authorities, Year Ending 31 March 1998.* London: Government Statistical Services.

Department of Health (1999g) *A New Framework for Assessment of Children in Need and Families (consultation document).* London: Department of Health.

Department of Health (1999h) *Adoption Now: Messages from Research.* Chichester: Wiley.

Department of Health (1999i) *National Service Framework for Mental Health: Modern Standards and Service Models.* London: Department of Health.

Department of Health (1999j) *Promoting Health for Looked After Children: A Guide to Health Care Planning, Assessment and Monitoring.* London: Department of Health.

Department of Health (1999k) *Mental Health of Children and Adolescents in Britain.* London: The Stationery Office.

Department of Health (2000a) *Children's Services Planning, Draft Guidance.* London: Department of Health.

Department of Health (2000b) *Children in Need in England: First Results of a Survey of Activity and Expenditure as reported by Local Authority Social Services' Children and Families Teams for a Survey Week in February 2000.* London: Department of Health.

Department of Health (2000c) *Assessing Children in Need and their Families: Practice Guidance.* London: The Stationery Office.

Department of Health (2000d) *Studies which Inform the Development of the Framework for the Assessment of Children in Need and their Families.* London: The Stationery Office.

Department of Health (2000e) *Integrated Children's System: Briefing Paper No. 1.* London: Department of Health.

Department of Health (2001a) *Children's Social Services: Core Information Requirements: Process Model, Version 2.0.* London: Department of Health.

Department of Health (2001b) *Children's Social Services: Core Information Requirements: Data Model, Version 2.0.* London: Department of Health.

Department of Health (2001c) *The Children Act Now: Messages from Research.* London: The Stationery Office.

Department of Health (2001d) *Children (Leaving Care) Act 2000: Regulations and Guidance.* London: The Stationery Office.

Department of Health (2001e) *Outcome Indicators for Looked After Children*. London: Department of Health.

Department of Health (2001f) *Information for Social Care: A Framework for Improving Quality in Social Care through Better Use of Information and Information Technology*. London: Department of Health.

Department of Health (2001g) *Carers and Disabled Children Act 2000: Policy and Practice Guidance*. London: Department of Health.

Department of Health (2001h) *Provision of Therapy for Child Witnesses Prior to a Criminal Trial: Practice Guidance*. London: Department of Health.

Department of Health (2001i) *Safeguarding Children in whom Illness is Fabricated and Induced by Carers with Parental Responsibilities*. London: Department of Health.

Department of Health (2001j) *Fair Access to Care Services: Policy Guidance (consultation draft)*. London: Department of Health.

Department of Health (2001k) *Co-ordinated Service Planning for Vulnerable Children and Young People in England*. http://www.doh.gov.uk/scg/childplan.htm

Department of Health (forthcoming) *Achieving Best Evidence in Criminal Proceedings: Guidance for Vulnerable or Intimidated Witnesses Including Children*.

Department of Health and Cleaver, H. (2000) *Assessment Recording Forms*. London: The Stationery Office.

Department of Health and Department of Education and Employment (1996) *Children's Services Planning Guidance*. Wetherby: Department of Health.

Department of Health and Department for Education and Employment (2000) *Guidance on the Education of Children and Young People in Public Care*. London: Department of Health.

Department of Health and Social Security (1981) *Observation and Assessment: Report of a Working Party*. London: The Stationery Office.

Department of Health and Social Security (1985) *Social Work Decisions in Child Care*. London: The Stationery Office.

Department of Health, Department for Education and Employment, Home Office (2000a) *Framework for the Assessment of Children in Need and Their Families*. London: The Stationery Office.

Department of Health, Department for Education and Employment, Home Office (2000b) *Safeguarding Children Involved in Prostitution: Supplementary Guidance to Working Together to Safeguard Children*. London: Department of Health.

Department of Health, Home Office, Department for Education and Employment (1999) *Working Together to Safeguard Children: A Guide to Inter-Agency Working to Safeguard and Promote the Welfare of Children*. London: The Stationery Office.

Department of Social Security (1997) *Households Below Average Income: A Statistical Analysis 1979–1994/5*. London: The Stationery Office.

Department of Social Security (1998a) *Households Below Average Income, 1979–1996/7*. Leeds: Corporate Documents Services.

Department of Social Security (1998b) *New Ambitions for our Country: A New Contract for Welfare*. Cm. 3805. London: The Stationery Office.

Department of Social Security (1999a) *Households Below Average Income, 1994/5–1997/8*. Leeds: Corporate Documents Services.

Department of Social Security (1999b) *Opportunity for All: Tackling Poverty and Social Exclusion*. Cm. 4445. London: The Stationery Office.

Department of Social Security (2000) *Opportunity for All – One Year On: Making a Difference. Second Annual Report*. Cm. 4865. London: The Stationery Office.

Department of Social Security (2000) *Households Below Average Income, 1994/5 – 1998/9*. London: The Stationery Office.

Department of Social Security (2001) *Households Below Average Income*. London: Stationery Office.

Department of the Environment, Transport and the Regions (1998) *Modern Local Government – In Touch with the People.* London: The Stationery Office.

Department of the Environment, Transport and the Regions (2000) *Regeneration Research Summary No 31: Indices of Deprivation 2000.* London: Department of the Environment, Transport and the Regions.

Department of the Environment, Transport and the Regions (2001) *Local Strategic Partnerships, Government Guidance.* London: Department of the Environment, Transport and the Regions.

Di Leonardi, J. and Yuan, Y. (eds.) (2000) 'Special Issue: Using Administrative Data in Child Welfare.' *Child Welfare League of America Journal of Policy, Practice, and Program,* LXXIX, 5 September/October.

Dobash, R.E. and Dobash, R.P. (1992) *Women, Violence and Social Change.* London: Routledge.

Dominy, N. and Radford, L. (1996) *Domestic Violence in Surrey: Towards an Effective Inter-Agency Response.* London: Roehampton Institutes/Surrey Social Services.

Donovan, N. (ed.) (1998) *Second Chances: Exclusion from School and Equality of Opportunity.* London: New Policy Institute.

Dorling, D. (1993) 'Children in Need.' *Roof,* September/October.

Downey, G. and Coyne, J. C. (1990) 'Children of Depressed Parents: An Integrative Review.' *Psychological Bulletin 108,* 50–76.

Doyal, L. and Gough, I. (1991) *A Theory of Human Need.* Basingstoke: Macmillan.

Driver, S. and Martell, L. (1998) *New Labour: Politics after Thatcherism.* Cambridge: Polity.

Dunn, B. (1993) 'Growing Up with a Schizophrenic Mother: A Retrospective Study.' *American Journal of Orthopsychiatry 63,* 2, 177–189.

Eames, M., Ben-Shlomo, Y. and Marmot, M. (1993) 'Social Deprivation and Premature Mortality: Regional Comparisons across England.' *British Medical Journal 307,* 1099–1102.

Elander, J. and Rutter, M. (1996) 'Use and Development of the Rutter Parents' and Teachers' Scales.' *International Journal of Methods in Psychiatric Research 6,* 63–78.

Erskine, A. (1996) 'The Burden of Risk.' *Social Policy and Administration 30,* 2.

Erwin, P. (1993) *Friendship and Peer Relations in Children.* London: Wiley.

Everitt, A. and Hardiker, P. (1996) *Evaluation for Good Practice.* Basingstoke: Macmillan.

Fajerman, L., Jarret, M. and Sutton, F. (2000) *Children as Partners in Planning.* London: Save the Children.

Falkov, A. (1996) *Department of Health Study of Working Together 'Part 8' Reports: Fatal Child Abuse and Parental Psychiatric Disorder.* Department of Health, ACPC Series Report No. 1.

Falkov, A. (1997) *Parental Psychiatric Disorder and Child Maltreatment – Part II: Extent and Nature of the Association. Highlight Series No. 149.* London: National Children's Bureau.

Falkov, A. (ed.) (1998) *Crossing Bridges: Training Resources for Working with Mentally Ill Parents and their Children: A Reader.* Brighton: Pavilion Publishing.

Falkov, A., Murphy, M. and Antweiler, U. (Forthcoming) *The 'Families And Mental Illness Initiative' – An Interagency Survey .*

Feighner, J., Robins, E., Guze, S.B., Woodruff, R.A., Winokur, G. and Munoz, R. (1972) 'Diagnostic Criteria for use in Psychiatric Research.' *Archives of General Psychiatry 26,* 57–63.

Fergusson, D., Horwood, L., and Lynskey, M. (1994) 'Structure of DSM-III-R Criteria for Disruptive Childhood Behaviours: Confirmatory Factor Models.' *Journal of Child Psychology and Psychiatry 33,* 1145–1154.

Field, F. (1995) *Making Welfare Work: Reconstructing Welfare for the Millennium.* London: Institute of Community Studies.

Flynn, R. and Biro, C. (1998) 'Comparing Developmental Outcomes for Children in Care with those for Other Children in Canada.' *Assessing Outcome in Childcare: An International Perspective. Special Issue Children and Society 12,* 228–233.

Fonagy, P., Steele, H and Steele, M. (1991) 'Maternal Representations of Attachment during Pregnancy Predict the Organisation of Infant–Mother Attachment at Age One.' *Child Development 62*, 891–905.

Fonagy, P., Steele, M., Steele, H., Higgett, A. and Targett, M. (1994) 'The Theory and Practice of Resilience: Emmanuel Millar memorial lecture.' *Journal of Child Psychology and Psychiatry 35*, 2, 231–257.

Forrest, R. and Kearns, A. (1999) *Joined-Up Places? Social Cohesion and Neighbourhood Regeneration.* York: Joseph Rowntree Foundation.

Forrester, R., (2000) 'Where the Money Goes.' *Society, The Guardian,* February 23.

Fowler, R.D. (ed.) (1996) 'Vulnerability and Resilience.' *The American Psychologist, 51*, 1, 22–27.

France, A., (2000) *Youth Researching Youth: The Triumph and Success Peer Research Project.* London: National Youth Agency.

France, A., (2001) 'Involving communities in the evaluation of programmes with "at risk" children and young people. Made to measure? Evaluating Community Initiatives for Children.' *Children and Society Special Issue 15*, 1, 39–45.

France, A., and Crowe, I., (2001) *Interim Report on the Evaluation of Three Communities that Care Demonstration Programmes in the UK.* York: Joseph Rowntree Foundation.

Franklin, A., and Madge, N., (2000) *In Our View: Children, Teenagers and Parents Talk about Services for Young People.* London: National Children's Bureau.

Fraser, M. (1989) 'Talking about Needs: Interpretive Contests as Political Conflicts in Welfare State Societies.' *Ethics 99*, 291–313.

Frawley, W., Piatetsky-Shapiro, G. and Matheus, C. (1992) 'Knowledge Discovery in Databases: An Overview.' *AI Magazine,* Fall, 213–228.

Freud, A. (1965) *Normality and Pathology in Childhood.* New York: International Universities Press.

Frost, N. and Stein, M. (1989) *The Politics of Child Welfare: Inequality, Power and Change.* Hemel Hempstead: Harvester Wheatsheaf.

Galbraith, J.K. (1993) *The Culture of Contentment.* Harmondsworth: Penguin.

Garbarino, J. (1982) *Children and Families in the Social Environment.* New York: Aldine.

Garmezy, N. (1993) 'Children in Poverty: Resilience Despite Risk.' *Psychiatry 56*, 127–136.

Garnett, L. (1992) *Leaving Care and After.* London: National Children's Bureau.

Gaudin, J.M., Shilton, P., Kilpatrick, A.C. and Polansky, N.A. (1996) 'Family Functioning in Neglectful Families.' *Child Abuse and Neglect 20*, 4, 363–377.

Ghate, D. 'Community based evaluations in the UK. Made to Measure? Evaluating Community Initiatives for Children.' *Special Issue Children and Society 15*, 1, 23–32.

Giddens, A. (1998) *The Third Way.* Cambridge: Polity.

Gilligan, R. (2001) 'Promoting positive outcomes for children in need: the assessment of positive factors.' In J. Horwarth (ed.) *The Child's World.* London: Jessica Kingsley.

Glaser, D. and Prior, V., (1997) 'Is the Term Child Protection applicable to Emotional Abuse?' *Child Abuse Review 6*, 315–329.

Glennerster, H. (1995) *British Social Policy Since 1945.* Oxford: Blackwell.

Glennester, H. (1983) *Planning for Priority Groups.* Oxford: Martin Robertson.

Goldman, H. (1982) 'Mental Illness and Family Burden: A Public Health Perspective.' *Hospital and Community Psychiatry 33*, 7, 557–560.

Goodman, A., Johnson, P. and Webb, S. (1997) *Inequality in the UK.* Oxford: Oxford University Press.

Goodman, R. (1997) 'The Strengths and Difficulties Questionnaire: A Research Note.' *Journal of Child Psychology and Psychiatry and Allied Disciplines 38*, 5, 581–586.

Goodman, R. (1999) 'The Extended Version of the Strengths and Difficulties Questionnaire as a Guide to Child Psychiatric Caseness and Consequent Burden.' *Journal of Child Psychology and Psychiatry and Allied Disciplines 40*, 5, 791–799.

Goodman, R., Meltzer, H. and Bailey, V. (1998) 'The Strengths and Difficulties Questionnaire: A Pilot Study on the Validity of the Self-report Version.' *European Child and Adolescent Psychiatry 7*, 3, 125–130.

Goodman, R. and Scott, S. (1999) 'Comparing the Strengths and Difficulties Questionnaire and the Child Behaviour Checklist: Is Small Beautiful?' *Journal of Abnormal Child Psychology 27*, 1, 17–24.

Gopfert, M., Webster, J. and Seeman M.V. (eds.) (1996) *Parental Psychiatric Disorder: Distressed Parents and Their Families.* Cambridge: Cambridge University Press.

Gordon, D. and Loughran, F. (1997) 'Child Poverty and Needs Based Allocation.' *Research, Policy and Planning 15*, 3, 28–38.

Gordon, D., Shaw, M., Dorling, D. and Davey-Smith, G. (eds.) (1999) *Inequalities in Health: The Evidence.* Policy: Bristol.

Gough, I. (1992) 'What are human needs?' In J. Percy-Smith and I. Anderson *Understanding Local Needs.* Leeds: Institute of Public Policy Research.

Gould, P. (1998) *The Unfinished Revolution.* London: Little, Brown and Co.

Graham, H. (1984) *Women, Health and the Family.* Brighton: Wheatsheaf.

Gregg, P., Harkness, S. and Machin, S. (1999) *Child Development and Family Income.* York: Joseph Rowntree Foundation.

Gregory, I., Southall, H. and Dorling, D. (2000) 'A Century of Poverty in England and Wales, 1989–1998: A Geographical Analysis.' In J. Bradshaw and R. Sainsbury (eds.) *Researching Poverty.* Aldershot: Ashgate.

Grunbaum, L. and Gammeltoft, M. (1993) 'Young Children of Schizophrenic Mothers: Difficulties of Intervention.' *American Journal of Orthopsychiatry 63*, 1, 16–27.

Guralnick, M.J. (ed.) (1997) *The Effectiveness of Early Intervention.* Baltimore: P.H. Brookes.

Hair, J., Anderson, R., Tatham, R. and Black, W. (1998) *Multivariate Data Analysis.* London: Prentice-Hall.

Hallett, C. and Stevenson, O. (1978) *Child Abuse: Aspects of Inter-Professional Co-operation.* Oxford: Blackwell.

Halpern, D. and Mikosz, D. (eds.) (1998) *The Third Way: Summary of the Nexus On-Line Discussion.* London: Nexus.

Halsey, A.H., Heath, A.F. and Judge, J. (1980) *Origins and Destinations.* Oxford: Clarendon.

Halsey, A.H., Lauder, H., Brown, P. and Wells, A.S. (eds.) (1997) *Education, Culture, Economy and Society.* Oxford: Oxford University Press.

Hamilton, M.A. and Orme, J.G. (1990) 'Examining the Construct Validity of Three Parenting Knowledge Measures using LISREL.' *Social Services Review*, March, 129–143.

Hardiker, P. (1994) 'Thinking and Practising otherwise: Disability and Child Abuse.' *Disability and Society 9*, 2, 257–264.

Hardiker, P. (1997) 'Children Still in Need, Indeed! Prevention Across Five Decades.' In O. Stevenson (ed.) *Child Welfare in the UK.* Oxford: Blackwell.

Hardiker, P. (1999) 'Children First: Bringing Disabled Children into the Child Welfare Fold.' *Practice 11*, 4.

Hardiker, P. and Barker, M. (1999) 'Implementing the New Community Care: The Role of Social Work Practice.' *Health and Social Care in the Community* 7, 2, 205–215.

Hardiker, P. and Everitt, A. (1996) *Evaluating for Good Practice.* Basingstoke: Macmillan.

Hardiker, P., Exton, K. and Barker, M. (1991a) *Policies and Practices in Preventive Childcare.* Aldershot: Avebury.

Hardiker, P., Exton, K. and Barker, M. (1991b) 'The Social Policy Contexts of Prevention in Childcare.' *British Journal of Social Work 21*, 4, 341–359.

Hardiker, P., Exton, K. and Barker, M. (1996) 'The Prevention of Child Abuse: A Framework for Analysing Services.' *Childhood Matters: Report of the National Commission of Inquiry into the Prevention of Child Abuse*, Vol. 2. London: The Stationery Office.

Hardiker, P., Seden, J. and Barker, M. (1995) 'Children First: Protection and Prevention in Services to Disabled Children.' *Child Care in Practice: Northern Ireland Journal of Multi-Disciplinary Child Care Practice 2*, 1, 1–17, Part I and *2*, 2, 1–9, Part II.

Harris, J., Sellers, T. and Westerby, M. (1997) *Developing a Whole Community Approach to Teenage Sexual Health. Participatory Appraisal in Hull.* Hull: University of Hull.

Harris, T., Brown, G. and Bifulco, A. (1987) 'Loss of Parent in Childhood and Adult Psychiatric Disorder: The Role of Social Class Position and Premarital Pregnancy.' *Psychological Medicine 17*, 163–183.

Hearn, B. and Sinclair, R. (1998) 'How effective are Children's Services Plans?' In D. Utting (ed.) *Children's Services Now and in the Future.* London: National Children's Bureau and Joseph Rowntree Trust.

Heywood, J.S. (1978) *Children in Care.* Third edition. London: Routledge and Kegan Paul.

Hill, M. (1999) 'Effective Professional Intervention in Children's Lives.' In M. Hill (ed.) *Effective Ways of Working with Children and their Families.* London: Jessica Kingsley.

Hill, M., Laybourn, A. and Borland, M. (1996) 'Engaging with Primary-aged Children about their Emotions and Well Being: Methodological Considerations.' *Children and Society 10*, 2.

Hogan, C.D. (1999) *Vermont Communities Count. Using Results to Strengthen Services for Children and Families.* Baltimore: Annie E. Casey Foundation.

Hogan, D.M. (1998) 'The Psychological Development and Welfare of Children of Opiate and Cocaine Users: Review and Research Needs.' *Journal of Child Psychology and Psychiatry 39*, 5, 609–620.

Home Office (1994) *Criminal Statistics for England and Wales 1993.* Cm. 2680. London: The Stationery Office.

Home Office (1998) *Supporting Families.* London: The Stationery Office.

Home Office (2001) *Prison Statistics England and Wales 2000.* London: The Stationery Office.

Horwath, J. (ed.) (2001) *The Child's World: Assessing Children in Need.* London: Jessica Kingsley.

Howarth, C., Kenway, P., Palmer, G and Street, C. (1998) *Monitoring Poverty and Social Exclusion.* York: Joseph Rowntree Foundation.

Howe, D. (1995) *Attachment Theory for Social Workers.* Basingstoke: MacMillan.

Howe, D., Brandon, M., Hinings, D. and Schofield, G. (1999) *Attachment Theory, Child Maltreatment and Family Support: A Practice and Assessment Model.* Basingstoke: MacMillan.

Hudson, B. (1987) 'Collaboration in Social Welfare: A Framework for Analysis.' *Policy and Politics 15*, 175–182.

Hudson, B., Hardy, B, Henwood, M. and Wistow, G. (1999) 'In Pursuit of Inter-agency Collaboration in the Public Sector: What is the Contribution of Theory and Research?' *Public Management: An International Journal of Research and Theory 1*, 2, 235–260.

Ignatieff, Michael (1984) *The Needs of Strangers.* London: Vintage.

Innes, M. (1998) *Guardian*, October 27.

Isaac, B., Minty, E.B. and Morrison, R.M. (1986) 'Children in Care – The Association with Mental Disorder in Parents.' *British Journal of Social Work 16*, 325–329.

Jacelon, J.S. (1997) 'The Trait and Process of Resilience.' *Journal of Advanced Nursing 25*, 123–129.

Jack, G. (1997) 'An Ecological Approach to Social Work with Children and Families.' *Child and Family Social Work 2*, 109–120.

Jack, G. (2001) 'Ecological perspectives in assessing children and families.' In J. Horwath (ed.) *The Child's World: Assessing Children in Need.* London: Jessica Kingsley Publishers.

Jackson, S. (1989) 'Education of children in care.' In B. Kahan (ed.) *Child Care Research, Policy and Practice.* London: Hodder and Stoughton.

Jacobs, M. (1998) *The Presenting Past.* Buckingham: Open University Press.

Jenkins, J.M. and Smith, M.A. (1990) 'Factors Protecting Children Living in Disharmonious Homes: Maternal Reports.' *Journal of the American Academy of Child Adolescent Psychiatry 29,* 1, 60–69.

Jones, D. (1987) 'The Untreatable Family.' *Child Abuse and Neglect,* 409–420.

Jones, D. (1991) 'The Effectiveness of Intervention.' In M. Adcock, R. White and A. Hollows (eds.) *Significant Harm.* Croydon: Significant Publications.

Jones, D. (1997) 'Treatment of the Child and the Family where Child Abuse or Neglect has Occurred.' In R.Helfer, R. Kempe and R. Krugman (eds.) *The Battered Child.* Fifth edition. Chicago: University of Chicago Press.

Jones, D. (2001) 'The Assessment of Parental Capacity.' In J. Horwath (ed.) *The Child's World: Assessing Children in Need.* London: Jessica Kingsley.

Jones, D.P.H. and Ramchandani, P. (1999) *Child Sexual Abuse: Informing Practice from Research.* Oxon: Radcliffe Medical Press.

Jones, H., Clark, R., Kufeldt, K. and Norman, M. (1998) 'Looking After Children: Assessing Outcomes in Child Care: The Experience of Implementation.' *Assessing Outcome in Child Care: An International Perspective. Special Edition Children and Society 12,* 3, 212–222. (1995) *Joseph Rowntree Foundation Inquiry into Income and Wealth* York: Joseph Rowntree Foundation.

Joseph Rowentree Foundation (1995). *Joseph Rowntree Foundation Inquiry into Income and Health.* York: Joseph Rowntree Foundation.

Katz, I. (1997) *Current Issues in Comprehensive Assessment.* London: NSPCC.

Keane, A. (1983) 'Behavioural Problems Among Long-term Foster Children.' *Adoption and Fostering 7,* 3.

Kellner, P. (1999) 'Bring Back the E-word.' *New Statesman* 13 December.

Kelmer Pringle, M. (1980) *The Needs of Children.* London: Hutchinson.

Kinard, E.M. (1998) 'Psychological Issues in Assessing Resilience in Maltreated Children.' *Child Abuse and Neglect 22,* 7, 669–677.

Knight, J. (1995) 'The Resilience of Children.' *Probation Journal 42,* 3, 156–159.

Kufeldt, K., Vachon, J. and Simard, M. (2000) *Looking After Children in Canada: Final Report.* New Brunswick: Maria Fergusson Centre, University of New Brunswick.

Kumar, V. (1993) *Poverty and Inequality in the UK: The Effects on Children.* London: National Children's Bureau.

Labour Party (1997) *New Labour: Because Britain Deserves Better.* London: Labour Party.

Labour Party (2001) *Ambitions for Britain.* London: Labour Party.

Lambert, L., Essen, J. and Head, J. (1977) 'Variations in Behaviour Ratings of Children who have been in Care.' *Journal of Child Psychology and Psychiatry 18,* 335–346.

Landerman, R., George, L. and Blazer, D. (1991) 'Adult Vulnerability for Psychiatric Disorders: Interactive Effects of Negative Childhood Experiences and Recent Stress.' *Journal of Nervous and Mental Disease 179,* 11, 656–663.

Laucht, M., Esser, G. and Schmidt, M. (1994) 'Parental Mental Disorder and Early Child Development.' *European Child and Adolescent Psychiatry 3,* 125–137.

Layard, R. (1997) *What Labour Can Do.* London: Warner.

Le Grand, J. (1982) *The Strategy of Equality.* London: Allen and Unwin.

Lewis, J. (2001) *The Role of Evidence in Practice Change.* Paper presented to the Health Development Agency/Kings Fund Conference on Evidence into Practice, 3 April.

Little, M. and Mount, K. (1999) *Prevention and Early Intervention with Children in Need.* Aldershot: Ashgate Publishing Ltd.

Little, M., Ryan, M. and Tunnard, J. (1999) *Matching Needs and Services for Children Supported at Home.* Dartington: Dartington Social Research Unit.

Lupton, C., Parves, K., North, N. and Lacey, D. (1997) *The Role of Health Professionals in the Child Protection Process.* Portsmouth: University of Portsmouth.

Luthar, S. and Zigler, E. (1991) 'Vulnerability and Competence: A Review of Research on Resilience in Childhood.' *American Journal of Orthopsychiatry 61,* 1, 6–23.

Lyons, R. A., Sibert, J., McCabe, M. (1999) 'Injury Surveillance Programmes, Ethics and the Data Protection Act.' *British Medical Journal 319,* 372–374.

Macdonald G. (1999) 'Evidence Based Social Care: Wheels off the Runway?' *Public Money and Management 19,* 1, 25–32.

Macfarlane, A and Mugford, M. (1984) *Birth Counts: Statistics of Pregnancy and Childbirth.* London: The Stationery Office.

Malek, M. (1993) *Passing the Buck: Institutional Responses to Controlling Children with Difficult Behaviour.* London: The Children's Society.

Maluccio, A. (ed.) (1981) *Promoting Competence in Clients: A New/Old Approach to Social Work Practice.* New York: The Free Press.

Mandelson, P. (1997) *Labour's Next Steps: Tackling Social Exclusion.* London: Fabian Society.

Marchant, R., Jones, M., Giles, A. and Julyan, A. (1999) *Listening on All Channels: Consulting with Disabled Children.* Brighton: Triangle.

Maslow, A.H. (1943) 'A Theory of Human Motivation.' *Psychological Review 50,* 370–378.

Maslow, A.H. (1968) *Towards a Psychology of Being.* Second edition. New York: Van Nostrad Reinhold.

Masten, A.S. and Coatsworth, J.D. (1998) 'Development of Competence in Favourable and Unfavourable Environments.' *American Psychologist 53,* 2, 205–220.

McCann, J., James, A., Wilson, S. and Dunn, G. (1996) 'Prevalence of Psychiatric Disorders in Young People in the Care System.' *British Medical Journal 313,* 1529–1530.

Meadows, P. (1996) 'I Spend, Therefore I am.' *Prospect,* December, 14–15.

Middleton, S., Ashworth, K. and Braithwaite, I. (1997) *Small Fortunes: Spending on Children, Childhood Poverty and Parental Sacrifice.* York: Joseph Rowntree Foundation.

Milham, S., Bullock, R., Hosie, K. and Haak, M. (1986) *Lost in Care: The Problem of Maintaining Links between Children in Care and their Families.* Aldershot: Gower.

Miller, I.W., Kabacoff, R.I., Epstein, N.B., Bishop, D.S., Keitner, G.I., Baldwin, I.M. and Van der Spey, N.I.J. (1994) 'The Development of a Clinical Rating Scale for the McMaster Model of Family Functioning.' *Family Process 33,* 1, 53–65.

Moffitt, T. (1993) 'Adolescence-limited and Life-course-persistent Anti-social Behaviour: A Developmental Taxonomy.' *Psychological Review 100,* 674–701.

Moffitt, T.E. and Caspi, A. (1998) 'Implications of Violence between Intimate Partners for Child Psychologists and Psychiatrists.' *Journal of Child Psychology and Psychiatry 39,* 2, 137–144.

Mooney, J. (1994) *The Hidden Figure: Domestic Violence in North London.* London: Islington Council.

Morton, N. and Browne, K.D. (1998) 'Theory and Observation of Attachment and its Relation to Child Maltreatment: A Review.' *Child Abuse and Neglect 22,* 11, 1093–1104.

Moss, P. and Petrie, P. (1996) *Time for a New Approach: A Discussion Paper.* London: Thomas Coram Research Unit.

Moyers, S. (1996) *Looking After Children: Audit of Implementation in Year One (1995–6).* Dartington: Dartington Social Research Unit.

Moyers, S. and Mason, A. (1995) 'Identifying standards of parenting.' In H. Ward (ed.) *Looking After Children: Research into Practice.* London: The Stationery Office.

Murphey, D.A. (2000) 'Citizen Engagement as Well Being.' Unpublished paper. Vermont Agency of Human Services.

Murray, L. and Cooper, P.J. (1997) 'Post-partum Depression and Child Development.' *Psychological Medicine 27*, 253–260.

National Statistics (2001) *Neighbourhood Statistics.* Http://www.statistics.gov.uk/neighbourhood/home.asp

NCH Action For Children (1994) *The Hidden Victims: Children and Domestic Violence.* London: NCH Action for Children.

Nelson, D. (1996) *The Building Blocks of Neighbourhoods that Support Families.* Paper to a seminar of the International Initiative, Baltimore, USA.

Netten, A. and Curtis, L. (2000) *Unit Costs of Health and Social Care.* Canterbury: PSSRU.

Newman, T. (1999) 'Evidence-based Childcare Practice.' Highlight no. 170. London: National Children's Bureau.

Nicholson, D and Ward, H. (1999) *Looking After Children: Good Parenting. Good Outcomes: Report of an Audit of Implementation in Eleven Local Authorities in Wales.* Loughborough: Loughborough University.

Nicholson, J., Geller, J., Fisher, W. and Dion, G. (1993) 'State Policies and Programs that Address the Needs of Mentally Ill Mothers in the Public Sector.' *Hospital and Community Psychiatry 44*, 5, 484–489.

Nissan, D. and Le Grand, J. (2000) *A Capital Idea: Start-up Grants for Young People.* Policy Report No. 49. London: Fabian Society.

Noble, M. and Smith, T. (1994) 'Children in Need: Using Geographical Information Systems to Inform Strategic Planning for Social Service Provision.' *Children and Society 8*, 4, 360–376.

Nocon, A. and Qureshi, H. (1996) *Outcomes of Community Care for Users and Carers.* Buckingham: Open University Press.

O'Driscoll, C. (1993) 'The TAPS Project 7: Mental Hospital Closure – A Literature Review on Outcome Studies and Evaluative Techniques.' *British Journal of Psychiatry 162*, (suppl 19) 7–17.

Office for National Statistics (1997) *Living in Britain: Preliminary Results from the 1996 General Household Survey: A Survey carried out by Social Services Division/Office for National Statistics.* London: The Stationery Office.

Office for National Statistics (1999) *Living in Britain: Results from the 1997 General Household Survey.* London: Stationery Office.

Office of Population and Censuses and Surveys (1996) *The Prevalence of Psychiatric Morbidity among Adults Living in Private Households.* London: The Stationery Office.

Oldfield, N. and Yu, A. (1993) *The Cost of a Child: Living Standards for the 1990s.* London: Child Poverty Action Group.

Oliver, J. E. (1985) 'Successive Generations of Child Maltreatment: Social and Medical Disorders in the Parents.' *British Journal of Psychiatry 147*, 484–490.

Oliver, J. E. (1988) 'Successive Generations of Child Maltreatment: The Children.' *British Journal of Psychiatry 153*, 543–553.

Oppenheim, C. and Harker, L. (1996) *Poverty – The Facts.* London: Child Poverty Action Group.

Orford, J. and Velleman, R. (1990) 'Offspring of Parents with Drinking Problems: Drinking and Drug-taking as Young Adults.' *British Journal of Addiction 85*, 779–794.

Packman, J., Randall, J. and Jacques, N. (1985) *Who Needs Care?* Blackwell: Oxford.

Page, R.M. (1991) 'Social welfare since the war.' In N. Crafts and N. Woodward (eds.) *The British Economy Since 1945.* Oxford: Oxford University Press.

Page, R.M. (1999) 'Social policy.' In M. Haralambos (ed.) *New Developments in Sociology*, vol.15. St Helens: Causeway.

Page, R. M. and Silburn, R. (eds.) (1998) *British Social Welfare in the Twentieth Century.* Basingstoke: MacMillan.

Paris, J. and Frank, H. (1989) 'Perceptions of Parental Bonding in Borderline Patients.' *American Journal of Psychiatry 146,* 1498–1499.

Parker, R., Ward, H., Jackson, S., Aldgate, J. and Wedge, P. (1991) *Looking After Children: Assessing Outcomes in Child Care.* London: The Stationery Office.

Parsons, D. (1910) *Report on the Condition of the Children who are in Receipt of the Various forms of Poor Relief in Certain Parishes in Scotland,* pp.1910. vol .LII: Royal Commission on the Poor Laws.

Peel, M. (1997) *Looking After Children: Audit of Implementation in Year Two (1996–7).* Leicester: University of Leicester.

Peel, M. and Ward, H. (1997) *The Refocusing Children's Services Initiative: A Literature Review.* Unpublished report. Leicester: Leicester University.

Peel, M. and Ward, H. (2000) *North Lincolnshire Parenting Project: Final Report.* Loughborough: Loughborough University.

Percy-Smith J. (1996) *Needs Assessments in Public Policy.* Buckingham: Open University Press.

Percy-Smith, J. and Sanderson, I. (1992) *Understanding Local Need.* Leeds: Institute of Public Policy Research.

Perry, B.D. (1993) 'Neurodevelopment and the Neurophysiology of Trauma.' *The Advisor.* American Professional Society on the Abuse of Children *6,* 1, 14–19.

Phillimore, P., Beattie, A. and Townsend. P. (1994) 'Widening Inequality of Health in Northern England, 1981–91.' *British Medical Journal 308,* 1125–1128.

Piachaud, D. (1979) *The Cost of a Child.* London: Child Poverty Action Group.

Piachaud, D. (1981) *Children and Poverty.* Poverty Pamphlet No.43. London: Child Poverty Action Group.

Piachaud, D. (1984) *Round About Fifty Hours a Week.* London: Child Poverty Action Group.

Piachaud, D. (1991) 'Revitalising Social Policy.' *The Political Quarterly 62,* 204–224.

Piachaud, D. and Sutherland, H. (2001) 'Child poverty and the New Labour Government.' *Journal of Social Policy 30,* 1, 95–118.

Pinnock, M. and Soper, M. (1996) *Putting Children on the Map.* Paper to the Association of Geographical Information Annual Conference (1996): Children in Need Assessment Project.

Plant, R., Lesser, H. and Taylor-Gooby, P. (1980) *Political Philosophy and Social Welfare: Essays on the Normative Basis of Welfare Provision.* London: Routledge.

Poor Law Commissioners (1834) *Report from the Commissioners on the Administration and Practical Operation of the Poor Laws.* pp.1834, Vol. XXXVI.

Powell, M. (ed.) (1999) *New Labour, New Welfare State?* Bristol: Policy.

Power, A. (1987) *Property Before People: The Management of Twentieth Century Council Housing.* London: Allen and Unwin.

Power, S., Whitty, G. and Youdell, D. (1995) *No Place to Learn – Homelessness and Education.* London: Shelter.

Prilleltensky, I. and Nelson, G. (2000) 'Promoting Child and Family Wellness: Priorities for Psychological and Social Interventions.' *Journal of Community and Applied Social Psychology 10,* 85–105.

Pugh, E. (1968) *Social Work in Child Care.* London: Routledge and Kegan Paul.

Puttnam, F. (1998) 'The Effect of Maltreatment on Early Brain Development.' APSAC Conference.

Quadrel, M.J., Fischhoff, B. and Davis, W. (1993) 'Adolescent (in)vulnerability.' *Journal of the American Psychological Association,* February, 102–116.

Queralt, M and Witte, A.D. (1998) 'A Map for You? Geographic Information Systems in the Social Services.' *Social Work 43,* 455–468.

Quinton, D. (1996) 'Cultural and Community Influences.' In M. Rutter and D. Hay (eds.) *Development Through Life.* London: Blackwell.

Quinton, D., Pickles, A., Maughan, B. and Rutter, M. (1993) 'Partners, Peers and Pathways: Assortative Pairing and Continuities in Conduct Disorder.' *Development and Psychopathology. 5,* 763–783.

Quinton, D., Rushton, A., Dance, C. and Mayes, D. (1998) *Joining New Families: A Study of Adoption and Fostering in Middle Childhood.* London: John Wiley.

Quinton, D. and Rutter, M. (1985) 'Family Pathology and Child Psychiatric Disorder: A Four Year Prospective Study.' In A.R. Nicol (ed.) *Longitudinal Studies in Child Psychology and Psychiatry.* London: John Wiley and Sons Ltd.

Quinton, D. and Rutter, M. (1988) *Parenting Breakdown: The Making and Breaking of Intergenerational Links.* Aldershot: Avebury.

Quinton, D., Rutter, M. and Gulliver, L. (1990) 'Continuities in Psychiatric Disorders from Childhood to Adulthood in the Children of Psychiatric Patients.' In L. Robins and M. Rutter (eds.) *Straight and Devious Pathways from Childhood to Adulthood.* New York: Cambridge University Press.

Reich, R. (1999) 'Give £50,000 to Every Boy and Girl.' *New Statesman,* 14 June, 15–16.

Rickford, F. (2001) 'Right up your street.' *Community Care,* 18–24 January, 18–19.

Rolf, J., Masten, A.S., Cicchetti, D., Nuechterlein, K. and Weintraub, S. (eds.) (1990) *Risk and Protector Factors in the Development of Psychopathology.* Cambridge University Press.

Rose, W. (1992) 'Foreword.' In J. Gibbons (ed.) *The Children Act 1989 and Family Support: Principles into Practice.* London: The Stationery Office.

Rose, W. and Aldgate, J. (2000) 'Knowledge Underpinning the Assessment Framework.' In Department of Health *Assessing Children in Need and their Families: Practice Guidance.* London: The Stationery Office.

Rosenstein, P. (1995) 'Parental Levels of Empathy as Related to Risk Assessment in Child Protective Services.' *Child Abuse and Neglect 19,* 11, 1349–1360.

Rowe, J., Hundleby, M. and Garnett, L. (1989) *Child Care Now.* Research Series 6. London: British Agencies for Adoption and Fostering.

Russell, P. (1994) Review of Thompson, T. and Hupp, S. C. (eds.) *Saving Children at Risk: Poverty and Disability.* London: Sage.

Rutter, M (1966) *Children of Sick Parents: An Environmental and Psychiatric Study.* Institute of Psychiatry Maudsley Monographs No. 16. London: Oxford University Press.

Rutter, M. (1987) 'Psychosocial Resilience and Protective Mechanisms.' *American Journal of Orthopsychiatry 57,* 3, 316–329.

Rutter, M. (1989) 'Pathways from Childhood to Adult Life.' *Journal of Child Psychology and Psychiatry 30,* 23–51.

Rutter, M. (1990) 'Psychosocial Resilience and Protective Mechanisms.' In J. Rolf, A.S. Masten, D. Cicchetti, K.H. Neuchterlein and S. Weintraub (eds.) *Risk and Protective Factors in the Development of Psychopathology,* 79–101. New York: Cambridge University Press.

Rutter, M. (1992) 'Resilience.' *Journal of Adolescent Health 13,* 451–460.

Rutter, M. (1993) 'Resilience: Some Conceptual Considerations.' *Journal of Adolescent Health 14,* 626–631.

Rutter, M. (1999) 'Resilience Concepts and Findings: Implications for Family Therapy.' *Journal of Family Therapy 21,* 119–144.

Rutter, M. and Day, D. (eds.) (1996) *Development Through Life.* London: Blackwell.

Rutter, M. and Quinton, D. (1984) 'Parental Psychiatric Disorder: Effects on Children.' *Psychological Medicine 14,* 853–880.

Rutter, M., Taylor, E. and Hersov, L. (1995) *Child and Adolescent Psychiatry.* London: Blackwell.

Ryan, M. (2000) *Working with Fathers.* Abingdon: Radcliffe Medical Press.

Saleeby, D. (ed.) (1997) *The Strengths Perspective in Social Work Practice.* New York: Longman.

Sanderson, M. (1999) 'Education.' In R.M. Page and R.L. Silburn (eds.) *British Social Welfare in the 20th Century.* London: Macmillan.

Satir, V (1972) *Peoplemaking.* London: Souvenir Press.

Saunders, B.E., Berliner, L. and Hanson, R.F. (2001) *Guidelines for the Psychological Treatment of Intrafamiliar Child Physical and Sexual Abuse* (draft). http://www.musc.edu/cvc/

Sayce, L. (1999) 'Parenting as a Civil Right: Supporting Service users who Choose to Have Children.' In A. Weir and A. Douglas (eds.) *Child Protection and Adult Mental Health: Conflict of Interest?* Oxford: Butterworth Heinemann.

Schorr, L.B. (1998) *Within our Reach: Breaking the Cycle of Disadvantage.* New York: Anchor/Doubleday.

Scott, J. (1999) *Looking After Children: Audit of Implementation in Year Three (1997–8).* Leicester: University of Leicester.

Seden, J., Hardiker, P. and Barker, M. (1996) 'Child Protection Revisited: Balancing State Intervention and Family Autonomy through Social Work Processes.' *Child and Family Social Work 1,* 1, 57–66.

Senge, P. (1990) *The Fifth Discipline: The Art and Practice of the Learning Organization.* New York: Doubleday.

Sergeant, J. and Steele, J. (1998) *Consulting the Public. Guidelines and Good Practice.* London: Policy Studies Institute.

Shaw, M., Dorling, D., Gordon, D. and Davey Smith, G. (1999) *The Widening Gap.* Bristol: Policy.

Sheppard, M. (1993) 'Maternal Depression and Childcare: The Significance for Social Work Research.' *Adoption and Fostering 17,* 10–15.

Sheridan, M. (1997) *From Birth to Five Years.* London: Routledge.

Silverman, M. (1989) 'Children of Psychiatrically Ill Parents: A Prevention Perspective.' *Hospital and Community Psychiatry 40,* 1257–1265.

Simon, H (1997) *Administrative Behaviour: A Study of Decision-Making Processes in Administrative Organizations.* Fourth edition. New York: The Free Press.

Sinclair, I. and Gibbs, I. (1998) *Children's Homes: A Study in Diversity.* Chichester: Wiley.

Sinclair, R. (1998) 'Developing Evidenced-based Policy and Practice in Social Interventions with Children and Families.' *International Journal of Social Research Methodology 1,* 2,169–176.

Sinclair, R. (1999) *The Language of Need: Social Workers describing the Needs of Children.* London: Department of Health.

Sinclair, R. (2000) 'Developing a Taxonomy for Children in Need.' *Children Now,* Issue 4, 12. London: National Children's Bureau.

Sinclair, R. and Carr-Hill, R. (1996) *The Categorisation of Children in Need: A Report to the Department of Health.* London: National Children's Bureau.

Sinclair, R., Garnett, L. and Berridge D. (1995) *Social Work and Assessment with Adolescents.* London: National Children's Bureau.

Siporin, M. (1975) *Introduction to Social Work Practice.* New York: Macmillan.

Skuse, T., Macdonald, I. and Ward, H. (2001) *Looking After Children: Transforming Data into Management Information: Report from the Second Round of Data Collection.* Loughborough: Loughborough University.

Smith, T. 'Neighbourhood and Preventive Strategies with Children and Families: What Works?' *Children and Society 13,* 4, 265–277.

Smith, C. and Carlson, B.E. (1997) 'Stress, Coping and Resilience in Children and Youth.' *Social Services Review 71,* 2, 231–256. Chicago: University Press.

Smith, G. and Noble, M. (2000) 'Developing the Use of Administrative Data to Study Poverty.' In J. Bradshaw and R. Sainsbury (eds.) *Researching Poverty.* Aldershot: Ashgate.

Smith, P. (ed.) (1996) *Measuring Outcome in the Public Sector.* London: Taylor and Francis.

Smith, T. (1996) *Family Centres: Bringing Up Young Children.* London: The Stationery Office and The Children's Society.

Social Exclusion Unit (1998a) *Truancy and School Exclusion.* Cm. 3957. London: The Stationery Office.

Social Exclusion Unit (1998b) *Bringing Britain Together: A National Strategy for Neighbourhood Renewal.* Cm. 4045. London: The Stationery Office.

Social Exclusion Unit (1999) *Teenage Pregnancy.* Cm. 4342. London: The Stationery Office.

Social Exclusion Unit (2001) *Preventing Social Exclusion.* London: The Stationery Office.

Social Information Systems (1993) *Children in Need, Definition, Management and Monitoring.* London: Health Publication Unit.

Social Services Inspectorate (1986) *Inspection of the Supervision of Social Workers in the Assessment and Monitoring of Cases of Child Abuse.* Heywood: Department of Health and Social Security.

Social Services Inspectorate (1997) *Responding to Families in Need: Inspection of Assessment, Planning and Decision-making in Family Support Services.* London: Department of Health.

Social Services Inspectorate (2001a) *Quality on the Way: Report of an Inspection of Service Quality Improvements in Social Care.* London: Department of Health.

Social Services Inspectorate (2001b) *Modern Social Services: A Commitment to Deliver, The 10th Annual Report of the Chief Inspector.* London: Department of Health.

Social Services Inspectorate and Audit Commission (1999) *Getting the Best From Children's Services. Findings from the Joint Reviews of Social Services 1998/9.* Oxon: Audit Commission Publications.

Sonuga-Barke, E. (1998) 'Categorical Models of Childhood Disorder: A Conceptual and Empirical Analysis.' *Journal of Child Psychology and Psychiatry 39,* 115–133.

Spaccarelli, S. and Kim, S. (1995) 'Resilience Criteria and Factors associated with Resilience in Sexually Abused Girls.' *Child Abuse and Neglect 19,* 9, 1171–1182.

Child Abuse Review (1995) Special Issue on Fatal Child Abuse 4, 309–392.

Spencer, N. (1996) *Poverty and Child Health.* Oxford: Radcliffe.

'Spotlight on Practice on Child Maltreatment Fatalities.' *Child Abuse and Neglect,* 1995, 19, 843–883.

Stein, E., Evans, B., Mazumdar, R. and RaeGrant, N. (1996) 'The Mental Health of Children in Foster Care: A Comparison with Community and Clinical Samples.' *Canadian Journal of Psychiatry-Revue Canadienne De Psychiatrie 41,* 6, 385–391.

Stein, M. (1990) *Living Out of Care.* Ilford: Barnardo's.

Stein, M. and Carey, K. (1986) *Leaving Care.* Oxford: Blackwells.

Stevens, A. and Gillam, S. (1998) 'Needs Assessment from Theory to Practice.' *British Medical Journal 316,* 1448–1451.

Stevenson, O. (1998) *Neglected Children: Issues and Dilemmas.* Oxford: Blackwell Science.

Stones, C. (1996) *Focus on Families.* Basingstoke: Macmillan.

Stroud, J. (1997) 'Mental Disorder and the Homicide of Children.' *Social Work and Social Sciences Review: An International Journal of Applied Research 6,* 3, 149–162.

Sugarman, L. (1986) *Life-Span Development: Concepts, Theories and Interventions.* London: Routledge.

Sutton, P. (1995) *Crossing the Boundaries.* London: National Children's Bureau.

Sutton, P. (1997) 'All in the same boat – rowing in the same direction? Influences on collaboration over children's services.' In B. Cohen and U. Hagen (eds.) *Children's Services: Shaping Up for the Millennium.* Edinburgh: The Stationery Office.

Swadi, H. (1994) 'Parenting Capacity and Substance Misuse: An Assessment Scheme.' *ACPP Review and Newsletter 16,* 5, 237–244.

Sylva, K. and Lunt, I. (1982) *Child Development: A First Course.* Oxford: Blackwell.

Taylor, P. and Gunn, J. (1999) 'Homicides by People with Mental Illness: Myth and Reality.' *British Journal of Psychiatry 174*, 9–14.

The Government's Annual Report 97/98 (1998). Cm. 3969. London: The Stationery Office.

Thoburn, J., Wilding, J. and Watson, J. (2000) *Family Support in Cases of Emotional Maltreatment and Neglect.* London: The Stationery Office.

Thomas, M. (1976) *The Language of Botany: A Dictionary of Terms used by Linnaeus.* London: B. and J. White.

Thorpe, D. (1998) *Report for Northamptonshire Social Services Department on the Pilot Child Protection Project in Wellingborough.* Lancaster: University of Lancaster.

Titmuss, M.R. (1974) *Social Policy: An Introduction.* London: Allen and Unwin.

Townsend, P. and Davidson, N. (eds.) (1982) *Inequalities in Health.* Harmondsworth: Penguin.

Townsend, P., Phillimore, P. and Beattie, A. (1988) *Health and Deprivation: Inequality and the North.* London: Croom Helm.

Tunstill, J. (1992) 'Local authority policies on children in need.' In Gibbons (ed.) *The Children Act and Family Support: Principles into Practice.* London: The Stationery Office.

Tunstill, J. and Aldgate, J. (2000) *Services for Children in Need: From Policy to Practice.* London: The Stationery Office.

Tweed, S.H. (1991) 'Adult Children of Alcoholics: Profiles of Wellness amidst Distress.' *Journal of Studies on Alcohol 52*, 2, 133–141.

United Nations (1989) *United Nations Convention on the Rights of the Child.* Geneva: Office of the United Nations High Commissioner for Human Rights.

Utting, D. (Ed.) (1995) *Family and Parenthood: Supporting Families Preventing Breakdown: A Guide to the Debate.* York: Joseph Rowntree Foundation.

Utting, D. (2001) 'Made to measure? Evaluating Community Initiatives for Children.' *Children and Society 15*, 1, 53–54.

Utting, Sir W. (1997) *People Like Us: The Report of the Review of the Safeguards for Children Living Away from Home.* London: The Stationery Office.

Varma, V. (1993) *How and Why Children Fail.* London: Jessica Kingsley.

Veit-Wilson, J. (1994) *Dignity Not Poverty.* London: Institute for Public Policy Research.

Veit-Wilson, J. (1998) *Setting Adequacy Standards.* Bristol: Policy.

Velleman, R. (1993) *Alcohol and the Family.* London: Institute of Alcohol Studies.

Vostanis, P., Cumella, S., Gratton, E. and Winchester, C. (1996) *The Impact of Homelessness on the Mental Health of Children and Families.* Birmingham: University of Birmingham.

Wade, J., Biehal, N., Clayden, J. and Stein, M. (1998) *Going Missing: Young People Absent from Care.* Chichester: Wiley.

Waller, B. (1996) Mimeo Paper. Unpublished.

Ward, H. (1995) (ed.) *Looking After Children: Research into Practice.* London: The Stationery Office.

Ward, H. (1998) 'Using a Child Development Model to Assess the Outcomes of Social Work Interventions with Families.' *Assessing Outcome in Child Care: An International Perspective. Special Issue Children and Society 12*, 3, 202–211.

Ward, H. (1999) 'Parental Responsibilities and the Children Act 1948.' *Practice 11*, 2, 27–34.

Ward, H. (2000) 'Poverty and family cohesion.' In J. Bradshaw and R. Sainsbury *Getting the Measure of Poverty: the Early Legacy of Seebohm Rowntree.* Aldershot: Ashgate.

Ward, H. (forthcoming) 'Current initiatives in the development of outcome-based evaluation of children's services in England and Wales.' In A.N. Maluccio, C. Canali and T. Vecchiato *Outcome Based Evaluation in Child and Family Services – Cross-National Perspectives.* New York: Aldine de Gruyter.

Ward, H., Garnett, L. and Everett, G. (forthcoming) *Report on Piloting of Inter-Agency Assessment Protocol 2000–2001.* Loughborough: Loughborough University.

Ward, H., Macdonald, I., Pinnock, M. and Skuse, T. (forthcoming) 'Monitoring and Improving Outcomes for Children in Out of Home Care.' In K. Kufeldt and B. McKenzie (eds.) *Child Welfare: Connecting Research, Policy and Practice.* Waterloo, Ontario: Wilfrid Laurier Press.

Ward, H., Skuse, T. and Pinnock, M. (1998) *Looking After Children: Using Data as Management Information: Interim Report to Research Advisory Group.* Leicester: University of Leicester.

Ward, H. and Skuse, T. (1999) *Looking after Children: Transforming Data into Management Information: Report from the First Year of Data Collection.* Totnes: Dartington Social Research Unit.

Ward, H. and Skuse, T. (2001) 'Performance Targets and Stability of Placements for Children Long Looked After away from Home.' *Children and Society 15,* 5, 333–346.

Ware, A. and Goodin, R.E. (eds.) (1990) *Needs and Welfare.* London: Sage.

Waterhouse, R. (2000) *Lost in Care: Report of the Tribunal of Inquiry into the Abuse of Children in Care in the Former County Council Areas of Gwynedd and Clwyd since 1974.* London: The Stationery Office.

Watt, N., Anthony, E.J., Wynne, L.C. and Rolf, J.E. (eds.) (1984) *Children At Risk For Schizophrenia: A Longitudinal Perspective.* Cambridge: Cambridge University Press.

Webb, S.A. (2001) 'Some Considerations on the Validity of Evidence-based Practice in Social Work.' *British Journal of Social Work 31,* 1, 57–79.

Weir, A. and Douglas, A. (eds.) (1999) *Child Protection and Adult Mental Health: Conflict of Interest?* Oxford: Butterworth Heinemann.

Werner, E.E. (1996) 'Vulnerable but Invincible.' *European Child and Adolescent Psychiatry 5,* 47–51.

Whitehead, M. (1988) *The Health Divide.* Harmondsworth: Penguin.

Widom, C.S. (1996) 'Understanding the Consequences of Childhood Victimisation.' Manuscript submitted to *American Journal of Orthopsychiatry.*

Wilczynski, A. (1997) *Child Homicide.* London: Greenwich Medical Media.

Williamson, H. and Butler, I. (1997) 'No One Ever Listens to Us.' In C. Cloke and M. Davies (eds.) *Participation and Empowerment in Child Protection.* Chichester: Wiley.

Willow, C. (1997) *Hear! Hear! Children and Young People's Democratic Participation in Local Government.* London: Local Government Information Unit.

Willow, C. (1998) 'Listening to children in local government.' In D. Utting (ed.) *Children's Services Now and in the Future.* London: National Children's Bureau and Joseph Rowntree Trust.

Wolkind, S. and Renton, G. (1979) 'Psychiatric Disorders in Children in Long-term Residential Care.' *British Journal of Psychiatry 135,* 129–135.

Wolkind, S. and Rutter, M. (1977) 'Children Who Have Been "In Care": An Epidemiological Study.' *Journal of Child Psychology and Psychiatry, 14,* 97–105.

Woodley Team Report (1995) *Report of the Independent Review Panel to East London and the City Health Authority and Newham Council, Following a Homicide in July 1994 by a Person Suffering with a Severe Mental Illness.* London: East London and City Health Authority.

World Health Organisation (1992) *ICD-10: The ICD-10 Classification of Mental and Behavioural Disorders: Clinical Descriptions and Diagnostic Guidelines.* Geneva: WHO.

Wright, J., Williams, R. and Wilkinson, J.R. (1998) 'Development and Importance of Health Needs Assessment.' *British Medical Journal 316,* 1311–1313.

Wright, T. (1996) *Socialisms Old and New.* London: Routledge.

6, Perri. (1997) *Escaping Poverty: From Safety Net to Networks of Opportunities.* London: Demos.

Contributors

Jane Aldgate is Professor of Social Care at the Open University. She has taught many students in social work education for over two decades. She has undertaken a wide range of research about children in need and their families spanning family support, children looked after and direct work with children and child maltreatment, and has worked closely with the Department of Health on a number of initiatives including the development of the PQ Award in Child Care and the *Framework for the Assessment of Children in Need.* She is co-author, with June Statham, of the Department of Health's overview of the Children Act 1989 research studies: *The Children Act Now – Messages from Research*, TSO 2001.

Hedy Cleaver is Professor of Social Work Research at Royal Holloway College, University of London and has been involved in the development of structured assessment records to encompass the *Framework for the Assessment of Children in Need and their Families.* Together with J. Unell and J. Aldgate she wrote *Children's Needs – Parenting Capacity* (1999). Her current research for the Department of Health explores the impact of the Assessment Framework on social work practice.

Adrian Falkov is a consultant child and adolescent psychiatrist, previously with the South London and Maudsley (NHS) Trust and now with the Bedfordshire and Luton Community (NHS) Trust. He has a long-standing interest in children's understanding of parental mental illness and the links between parenting, parental psychiatric disorder and child maltreatment. In 1995 he undertook a study of *Working Together* (Part 8 Reviews) assessing the association between parental psychiatric disorder and fatal child abuse. He co-ordinated the Department of Health sponsored development of multi-agency training materials to improve awareness, knowledge and skills about the impact of parental mental illness on children, entitled *Crossing Bridges.* He has established a family mental health liaison service with colleagues in Adult Mental Health and continues to promote the development of better services for children and their mentally ill parents.

Louise Garnett began her career in social research in 1985 and has contributed to several national child welfare research projects. She worked as a research officer for BAAF for three years on the Child Care Now Study and for four years as a research officer with the National Children's Bureau. She returned to Humberside in the early 1990s where she was employed within the county's Economic Development Unit. In 1995 she established the Children in Need Assessment Project, an innovative research project joint-funded by health and social services. Her research interests also encompass vulnerable adults and since 1998 she has been based in North Lincolnshire where she currently manages the Community Care Needs Assessment Project.

Jenny Gray trained as a social worker in New Zealand but has spent most of her professional career working in England. She has a child care background and joined the Social Services Inspectorate in 1990. Her current responsibility is to provide professional advice on child protection within the Department of Health. She has lead responsibility for the Framework Assessment of Children in Need and their Families.

Pauline Hardiker has recently retired from her post as senior lecturer in the School of Social Work at the University of Leicester. She has published extensively on the theory of social work, social work practice and social policy. The Framework for Conceptualising Need which she developed has influenced policy at national and local levels.

Michael Little is a researcher at the Dartington Social Research Unit and the Chapin Hall Centre for Children at the University of Chicago. He has published extensively on social policy aspects of services for children in need. His current work is primarily concerned with aspects of child development in the context of extensive separation from relatives.

Clare Murray is a senior researcher in the Family and Child Psychology Research Centre at City University where she gained her PhD. for work on eating disorders. She is currently involved in work on parenting and child development in non-traditional families and assisted reproduction.

Robert Page is a reader in Democratic Socialism and Social Policy at Birmingham University. He is the author of *Stigma* (Routledge & Kegan Paul 1984) and *Altruism and the Welfare State* (Avebury 1996) and the joint editor of *British Social Welfare in the Twentieth Century* (with Richard Silburn, Macmillan 1999) and *Understanding Social Problems* (with Margaret May and Edward Brunsdon, Blackwell 2000). He is a member of the editorial board of *The Journal of Social Policy* and *Benefits.*

Mark Peel worked as a social worker and manager in the statutory and voluntary sectors prior to becoming involved with social work research and teaching. He has previously worked at the universities of Sheffield, Leicester and Loughborough, and is presently Director of Social Work Studies at the Open University. As a Research Fellow, Mark worked closely with a wide range of professionals, parents and children in the research area.

Michael Pinnock began his career in 1973 as a social worker carrying a generic caseload. He went on to specialise in work with young people in trouble and to manage various childcare services. In 1990 he moved into policy development, planning and performance review. He assisted the Department of Health in early work on children's services planning and is currently employed as Performance Manager by North Lincolnshire Social and Housing Services. He is seconded part time to work at Loughborough University on research into the use of outcome-based data in developing children's services. He is an Honorary Fellow in Social Work at the University of Hull.

David Quinton is Professor of Psychosocial Development in the School for Policy Studies at the University of Bristol. Prior to this he worked for many years at the Institute of Psychiatry and in the MRC Child Psychiatry Unit, specialising in the long-term outcomes for children from high psychosocial risk backgrounds. He is academic co-ordinator of the Department of Health's initiative on Supporting Parenting and is Director of the new Hadley Centre for Adoption and Foster Care studies at Bristol.

Wendy Rose is a senior research fellow at the Open University. She worked for 11 years in the Department of Health as Assistant Chief Inspector (Children's Services) advising on the development and implementation of childcare policy. She has a background in social services practice, policy and management in local authority and NHS settings. She has been working with the Department of Health to develop guidance and associated resources publications and research on assessing children in need and their families.

Janet Seden is a lecturer in Health and Social Welfare at the Open University. She has worked as a probation officer and a social worker and lectured at Leicester University before taking up her present post in 1999. She is the author of *Counselling Skills in Social Work Practice*, and has also published on the assessment of children in need and their families, the provision of services for children and their families, social work processes, children and spirituality and practice teaching. She is also a counselling tutor and supervisor.

Ruth Sinclair is Director of Research at the National Children's Bureau. She has many years' experience in research on children and children's services. Previously she worked at Loughborough University and as Head of Research at Leicestershire Social Services Department. She has a particular interest in the assessment of need and planning to meet need, both for individual children and for groups of children and is author or co-author of many publications in this area.

Jo Tunnard works with both Dartington and RTB (Ryan Tunnard Brown) on projects commissioned by local and health authorities and voluntary organisations. Her main focus of work is the auditing of need, the development and evaluation of services in response to needs identified, and new ways of recording and analysing need in individual families. As a researcher, writer and editor she has worked for both adult and children's divisions of the Department of Health. She has a long experience of working in NGOs concerned with enabling families to have a voice in decisions made by social services departments and the courts about their children and young relatives.

Harriet Ward is Director of the Centre for Child and Family Research and a senior research fellow in the Department of Social Sciences at Loughborough University. Since 1992 she has directed the research and development for the Department of Health programme for assessing outcome for children looked after away from home (the Looking After Children project). Her current research programme includes cohort studies of children looked after away from home, studies of the costs of services, and issues concerning inter-agency work and data analysis in local authorities.

Subject Index

Author Index